DATE DUE

Performing O'Neill

Other Books by Yvonne Shafer

American Women Playwrights, 1900–1950

August Wilson

The Play's the Thing (with Marvin Carlson)

Henrik Ibsen: Life, Work, and Criticism

Approaches to Teaching Ibsen's "A Doll's House"

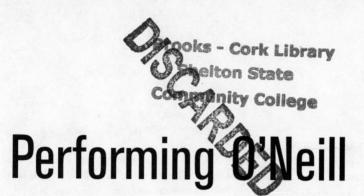
Performing O'Neill

Conversations with Actors and Directors

Yvonne Shafer

St. Martin's Press
New York

Library of Congress Cataloging-in-Publication Data

Performing O'Neill : conversations with actors and directors / [compiled by] Yvonne Shafer.
     p. cm.
    ISBN 0-312-22626-8
     1. O'Neill, Eugene, 1888-1953—Dramatic Production. 2. O'Neill, Eugene,
     1888-1953—Stage history. 3. Actors—United States—Interviews. 4. Theatrical producers
     and directors—United States—Interviews. I. Shafer, Yvonne, 1936-

PS3529.N5 Z773 2000
792.9'5—dc21

                                                        00-031131

Book design by Acme Art, Inc.
First edition: December 2000
10 9 8 7 6 5 4 3 2 1

*This book is dedicated to Jason Robards
with thanks for all the wonderful performances.*

Contents

Acknowledgements

As always Louis Rachow at the International Theatre Institute has been of great assistance from the beginning of the work to the end. Dr. Rod Bladel of the New York Public Library for the Performing Arts was extremely kind and helpful as I worked with the sadly crumbling clippings in the files for each of the actors and directors. My chairperson, Dr. Barbara Horn, was a great support throughout the work in many ways. Tom Shafer was both enthusiastic and helpful, as usual, as was Frederick C. Wilkins, the ebullient editor of *The Eugene O'Neill Review*. Robert Chamberlain was a great help, particularly in the last stages of the writing. My knowledgeable editor, Michael Flamini, was helpful and charming. My friend of many years, Don Brannan, read parts of the manuscript and gave welcome encouragement. I am grateful to St. John's University for allowing me a teaching reduction so that I could spend time writing. Mary Fama, Joanne Lamanno, Michelle Boccio, and Jaclyn Falco, at St. John's University, were patient and helpful with the transcribing and difficulties with the computer. My colleagues Dr. William Tipper and Dr. Azzedine Layachi were friends in my times of need. I owe a great debt to Ghislaine Boulanger and Charles Kaduchin, who loaned me their apartment so I could have access to the Lincoln Center files and interview actors in Manhattan. I particularly want to thank the actors and directors, all of them very busy working in the theatre, who were so generous with their time. Finally, thanks to Edward Petherbridge, who was so charming and witty during my interview with him for *The Eugene O'Neill Review* that I was inspired to write this book.

Performing O'Neill

1 | Introduction: Early Actors and Directors

The history of Eugene O'Neill plays onstage is filled with many triumphs and a number of terribly disappointing failures. What is surprising is the number of actors who achieved their greatest successes in plays by O'Neill. For many actors there were years of struggle in weak plays or vaudeville and then, finally, the opportunity to achieve a critical and popular success in an exciting role created by O'Neill. Although the plays have been revived, the initial presentation often created such a strong effect that the actor or actress is still identified with the role. After Fredric March died, his biographer Deborah Peterson quoted director José Quintero as saying, "I have seen other great, great actors perform James Tyrone in other productions of *Long Day's Journey into Night*. And with all due respect, I will have to tap them on the shoulder and say, 'Excuse me, your lordship. Let's step aside and let the one and only James Tyrone pass by.'"[1] Quintero is foremost among the later directors who brought the plays to the stage. In earlier times the directors who worked with O'Neill's major works were Robert Edmond Jones, Arthur Hopkins, and Philip Moeller. They contributed significantly to the success of many of the plays.

There are many myths and legends surrounding Eugene O'Neill. Many of these have to do with his relationships with actors. It is widely assumed that he hated actors and had no respect for their craft. A close look at the production history of his plays, interviews with actors and actresses, and interviews with O'Neill reveals a different picture. It is also widely accepted that he hated and had contempt for the theatre of his father's time, particularly his father's great hit *The Count of Monte Cristo*. In fact, he both learned from the theatre of his father's time (which was often noted by critics) and admired many of the actors. A background for the interviews with today's actors includes a picture of O'Neill's own experience as an actor, his views on acting, his work and friendship with actors, and the work of actors and directors in major performances of his plays in the first half of the twentieth century. Moving slightly into the second half of the century, there will be discussion of Quintero's production of *Long Day's Journey into Night* in 1956, a major turning point that led to a revival of interest in O'Neill's plays.

O'Neill's boyhood was spent hearing about theatre, seeing theatre, and often traveling with his father's company. When he wrote *The Fountain*, he actually visualized his father in the role. He often remarked that the actors in his father's time understood how to play the large-scale qualities of such a character as Ponce de Leon. Again, when he wrote *A Touch of the Poet*, he spoke of the great qualities of actors like his father and Maurice Barrymore, father of John and Lionel, who knew how to make an entrance (without having it built up by the playwright) and played with splendor and style. In 1933 he said to George Jean Nathan, "You can say what you want to about the theatre back in my old man's time, you can laugh at all those tin-pot plays and all that, but, by God, you've got to admit that the old man and all the rest of those old boys were actors!"[2]

O'Neill himself had no desire to be an actor. Early in his playwriting career O'Neill invented tales or elaborated on his acting experiences, and his stories were printed and reprinted, giving a muddled picture of actuality. He acted briefly in his father's company in the famous money-making play and found it a terrible experience. This, however, was during the period in which he had tried to commit suicide and his worldview was negative about most aspects of life. He played several small roles, some without lines, but he was so terrified and so embarrassed by wearing a costume, a fake moustache, and make-up that his performance was bad enough to cause laughter. The version of the tour that he gave in later years was that he was constantly drunk and that he and his brother Jamie pulled gags and generally disrupted the performances. An actor on the tour gave a different version, indicating that although Jamie's breath always smelled of liquor, there was no horseplay or drunkenness, and that O'Neill waited until after the play to drink. That O'Neill loved to embroider this experience to make people laugh is clear from the fact that he told at least one person that he and Jamie performed a song and dance at the intermission. As Arthur and Barbara Gelb note in their book *O'Neill,* he said, "Although I was only on the stage for minutes at a time, I imagine there are still people in this country who awake screaming in the night at the memory of it." If this experience affected his attitude toward actors, it must have been to awaken admiration for persons who could do what he could not. He probably was a very bad actor, but he loved to exaggerate and come up with funny things about the experience. For example, he often said that he was a terrible actor and had graduated from the Orpheum Circuit with the degree of Lousy Cum Laude. After this short stretch on the boards, he was certain that he would never act again.[3]

However, as he often wrote, fate pulls funny tricks. When he became involved in the Provincetown Players, he was a participant in all aspects of the productions, as were all the others. The organization was a "creative collective." So O'Neill helped paint scenery and arrange the settings and participated in rehearsals. For his first production, *Bound East for Cardiff,* he acted as director (knowledge of the theatre he gained working with his father would have been his only preparation for this), cast himself in the smallest role, and helped to create the setting in the tiny wharf theatre. As the Second Mate he had only to say, "Isn't this your watch on deck, Driscoll?"[4] Nevertheless, he must have suffered agonies, since even being the prompter made him very nervous. As the actors performed the very moving play, they could hear O'Neill breathing hoarsely and quickly behind the scenery where he stood holding the script. Later he acted in a larger role, that of a West Indian Sailor in his play *Thirst.* He and two others were in a boat without food or drink. When the Dancer died, he pulled out his knife and announced that the Gentleman and he would now have food and drink. Appalled by the cannibalism, the Gentleman pushed the Dancer's body into the water; the enraged Sailor stabbed the Gentleman, but both ended up in the shark-infested water. The last staged direction he performed reads, "The Sailor's black head appears for a moment, his features distorted with terror, his lips torn with a howl of despair. Then he is drawn under."[5] His final appearance with the Provincetown Players was less demanding. In *Before Breakfast* he played the offstage husband driven to suicide by the harangue of his wife. He had only two things to do. He had to reach his hand out to take a bowl of water: "It is a sensitive hand with slender fingers. It trembles and some of the water spills on the floor."[6] Later, he had to give a cry of pain that must have come easily. Fortunately for this shy, reserved man, his acting days were over.

The work with other actors, however, continued. O'Neill was deeply involved in the rehearsals for most of his plays except when he was living in Europe waiting for his divorce from Agnes Boulton so he could marry Carlotta Monterey. When he and Carlotta returned, they both attended rehearsals, causing Philip Moeller to joke about the challenge of directing an O'Neill play with the two O'Neills watching.

It is difficult to determine how much he or anyone else contributed to the direction of the plays in the "creative collective" of the Provincetown Players. Sometimes one person began directing and another took over. O'Neill later claimed that he had little to do in the rehearsals as he had not yet quit drinking and was consequently "pickled" most of the time. None of the actors were truly professionals in the early productions, but several went on to have modest careers in the theatre. As time passed, professional actors, including Charles Gilpin and Louis Wolheim, were brought in to play particular roles. But there still was a communal feeling of a group working together as committed amateurs.

O'Neill's first real experience working with a professional actor in the theatre occurred with *Beyond the Horizon*. Reading about Richard Bennett, the actor who played the leading role so successfully, one might suppose a baptism by fire for the young playwright. Bennett was forty-seven years old and had established himself both as a successful actor and as a man of some eccentricities. As an actor, he had performed in the daring play about syphilis, *Damaged Goods,* and had been praised for his role as John Shand opposite Maude Adams in *What Every Woman Knows.* Nevertheless, he had never really reached the top of his profession and had performed in many plays that were claptrap. He was widely perceived as a matinee idol with a limited range. As Burns Mantle wrote in his review of *Beyond the Horizon,* he was a good actor and the critic "had often wondered why he had not been popularly placed among the few big men of the theatre of his day."[7]

Although another critic described Bennett as a gentleman and a scholar, he had achieved a reputation as "one of the most colorful actors the Broadway stage has known" for his tirades during performances, in which he stepped out of character "to chastise an inattentive audience." The Bennett file at Lincoln Center is filled with accounts of bizarre behavior for which he was frequently in the news. Married three times, his third divorce attracted much attention. One article was headed, "Wife Says He Acts Too Realistically With a Gun Offstage." In court his wife claimed that he was a perfectionist and that when his role called for a weapon, he used it at home, "And I've got the scars to prove it!" She spoke of his maniacal moods and said that he had stabbed her cheek with a nail file and that the divorce action was set off by his striking her on the head with a gun. In the many stories covering the case, she was quoted as saying, "When he wasn't threatening to kill me, he was threatening to kill himself." After the divorce was granted, he sailed for England in disguise, in tourist class, to avoid arrest for nonpayment of alimony. On another occasion he appeared in court, suing a hotel because his thumb was injured in a door that was being repaired. It turned out that he was apparently giving the workmen some unasked-for advice, and he was severely chastised by the judge for showing little sense on the occasion of the injury and less in taking up the court's time.

Onstage, despite his serious approach to acting and his preference for worthwhile plays, it was said that he followed in the footsteps of actor Richard Mansfield in "making impromptu speeches." His amusing quips were often quoted in the papers and notice was taken when, for example, he stopped a performance to point out that the audience had paid to hear him, not noisy radiators, and to demand that they be fixed. When he performed in *On Borrowed Time* he got mad about a gate and announced to the audience that he was taking a moment "to join the stage hands union and show these men how to fix a gate so it will stay open." (A possible result of that was his departure from the cast the next week, reputedly because of illness.) His many speeches directed at noisy latecomers were credited with an improvement in the seating of latecomers. Bennett was the father of two actresses known for their own displays of temperament, but a newspaper article stated that Richard Bennett "completely eclipses Joan and Constance Bennett." He often invited the audience to stay in their seats at the second intermission while he gave vent to whatever was on his mind: Mussolini, social problems, or critics whom he frequently described as bastards and sons of bitches with infantile intelligence. These disturbances during the play and lectures at intermissions amused audiences, but probably not the playwrights in whose works he was performing. This, then, was the actor O'Neill would face as a playwright struggling for acceptance in the American theatre with his first full-length play.

In fact, the relationship between the two men was full of camaraderie and mutual satisfaction. Bennett came across the script for *Beyond the Horizon* while poking around in the office of his producer, John Williams. O'Neill had been waiting for two years for Williams to produce it and by chance Bennett read it, was moved, and wanted to play the part of the twenty-three-year-old protagonist. It would be done in special matinees, and would have to be rehearsed while he was giving twelve performances a week in another play.

O'Neill described the process of working with Bennett in letters to his wife Agnes. For him the first challenge was cutting the play. It is widely believed that O'Neill refused to cut a word of his scripts. The truth is that he usually worked with directors or actors to cut and revise scripts during the rehearsal period. In this instance he wrote to his wife that he "labored until two A.M. on the cuts," arriving at a considerably tightened script. Then he met with Bennett and Williams for a whole afternoon changing the script. Following that, he and Bennett worked all night on the script, drinking absinthe as they went over the play line by line. In the last few days of rehearsal, O'Neill cut more than half an hour from the script.[8] (The published text did not indicate these cuts.) O'Neill worked with the actors during the rehearsals and took pleasure in the process. He described himself to Agnes as "the only man in the auditorium, director of my own play! And I don't think I've made such a fizzle of it either! They all showed a noticeable improvement today, and also a marked improvement in their respect for me."[9] As far as his work with Bennett, they ultimately formed a mutual admiration society. During the second rehearsal they had a terrific fight because Bennett did what he wanted instead of following the directions in the text. After doing it O'Neill's way, Bennett said, "By God, you're right. Let's have a few more fights and this play will pick up 100%." As for O'Neill, his appreciation of Bennett's talent and intelligence was expressed in letters and conversation. He stressed how much he had learned and how useful it would be to him: "Bennett is really a liberal education all in himself. He has brains and he uses them every second."[10]

It was generally known that Bennett's enthusiastic response to the play and the playwright helped create the production that achieved such fame in American theatre history. One newspaper photograph of the play had the caption, "It was largely due to Bennett's courage that *Beyond the Horizon* was produced. Its success has been justified by its brilliant reception." Bennett was repaid for his courage and dedication by receiving the most positive reviews of his career and moving into the ranks of the best actors of the time.

The play opened with cheap, thrown-together settings (disappointing for O'Neill, as the visual aspect is always an enormously important aspect of his plays), after limited rehearsals, and only at matinees. Nevertheless, the critics came because they had been watching O'Neill's development and because Bennett and others had created interest by talking about the play. Heywood Broun was one of several critics who said that Bennett was playing better than ever before. Another critic wrote that the role was excellent for an actor "acting from within": "Mr. Bennett has never done finer work. His dreaming Rob of the first scene has something of an ethereal charm, and this is not entirely lost among the vicissitudes of the following scenes." While objecting (as critics often did) to the subject matter of the play, he said that the critics' specific praise for Bennett for his "extraordinarily detailed acting of Robert's struggle in the last act is richly deserved."

The phrase "acting from within" would often be used by critics for other actors in O'Neill plays. The plays seemed to present a particular challenge to actors, causing them to explore their own resources and delve deeper into the character than they had previously done. Bennett wrote an article called "Words Versus Situations" in which he described his approach to playing Robert. He stated that he had previously felt that the success of a play depended on its situations rather than its language. Here, he felt "the power of words which Mr. O'Neill has so adroitly woven into the big moments of this tragedy." He said that he realized that playing Robert called for a different technique than he had ever used before. "I gave myself up to the broad sweep and rugged strength of the realism which has been so effectively invested in it. The result was that I was carried into an entirely different field of expression than I have ever realized." Although he was twenty-four years older than the character, he was able to please audiences, critics, and Eugene O'Neill through his realistic acting. A caption under a photograph read, "This splendid actor has earned for himself a high place as an exponent of realism on our stage."

The success of the matinees led to regular performances in the evening, a long run (surprising to critics who felt the play was "too great to be popular"), and to the Pulitzer Prize for 1919-1920. Although all the critics praised Bennett, Alexander Woolcott was also prophetic in his review, saying, "Richard Bennett plays with fine eloquence, imagination and finesse, a performance people will remember." This proved true even as Bennett went on to win praise in challenging roles such as He in the Theatre Guild production of *He Who Gets Slapped* and Tony in another Pulitzer Prize winner, Sidney Howard's *They Knew What They Wanted*. In his account of the Pulitzer Prize plays, John L. Toohey indicates that Bennett continued his policy of eccentricity. Percy Hammond had praised him as the finest actor in the Western Hemisphere, but Bennett wrote to him to complain about his review. He concluded the letter by saying, "I do not doubt you think me a great actor, but I wish that hereafter you would, if possible, abstain from saying so."[11]

O'Neill was interested in realism in drama, and when he wrote plays with African American characters, he wanted to have the roles played by African American actors, which was almost unheard of in the early part of the century. Although he had played the "mulatto" character in *Thirst* (without make-up because of his black hair and deep tan), in succeeding plays he chose to have appropriate actors playing the demanding roles he had written. In 1919 the Provincetown Players presented O'Neill's *The Dreamy Kid,* a one-act play set in Harlem. This featured an "all-Negro" cast and was the most successful play of their fall season. In his 1921 review of the Provincetown Players' *The Emperor Jones,* Heywood Broun noted that if O'Neill had taken his play to another company, "we have little doubt that the manager would engage a white man with a piece of burnt cork to play Brutus Jones. They have done better in Macdougal Street. The emperor is played by a negro actor named Charles S. Gilpin who gives the most thrilling performance we have seen anywhere this season."

The Emperor Jones was presented in New York with Gilpin in the extraordinary leading role. Legends and anecdotes about him give the picture of a man with limited experience who was hired by some members of the Provincetown Players between floors in the elevator he was operating in Harlem. In fact, Gilpin was a thorough professional with experience in film and onstage. His extensive career is described by Erroll Hill in *The Cambridge Guide to World Theatre.*

Born in 1879, Gilpin took part in amateur productions in school, then left at the age of fourteen to tour with a Canadian minstrel show. He then joined the well-known Pekin Theatre in Chicago, then moved on to the Lafayette Theatre in New York. He starred in some silent films, described then as "colored cast pictures." He also made phonograph records that were popular because of his rich, melodious voice. Like many other actors past and present, when he had no role he worked at other jobs. He was a barber, a printer, a porter, and an elevator man. In 1917 he was part of a performance that drew great attention. The white writer Ridgely Torrence wrote three plays that were given by the Coloured Players at Madison Square Garden. These were directed by Robert Edmond Jones, who was a central figure in the Provincetown Players. When John Drinkwater's play *Abraham Lincoln* was to be presented on Broadway, the unusual decision was made to cast a black actor in the role of a former slave, based on Frederick Douglass.[12] Because of his fine work at the Lafayette Theatre, Gilpin was cast in the role. He played it for the entire run in 1919. It was a popular and successful play that lost the Pulitzer Prize to O'Neill's *Beyond the Horizon*. Given his success and visibility at the Lafayette Theatre and in *Abraham Lincoln,* Gilpin was the logical choice for the lead in *The Emperor Jones*. In the many different accounts of the Provincetown Players, various members claim credit for having decided to cast him.

The role is incredibly demanding. The actor is onstage almost all the time, and much of the play is a soliloquy. The actor must run, shout, crawl on the stage, and engage in other physical activities. An aspect the audience does not think of is the number of costume changes required for Brutus Jones. He starts out in a very grand costume with gold braid and patent leather boots with spurs. As he tries to escape the natives who are in revolt against him, the costume gets more and more torn so that at the end he is in little more than a loin cloth. The difficulty for the actor was to run offstage with a dramatic line, then get the costume changed and make his next entrance without pauses, which would break the rhythm and excitement of the play. In some moments he was offstage saying lines while someone helped him take off the clothes and put on more distressed ones. All in all, the actor playing the role has to have physical strength, an ability to maintain the moods within the scenes, and an excellent, well-trained voice. At the age of forty-one, Gilpin had all of those qualities. One critic noted that it would be possible to put on any one of the hit Broadway shows with another actor in the lead, but that it would be impossible to perform this play without Gilpin.

Word spread that the performance was going to be something special and the Provincetown Players were bombarded with requests for tickets and with new subscriptions as soon as the play opened, despite the fact that the reviewers were busy with "more important" premieres of now-forgotten plays. *The Emperor Jones* was so successful that it was moved to a theatre uptown, taken on tour in the United States and then to London. The reviewers generally praised Gilpin and there is unanimity in most of the reviews about his tremendous ability. Kenneth Macgowan wrote that it was "a magnificent piece of acting: from Harlem they brought a colored player, Charles Gilpin, to impersonate the emperor." He went on to catalog Gilpin's previous experience in smaller roles and the opportunity this role gave him to show his ability: "He shows not only a great power and a great image, in addition to his fine voice, but he displays an extraordinary versatility. It is a genuine impersonation, a being of flesh and blood and brain, utterly different from the actor's other work." He described at length the steady buildup of fright turning to terror throughout the latter part of the play, calling Gilpin's performance "the crown of a play that opens up the imagination of the American theatre."

Others also spoke of the superb acting and credited Gilpin with the success of the O'Neill play. One described it as an "amazing and unforgettable performance." Heywood Broun headed his review, "The Most Thrilling Play of the Season." He gave particular attention to the vocal qualities required for the long role: "Gilpin sustains the succession of scenes in monologues not only because his voice is one of a gorgeous natural quality, but because he knows just what to do with it." He said further that a critic probably shouldn't call an actor great on the basis of one role, but "there can be no question whatever that in 'The Emperor Jones' Gilpin is great. It is a performance of heroic stature. It is so good that the fact that it is enormously skillful seems only incidental." Each evening after the performance cheers and shouts greeted Gilpin as he took his bows wearing a bathrobe to cover his minimal costume.

In contrast to the rave reviews Gilpin generally received, there were a few reviewers who made negative comments about him. One cannot help wondering if Alan Dale's review of the production (after it had moved to the Selwyn Theatre) was clouded by racial prejudice. He criticized him generally, then specifically stated that he had limited powers and vocal monotony. He did say that he was at his best in the few moments of comedy—again, perhaps revealing a belief that blacks were incapable of anything but comedy. But Gilpin was to face a much clearer example of racial prejudice, even as he was praised for his acting.

Each year the Drama League held a dinner at which a number of actors were honored. In view of the notices Gilpin received, it was obvious that he should be among them. However, when some of the League members protested having a black man at their annual dinner, the invitation, amazingly, was withdrawn. O'Neill was outraged and, although painfully shy, got Macgowan to go with him to see the other actors who were to be honored and to ask them to boycott the dinner unless Gilpin was there. As a result, Gilpin was reinvited, but he did not enjoy the evening. Even worse than this event was the knowledge he had that he might never play such a role—or in fact any role in mainstream theatre—again. In interviews he expressed his appreciation for the opportunity O'Neill and the Provincetown Players had given him, but expressed at length the view that he was facing "stone walls" in the American theatre: "If I were white, a dozen opportunities would come to me as a result of a success like this. But I'm black. It is no joke when I ask myself, 'Where do I go from here?'"[13]

The many personal and professional problems Gilpin faced caused him to drink more and more. Furthermore, he objected to the use of the term "nigger" in the play and substituted other words for it. He also started stretching the comedy, causing O'Neill to call him "all ham and a yard wide." The demanding role required a sober actor in good health and O'Neill objected strenuously to Gilpin's behavior. In a widely quoted vile statement, he told Gilpin after an erratic performance, "If I ever catch you rewriting my lines again, you black bastard, I'm going to beat you up." In his own defense, O'Neill told the critic Mike Gold that he had put up with much more from Gilpin because of his race than he would have from a white man and that Gilpin had been drunk all of the last season.[14] In subsequent performances the role was taken by Paul Robeson, who was to create great excitement on the theatrical scene.

Not only did Gilpin lose the role and opportunities for further acting with the Provincetown Players, he suffered the indignity of seeing Robeson in his role. The Gelbs give an account of the occasion. After viewing the performance, he told a member of the Provincetown Players, "I feel kind of low. I created the role of the Emperor. That role belongs to me. That Irishman, he just wrote the play."[15] According to his obituaries, Gilpin retired to a farm in New Jersey, but the wish for money and the desire to act took him back to playing in stock. At the age of fifty he suffered a breakdown while acting in Woodstock, New York, and lost his magnificent voice. His wife cared for him until his death at the age of fifty-one. His voice mysteriously returned just before he died. Certainly this is a tragic story. The critic Theophilus Lewis wrote, "He rose from obscurity to the peaks, lived his hour of triumph, and returned again to the shadows."[16] O'Neill never forgot how wonderful Gilpin had initially been in the role. Twenty-five years later he told an interviewer, "As I look back on all my work I can honestly say there was only one actor who carried out every notion of a character I had in mind. That actor was Charles Gilpin as the Pullman porter in *The Emperor Jones*."[17]

Paul Robeson was an outstanding figure in sports, the musical world, and theatre. A fine student, he went to Rutgers, then Columbia, to get a law degree. He became disenchanted with the idea of being a lawyer, as he felt that a black man could not rise to the top as a lawyer in his time. His biographer Martin Duberman describes his growing interest in acting. In 1920, while still a law student, he performed with the Amateur Players in Harlem at the YWCA. He was in a revival of *Simon the Cyrenian,* one of the plays Ridgely Torrence had written for the Coloured Players. Because of his performance in that play, the people involved in a production called *Taboo* asked him to be in it. The play was written by a white woman named Mary Hoyt Wiborg and treated a familiar theme of superstitions and myth among black people. The production was directed by Augustin Duncan (brother of the famous dancer Isadora Duncan) and featured Margaret Wycherly, who had previously acted with the Provincetown Players. The play was produced on Broadway in 1922 by Sam Harris, with Charles Gilpin helping to coach the actors. Unfortunately the play was weak and closed after three days. Some critics gave positive attention to Robeson, but he must have been dismayed by Alexander Woolcott's review saying that he belonged almost anywhere except on the stage—the critic was probably carried away by his negative view of the play. Although the play had not been a success on Broadway, it was performed on tour in England with Robeson playing opposite the famous actress Mrs. Patrick Campbell.[18]

Robeson was determined to make a career in the theatre, however, so he persevered even as he finished his law studies. He wrote a letter to Otto Kahn, the millionaire with many interests in theatre who was one of the backers of the Provincetown Players. Duberman quotes Robeson as saying, "I want to get before any theatrical managers and playwrights, especially those who may possibly have Negro roles." He made specific reference to Eugene O'Neill. In 1923 he had finished the law degree but was still seeking a career in the theatre. He asked Augustin Duncan to write to O'Neill directly, suggesting that he use Robeson in a play.[19] In the fall of 1923 O'Neill began working on a play with a leading role for a black actor, *All God's Chillun Got Wings*. He had just suffered a failure with the play *Gold* in which the actor Willard Mack didn't know his lines and was extemporizing. O'Neill had admired Gilpin as an actor but did not want to use him again because of his drinking. Speaking to critic Mike Gold, he said he had got hold of a young man with "wonderful presence and voice, full of ambition and a damn fine man personally with real brains—not a ham. . . . I don't believe he'll lose his head if he makes a hit—as he surely will, for he's read the play for me."[20] Just before the rehearsals began, Robeson appeared with the Lafayette Players in a play called *Roseanne*. It was first done by white players in make-up, then with Rose McClendon and Charles Gilpin in an all-black cast. Gilpin had to be replaced and Robeson stepped into the role.

O'Neill was correct in anticipating a hit for Robeson. What he did not anticipate was the furor that preceded the opening of the play. The story is that of a talented black man studying to be a lawyer who falls in love with a white woman. Actually the play begins with them as childhood friends, naïve about racial prejudice. Their paths separate, she becomes a streetwalker, he cherishes his love for her, and finally they marry. The play deals with the difficulties they experience in a marriage with too much against it. (Later critics take this play as a disguised picture of O'Neill's parents.) The play was published before it was presented, so that many people were aware of the theme. There were also rumors that a black man and a white woman kissed each other in the play.

In her diary about the Provincetown Players, Edna Kenton wrote that the theatre was besieged by people demanding that the play be stopped. Articles were written in the papers predicting race riots if the play were presented. O'Neill, the Provincetown Players, and the actors received hate mail from racists. The Ku Klux Klan threatened to march on the city of New York. The lengthy struggle, and the letters written by O'Neill and others to the newspapers is a long story. In brief, the rehearsals went forward and the play was produced despite opposition and despite the fact that a last-minute effort by opponents kept the children from performing the early scene in the play. It was read by the stage manager. Mary Blair played the wife, and the mail was so terrible that the Provincetown Players staff opened all the letters to her and threw away the worst.[21] There was no physical romance in the play, but at one point Blair was to kiss Robeson's hand. She often said that when she died her obituaries would say that she was the actress who had kissed Robeson's hand in *All God's Chillun Got Wings*. She was right.

Mary Blair was an erratic actress, sometimes wonderful, sometimes disappointing, but O'Neill often insisted she be in his plays because of gratitude for her early allegiance to the Provincetown Players. Because she became ill, the production was postponed and it seemed a good idea to fill in with Robeson playing in *The Emperor Jones*. There were only two weeks of rehearsal for that play, which opened on May 6, 1924, followed swiftly by the opening of *All God's Chillun* on May 15.

Despite the almost impossible schedule he had to follow, Robeson was successful in both roles. His performance as the Emperor was described as "stirring" by one critic, who noted that it was an exacting part for which Robeson was suited because of his "extraordinary physique and a deep resonant voice." He compared the performance favorably to that of Gilpin, although observing that he lacked "mellowness that comes with experience." But he felt that Robeson compensated for that lack with vigor and virility arising from his youth and spirit. Most of the reviewers noted that the role had been made famous by Gilpin. One said it was difficult to remember the details of Gilpin's performance and so to compare the two, but that Gilpin's excellence was a matter of record and that Robeson was "gorgeous in the part." Almost all the critics described Robeson as a giant with a beautiful body and a magnificent voice, "just such a voice as *The Emperor Jones* demands." Another critic placed him higher than Gilpin because of his physique and a voice unmatched in the American theatre. Frank Vreeland wrote that Robeson was physically better for the role, "his towering bulk giving a touch of imperial dignity to the unstable ruler." His description of the action makes it clear how powerful Robeson was in the role: "As he alternately groveled and fled through the primeval forest from the rebellious natives, he sounded the rock bottom depths of terror, and he fired his revolver at the ghosts of his slain with such tremendous conviction that he seemed likely to blow out the sides of the tiny playhouse." One critic commented that both actors were so successful that he began to have fleeting suspicions that "it is the play rather than the player that so holds an audience." Alexander Woolcott had clearly changed his mind about Robeson since seeing the little-lamented *Taboo,* and said, "Robeson brings to the play a more primitive strength, a broader stroke of tone and gesture, a greater tumult of the immemorial fears which this voodoo play invokes from the deeps." He also wrote that people were fighting to get standing room at the Provincetown Players to see the production while other theatres were not even full. One article said that "smudgy urchins tried to sneak in but ushers flung them firmly outdoors." At the curtain there were cheers and applause for Robeson, who appeared in a checked bathrobe, looking like a boxer who had just won a match. Of course, O'Neill was pleased by Robeson's success, but, according to his biographer, Louis Scheaffer, said privately that Gilpin's acting had been better.[22]

O'Neill's head was full of the problems concerning the production of *All God's Chillun Got Wings*. Despite efforts of the Provincetown Players to defuse the controversy and insure a performance without riots or shooting, there was great anger in many circles about the production, with New York's Mayor John Hylan promising an investigation and refusing to allow the children to perform. Arthur Hornblow expressed the opinion after the opening, which went very smoothly, that after all the fuss the performance seemed tame. O'Neill was regarded as the most promising American playwright in 1924, but most critics found the play tedious and uninteresting. Heywood Broun, while making it clear that he just didn't like the play, bent over backwards to write positive comments. Like most of the critics he seized upon Robeson's performance as the saving grace of the evening. In an ironic reference to the bogus charges of provocative racial material in the play, he wrote, "Caucasian superiority does suffer a little because Paul Robeson is a far finer actor than any white member of the cast. Even in the dreary stretches of the play he sometimes drives his eloquence of voice and gesture through the fog." He praised Robeson's offstage singing of a spiritual, and concluded, "In the final scene of the first act where O'Neill helps him with some vigorous and brilliant writing, Robeson furnishes one of the finest moments in the present theatrical season." Arthur Hornblow called that scene (in which Robeson acted with another fine black actor, Frank Wilson, playing a "belligerent young Negro") the highlight of the play. Again the critics praised Robeson's physical characteristics and his talent as an actor. John Corbin could not praise the play as a whole, but said, "O'Neill shines in the creation of Jim's character and Paul Robeson, who creates the part, is a very able ally." Alexander Woolcott was high in his praise of the "heroic and noble figure of the negro—superbly embodied and fully comprehended by Paul Robeson. It is Robeson who is so magnificent in the title role of *The Emperor Jones,* that other O'Neill play which shares the week in Macdougal Street where Robeson is playing in repertory."

Robert Gilbert Welsh was one critic who liked both the play and Robeson's acting. He wrote, "The difficult role of the negro husband is played powerfully and with a convincing simplicity by Paul Robeson. . . . [T]he play is likely to take a permanent place in the American theatre." In the event, he was wrong about the play. It has rarely been revived. The most notable production was in 1975 at the Circle in the Square, directed by George C. Scott and starring Robert Christian as Jim.

Robeson, having achieved what no black actor had before, playing two leading roles in repertory for a white theatre company, went on to even greater success in the theatre. He played the next year as a boxer in *Black Boy*. In 1927 he played Crown in the Heywards' play *Porgy* with Frank Wilson as the lead. Another success was his role as Joe in *Showboat*. He played the latter in the London production and was cheered for his rendition of "Ol' Man River." With altered lyrics he used this song throughout his career as a protest against racial oppression. In 1931 he performed his third O'Neill role, that of the stoker in *The Hairy Ape*. He later broke records with his three productions of *Othello*. Hounded in his later years for alleged Communist activities, Robeson could get no work and had no income. In 1978 Phillip Hayes Dean wrote a play called *Paul Robeson*, which starred James Earl Jones. In recent years even more attention has been given to the great performer with a PBS program about his life and career. There was an exhibit in 1999 at the Museum of the City of New York that included photos of his appearances in O'Neill plays. When he appeared in those plays, the demanding critic George Jean Nathan wrote, "with relatively little experience and with no training to speak of, Robeson is one of the most thoroughly eloquent, impressive, and convincing actors that I have looked at and listened to in almost twenty years of professional theatre-going."

Robeson was one of the most convincing actors of this period. One of the most convincing actresses of the early twentieth century was Pauline Lord. She is credited with contributing to the development of realistic acting. Her biographer, Nelda K. Balch, wrote that "when the Moscow Art Theatre was leading the way in realistic acting and when many American actresses were bringing their personalities to the stage, Pauline Lord was developing her unique kind of realistic portrayal of emotion."[23] It took Lord many years, however, to find the play that would allow her to achieve the success she deserved. She first acted in school plays at the Holy Rosary Academy near San Francisco. Her desire to act was whetted by her frequent trips to matinees in the city. She studied acting at the Alcazar Theatre School there and made her debut at the age of thirteen, playing an adult role. From that time on she performed in plays and in vaudeville, making her New York debut at the age of twenty-two in a light comedy. Her luck was not good in the next few years, as she appeared in seven unsuccessful plays. She impressed Arthur Hopkins while acting the role of a woman of the streets in *The Deluge* (which lasted only a few weeks in 1917) and he took an interest in developing her career. Hopkins put her in a number of plays, but she never achieved the renown he was sure she should have.

Similarly, Eugene O'Neill's play *Chris Christopherson* failed to find the success he thought it would have. His father's old friend George Tyler was to produce it, but he kept delaying. Finally, following the success of *Beyond the Horizon,* he decided to move quickly and try the play out in Atlantic City, take it on tour, then bring it to New York. O'Neill attended some rehearsals and was discontent with the casting, which he discussed in letters to his wife. Lynn Fontanne was to play Anna, but O'Neill was unconvinced that she was the right actress for the role.[24] Tyler wanted him in Atlantic City for extensive rewrites, but O'Neill preferred to do the work in Provincetown, so he was not closely involved in the production. The reviews were fairly positive, but the audiences didn't like the play. Tyler had made extensive cuts, as O'Neill had before the rehearsals began. When the play went to Philadelphia, the reviews were mixed and Tyler wanted O'Neill to join the company and rewrite. At this point, fortunately, as it turned out, O'Neill decided the play was not worth saving with mere revisions and told Tyler to throw it in the ash barrel as he was going to start over.[25] By 1921 Hopkins was interested in O'Neill and may have hoped to find a suitable role for Lord in one of his plays. The match proved perfect. O'Neill had nearly written a new play, far superior to the first version, which was called *Anna Christie.* This play brought tremendous success to Lord, praise for direction to

Hopkins, and another Pulitzer Prize to O'Neill. O'Neill knew Lord's work, but also knew her personally, as did Jamie. O'Neill's brother liked to say that Polly was the only woman he had ever loved—especially when he was drunk and sentimental—but this seems to have been self-dramatization on Jamie's part.

One of the interesting things in the Lincoln Center file on Pauline Lord is an article called "My Anna Christie," in which she discussed her approach to the role. Because she was almost as shy as O'Neill, she was reluctant to write about herself or the role. Unlike many other actresses, she was reclusive and far from a public figure. Lord was only five feet, two inches tall, with light brown hair, and a soft voice. A description of her by Balch could almost be a description of O'Neill: "hesitant, at times timid and vague, with an elusive quality."[26] In the article, Lord said that when she read the first act, she felt she could not play the role because she wasn't the right type. O'Neill had described a woman who was a gorgeous Swede, "a goddess of the flesh, of deep bosomed strength and golden hair. I couldn't manage that. I am not a goddess." Still, she continued to read and to feel pity for the character. Finally she decided she could play the role, working from the inside. "I knew when I got her and cared for her that I could do her as a poor girl whom the audience would love and pity,—so there was the end of the first goddess Anna and the beginning of the Anna I do." Knowing that her own background as a convent student would not serve her, her first idea was to study the prostitutes she saw on 10th Avenue. She talked to them and concluded, "They seemed to me for the most part silly and half-frightened. There was nothing about their talk that seemed especially revolting or even from the standpoint of reproducing it, particularly racy." When the time came to rehearse, Lord actually was more influenced by the character of a department store clerk who seemed utterly defeated, "a beaten soul, tired to death." She said she used a hoarse voice ("which sometimes leaves me at the end of a performance with scarcely any voice at all"), and selected various mannerisms to express her despair. "All her little mannerisms have now come to seem as real to me as if they had always existed. The other characters are real, too—is there any other American playwright to compare with Eugene O'Neill for putting life bodily on the stage?"

Certainly, realism was the keynote of the reviews for Lord's performance. Louis V. de Foe wrote under the heading, "Another Grim O'Neill Drama" that some people "might find the characters brutal and repellent" but that the acting made them tolerable. "Miss Lord gave a really remarkable impersonation of this girl in her struggle from the depths. She played the role with unyielding realism. She softened none of its ignoble traits." Percy Hammond assured readers that when they left the theatre they would ask themselves if there were any better acting that that of Miss Pauline Lord as "the weary ex-prostitute. She does not utter one sound or make one gesture that you do not believe." Another critic wrote that the actress "does vividly realistic work as Anna, world-weary, men-weary, and happy in the cloak of the fog." Yet another said that no performance except Minnie Maddern Fiske's in *Salvation Nell* approached Lord's in truthfulness and that Lord was better. "Skill is too slight a word. This is the spirit lived spontaneously before our very eyes. . . . The strange inner bloom of life is on the lips of this woman of the streets and the broken suffering of life is in her voice." Another comment on the realism was offered by J. Ranken Towse, who said, "Pauline Lord furnished a realistic sketch of the soiled and hardened Anna and delivered her passionate outburst in the third act with the proper hysterical intensity." Percy Hammond with so many others praised this scene, giving some details of what she did in it. Indicating that she had told her father and Matt that she had "sold herself many times in the St. Paul flesh market," he said, "It is a fine speech with a wallop in every syllable, spoken in the racy lingo and the flat monotonous tones of the Minnesota underworld, by a desperate, forthright, forlorn, and reluctant practitioner of sin."

Arthur Hornblow put his finger on one of the aspects of the performance that was deliberately devised by Lord: "Noteworthy was the frugality of her gestures, the gestures of a woman who has lost hope." Kenneth Macgowan noted that in the role she "commands comedy as well as badgered and inarticulate desperation." He went on to signal a view held by many critics that Pauline Lord was the finest actress of her time and that this play had revealed it. "She plays this particular role as no other American actress of a generation has played anything remotely approaching it." Burns Mantle, who published the ten best plays each year, wrote that the ugliness of the subject matter was turned into art by the writing and the performances and that people would long boast of having seen the play. "There have been several fine characterizations achieved in the theatre this season, but none of them has been more vivid, more vibrantly human, more impressively real than that of Pauline Lord. Discounting the aid she had from Mr. O'Neill and the sympathy the role naturally carries, she was still entitled to the cheers her audience gave her."

What a thrill the opening night must have been for Hopkins and Lord! O'Neill was far away in Provincetown. Like many other playwrights, including Moss Hart and S. N. Behrman, he was unable to bear the torture of opening nights, but eager to hear about the response and the reviews. It must have been particularly sweet to him, as an Ibsen admirer, to read that "Between Mr. O'Neill and Miss Lord, Anna Christie is as living and absorbing as Hedda Gabler." For Hopkins, there was the satisfaction in the "multitudinous cheers" of the audience, knowing he had been right in predicting stardom for Lord and in reading that his choice of the actress for the part was an inspiration. The critics noted again and again how ecstatic the response to her acting was. One critic wrote that she played the role with fire and "it brought her the noisiest acclaim that any actress has received this year." Another said, "Not even famous stars often receive such an ovation as the cheers Miss Lord heard."

For the trio, the best was yet to come. The cast was to perform in England, where Lord had to overcome three obstacles to be accepted there: first, she was an American actress; second, she was in a play by an American playwright; and third, she was (as one reviewer put it) "handicapped by a Swedish accent-cum-Yankee Slang." English critics noted that she played with naturalism, moving from an "almost inadequate first entrance," playing with a sort of repressive quality as if fearing to let anything become emotional, and then releasing the repression "into a tremendous tirade of a speech in which she shows a very considerable emotional power." American papers proudly reprinted the notices saying, for example, that Lord's Anna was a triumph and as poignant a picture that one could see as "the pitiful husk of a woman warmed into womanhood by love and in danger of slipping back." The greatest source of pride was the tremendous ovation she received: the ovation lasted half an hour, and the audience sang "For She's a Jolly Good Fellow." She had received, according to one critic, "an ovation rarely equaled in recent London stage history" and her dressing room after the performance was a mob scene.

This response is particularly impressive when compared to the reception of *One Night in Rome* in April 1920. Laurette Taylor starred and Lynn Fontanne played a small role. Her biographer, Jared Brown, describes the opening night as a riot, with booing and with shouts to Taylor, "Go back to America! We don't want you here!" It appeared that the unsatisfactory scenery had ignited latent anti-American feeling.[27] Lord's welcome less than a year later was completely different in the theatre and in the press. One review in particular must have pleased Hopkins and Lord after their years of working together for this success: "The play and the performance prove that out of the ranks there steps ever and anon something of flesh and blood and brains, and patiently acquired technique, and passionate heart appeal; an actress who epitomizes the art and charm of the most alluring of all arts." The rest of Lord's career proved that this was no flash in the pan. The next year she was successful in another Pulitzer Prize winner, Sidney Howard's *They Knew What They Wanted*, sharing the stage with Richard Bennett. Later she played as a replacement for vacationing Lynn Fontanne in *Strange Interlude*, commenting to the press that after acting in this long play, the equivalent of a matinee and evening performance every day, the earlier cast needed a rest. Lord was later praised for her role in the stage adaptation of Edith Wharton's *Ethan Frome* with Raymond Massey and Ruth Gordon. In 1944 she again played Anna, this time on the radio for "Arthur Hopkins Presents." Her haunting voice is very moving on the existing tape of this performance. O'Neill wrote to Hopkins, "Polly in *Anna Christie* again certainly brings back a host of pleasant memories. I wish I could have heard her in it. I don't think it is just a man of fifty-five looking back on the good old days. There *were* uncompromising idealists with a real love for what the American theatre might become."[28] Lord also played Amanda in *The Glass Menagerie* on tour. When she died at the age of sixty, the obituaries stated that she would probably be best remembered as the star of Eugene O'Neill's *Anna Christie*.

Unlike Pauline Lord, Louis Wolheim came to the stage late and after a life filled with many other types of activities. His appearance in O'Neill's *The Hairy Ape* was not his first stage appearance, but it was the first time most people were aware of him as an actor. He seemed so very much the part of the rough, physically frightening stoker that one theatregoer said, "He must have been caught and tamed in the wilds of Pago-Pago, Samoa and imported especially to play his part." In later years he was known as the ugliest man in films, but also as one of the screen's best actors. O'Neill chose him for the role and felt very much at home with him during the rehearsals and performance.

Wolheim was in fact a peculiar combination of the rough character O'Neill had created and an educated gentleman. He was described as a gentle, soft-spoken, scholarly man with a good education. He was born in 1880 to a Jewish family in Brooklyn. He was only a few years older than O'Neill and shared with him a love of adventure. He attended City College of New York and then went to Cornell to get a degree in math, but at the age of thirty he decided to go to Mexico, where he was a mechanical engineer for three years. He spoke French, German, Spanish, and Yiddish, and had translated several plays. His family was very proud of him, but his mother wanted him to have plastic surgery on his nose after it was smashed playing football. Naturally, the unusual background of this strange-looking actor fascinated columnists. Alexander Woolcott wrote, "Louis Wolheim, who plays the stoker, makes a genuine contribution to *The Hairy Ape*. Once he was a football player at Cornell, on whose gridiron he came honorably by the broken nose that is so useful a part of his present make-up. Later he taught at Cascadilla and engineered in Mexico and finally sidled into the theatre under the guidance of Lionel Barrymore. He is doing himself proud in his first important role."

Whereas most actors struggle to make a career in the theatre and have some sort of training, Wolheim just fell into a theatrical career. While he was at Cornell getting a Ph.D. and teaching math, he met Lionel Barrymore by chance. According to legend, Barrymore said, "With that mug of yours you could make a fortune in the theatre." (There are numerous versions of this conversation, which probably took place while Barrymore and Wolheim were knocking back drinks.) The upshot was that Wolheim finished his Ph.D. but (probably to his mother's dismay) followed Barrymore to Hollywood where he played in films. Talking to an interviewer in Toledo while touring *The Hairy Ape,* he said, "It sounded like an adventure and I went and damme if I didn't seem to click." He acted in *Sherlock Holmes* with John Barrymore and helped translate and adapt the play *The Claw* for the Barrymores. Lionel Barrymore asked him to play the role of his brother in *The Jest,* which Arthur Hopkins was producing. Attracted to the idea, the modest Wolheim nevertheless found the role too daunting and was glad when a picture commitment kept him from it. When he finished his film, he went to New York and hung around rehearsals observing Lionel Barrymore's approach to acting. Ultimately, he played a small role and became for O'Neill and others a "Hopkins actor"—high praise.

O'Neill's interest in Wolheim predated his completion of *The Hairy Ape.* He thought the actor might be fine for the role, but was worried on two counts. First, he felt Wolheim hadn't had enough stage experience, and, second, the shy O'Neill was embarrassed to ask him to play such an ugly, unattractive character for fear of insulting him. Later Wolheim said that he met O'Neill and his wife Agnes by chance at a supper given by the Barrymores to celebrate the opening of *The Claw.* Given the fact that O'Neill hated such occasions and was embarrassed to eat in public because of his shaky hands, it is more likely that O'Neill asked one of the brothers to invite him with the purpose of meeting Wolheim. The double connection of the actor to Hopkins, whom O'Neill admired so much, and to John and Lionel, whom he always hoped to attract to one of his plays, was a strong recommendation. When O'Neill met him, they talked about a number of things, but not his next play, as Wolheim told interviewer Ashton Stevens. Apparently O'Neill took to Wolheim immediately and soon Wolheim was offered the role by the Provincetown Players.

So, it would seem everything was set. However, Wolheim was overwhelmed by reading the play and in the interview with Stevens he described his reaction: "I didn't want to take the part at first. It was too damn important. Hell, why give it to me and take a chance on wrecking the whole damn production?" He told another interviewer that he said to Hopkins, "Why in God's name a dub like me? I've had no experience but four or five bum parts; I'll be a holy stench. Whynhell should I be picked. . . . Here was great stuff, here was something that needed telling. It called for trumpets. I told Hopkins why give it to a pennywhistle like me?" Apparently, Hopkins was very persuasive, because Wolheim concluded, "That's the way I talked," smiling, "and then I surrendered to better judgment."

During rehearsals O'Neill and Wolheim became friends, enjoying exchanging stories of their adventures. Although he rarely laughed, O'Neill loved funny stories and Wolheim was famous for his witty Yiddish dialect anecdotes. He was very proud of his Jewish heritage and had great contempt for people in the theatre who changed their Jewish names. Both were men who enjoyed a fight (once, when Wolheim was fighting, it took four policemen to stop him). O'Neill liked a brawl and on the opening night of *All God's Chillun Got Wings* he was careful not to drink so he would be in shape if there were a fight. (He was disappointed when everything went so tamely!) In restaurants and bars after rehearsals and performances, Wolheim would outdrink O'Neill and entertain him with discussions of the work on the play.

Although Wolheim had not acted extensively or had much training and although he was very modest about his ability, he was quite certain about the appropriate approach to acting. He was a great admirer of Lionel Barrymore and said everything he knew about acting he had learned from him. Wolheim was always ready to discuss his acting approach with interviewers. In an interview in Toledo, he told Grace Wilson that he had come upon Barrymore looking old and exhausted and chastised him for not taking better care of himself. Barrymore pulled himself up and said he had just thought himself into that physical state for his role. Wilson asked Wolheim if he had studied types like Yank to prepare for the role and he promptly answered, "No, I studied it as every actor must do—subconsciously." He then discussed his theory that every man has all of the different human characteristics within himself, that he is a cross section of the human race. An actor must draw from within himself the characteristics he needs and think himself into exhibiting them. "Lionel Barrymore considers this a form of self-hypnosis and I agree. That's why an actor can forget his most intense pain while he is acting. He is, for the time being, someone else." In the same interview Wolheim exhibited his own sensitivity about his looks. He was asked if he had always been cast in roles like Yank and answered with a dreamy look, "The Prince Regent of England in 'The Fair Circassian'? I guess that's about as different a type from Yank as you can imagine."

Rehearsals progressed well, although it is unclear who actually did all the directing. O'Neill originally wanted a "Hopkins man" to direct, but he was on tour, so James Light, a member of the Provincetown Players, took over. However, some critics credited O'Neill with the direction. In his second review, Alexander Woolcott gave credit for it to Arthur Hopkins, although it was produced by the Provincetown Players. He said that Hopkins was "lurking around its rehearsals, with perhaps a proprietary interest." Following its success downtown, Hopkins took most of the cast and produced the play uptown. He replaced Mary Blair with Carlotta Monterey in the role of Mildred.

The play opened to terrific reviews for Wolheim, but many critics were baffled or irritated by the Expressionistic play. Lawrence Reamer wrote that Wolheim was "physically and artistically striking." One critic wrote, "What Gilpin was to *The Emperor Jones,* Louis Wolheim is to *The Hairy Ape.* As Yank Smith he bears the burden of the play. Physically suited for the part, he carries it through with a somber naturalism and the tragic force of one who is mid-way between man and beast and is rejected by both." Kenneth Macgowan wrote that "the theatrical success of *The Hairy Ape* is considerably strengthened by the illusion of brute force created by Louis Wolheim under the excellent direction of O'Neill himself." Not only the critics and audiences were awed by Wolheim's brute force. Mary Blair played the society girl who comes upon the stoker and faints from fear. She told an unidentified interviewer after Wolheim's death that "I was always a bit alarmed that he would let me have the shovel full in the face. I stood only about two feet from him in the boiler room. He seemed fierce, as if he were expressing a vast social resentment."

So popular and well known was the play that satires were written on it, including one performed by, of all people, Mae West. According to her biographer, she burlesqued the character, noting that "Yank was the very sort of brutish cave-man type Mae West favored as a foil to play against, onstage and off: in O'Neill's hands a somber and powerful archetype, and in hers a comic cartoon rendered with broad strokes." Backed by a chorus line and a black orchestra, she sang, "Eugene O'Neill, You've Put a Curse on Broadway" and bellowed "Yank-style" lines including, "She don me doit! Lemme up! I'll show her who's an ape."[29] Some combination: Mae West, Louis Wolheim, and Eugene O'Neill.

Following the success in New York, Wolheim toured the country in the play, and his file at Lincoln Center is filled with interviews given in many cities. Despite his success, he remained strangely modest about his performance. Tracy Hammond Lews quoted him as saying, "I don't measure up to the part and I know it as well as anyone else." He was described by Grace Wilson as "the most natural, unpretentious, untheatrical actor I ever met." Naturally, he was asked what he would play after *The Hairy Ape* because he seemed a hard type to cast. He told Wilson, "I am quite aware that plays like *The Hairy Ape* aren't written every day; and I'm going to take any old part that comes my way. By golly, you won't find me hanging around till I'm an old white-headed man saying 'You ought to have seen me, thirty years ago in *The Hairy Ape.*'" He was in a position strangely similar to Gilpin's: a great O'Neill role had brought him success, but he saw no great future as an actor. He told an unidentified writer, "I bet after *The Ape* is over I'll recede into the ranks of among those present." Still, he took everything philosophically, saying, "What the hell—anyone who is foolish enough to want to be an artist can damn well paint miniatures."

He was not condemned to miniature roles or to fading into the crowd. In 1924 he scored a huge success as a rough-talking soldier in Arthur Hopkins' production of *What Price Glory?* He and O'Neill remained on friendly terms but their paths were parted. In 1926 O'Neill wrote to Macgowan that he hoped for a revival of *The Hairy Ape* "with a chance of getting Wolly that late in the season."[30] Instead Wolheim returned to films where he was known as one of the best-liked players in Hollywood. He had an appealing personality, but was also liked for his generosity. While filming in Truckee, California, he once provided food for more than 200 men. This and other stories about him were widely reported and he was the delight of the cartoonists.

Fun for the cartoonists, however, was not so much fun for him. His appearance continued to bother him and he felt it limited his career. In Lew's article "Louis Wolheim's Nose Caused Much Trouble," it was reported that early in his career, at his mother's insistence, he had his nose fixed. Wishing to celebrate the success of the operation, he went to a saloon, got into a fight, and had his nose again flattened by a longshoreman. After his return to Hollywood he decided he would try another operation so that he could play a wider range of roles. All of the newspapers printed pictures or caricatures with the story. An article called "Kept Ugly by Contract" revealed that in 1927 United Artists brought an injunction to keep him from this "beautification" because his appearance was what they wanted when he signed the contract. So "he surrendered to his fate."

He didn't have long to enjoy the success that began with a role he didn't feel qualified to play in 1923. In 1931 he was cast as the wily newspaper editor in a film version of *The Front Page.* He went on an intense diet, collapsed, and was taken to the hospital. There he was found to have stomach cancer and died quite suddenly. His death saddened the country and the obituary notices praised him personally and noted his fame as Yank. As Grace Wilson had written years before, "He was a simple-hearted, modest-minded star who has been an actor only a few years, but who impresses you as having been very much of a man, always." O'Neill would probably have said the same thing. He refused to go see the film of *The Hairy Ape* with William Bendix in the lead. Writing to Theresa Helburn in 1944, he described the production as one of his most satisfying times in the theatre. "I remember Wolheim was practically perfect as Yank and was also a pal of mine. I don't want to have that memory spoiled."[31] Similarly, he wrote Hopkins that he would give the picture "a wide miss" because "my memories of Wolly in the original production are too close, and the play remains one of my favorites."[32]

Like Wolheim, Walter Huston found that success in an O'Neill role was the turning point in his career and, like Wolheim, he achieved it rather late. When he was in *Desire Under the Elms* at the age of forty, he had, as his biographer John Weld put it, "his first honest-to-God hit."[33] Huston was born in Toronto. He decided to try acting, but had little success at first. He was cast in a play with the great Richard Mansfield in 1902. In later years he told interviewers that he was fired after the first night for fluffing his three lines. He returned to school, worked as an engineer, and then turned to vaudeville for fifteen years. According to a clipping in the Huston file, he played drums, danced, sang, "and spent a lot of time thinking up mechanical effects. He patented a face painted on a piece of rubber, with strings attached behind to use in a trick sketch called 'Spooks.'" His chance to move to Broadway came when his sister, Margaret Carrington, backed Zona Gale's *Mr. Pitt*. (She was a wealthy widow who later married Robert Edmond Jones and was a voice coach to John Barrymore among others). In it he faced a great challenge: he had to interest the audience in a traveling pickle salesman so boring and dense that he causes his wife to run away with a saxophone player. The play only ran six weeks, but Huston was highly praised and his career on Broadway was launched. His next play, however, did not take him forward. As Weld stated, "It looked as if Walter would go on for the balance of his professional life playing good-natured simpletons."[34]

But fate had something else in store. Kenneth Macgowan, Robert Edmond Jones, and O'Neill were impressed by his work in *Mr. Pitt* and he was asked if he would be interested in playing the lead in *Desire Under the Elms*. In a letter to Huston years later, O'Neill remembered their first meeting at the Greenwich Village Theatre. He remembered Huston and his son John appearing in fancy attire, with fawn-colored hats and wearing spats. Ephraim

Cabot was a hard, penny-pinching, sweaty farmer, but, O'Neill said, "It flashed across my mind that you were born to play Cabot, the leading role. I said, 'I believe you'd be fine.'"[35] Huston read the script, then passed it on to his eighteen-year-old son. As John Huston remembered in his autobiography *An Open Book,* he told his father, "I think it is one of the greatest things I ever read."[36] His father said he thought so, too, and signed at $300 a week, a big salary to the producers, but a small salary compared to Huston's previous earnings.

The rehearsals are charmingly described by John Huston, who remembered O'Neill as a quiet man with a delicate appearance who sat with the actors and the director, Jones, around a table. He spoke in such a low voice when the actors asked him questions that it was hard to hear the answer. As the rehearsals progressed he sat in the orchestra and occasionally passed notes up to the stage.[37] With this close involvement in the rehearsals, naturally O'Neill came to know Walter Huston and liked him. Their friendship lasted through the years.

It is strange to consider the initial response to the play, which has become a classic and has often been revived with success on the professional and the amateur stage in America and abroad. An unidentified clipping headed "Huston Good in Bad Drama" summed up the response of many of the critics. This reviewer said that the play "leaves the spectator with no desire to again witness such a performance." Another wrote, "Even the most hardened of Mr. O'Neill's disciples last night shuddered at its honest terrors and were subdued." Yet another unidentified critic wrote that leaving an O'Neill play was a fine experience: "I leave his plays with a song on my lips, congratulating myself that my glooms are comparatively insignificant." Robert Benchley called the play a "terrific catastrophe." Other critics felt the play was salacious. The play was banned in England and was not allowed a production for sixteen years, at which time one critic wrote, "It is strong with the strength of over-ripe cheese [but] need everyone be quite so loutish?"

However, some of the critics praised the play and almost all praised Huston. A major critic, Stark Young, wrote that he was "everywhere trenchant, gaunt, fervid, harsh as he should be in the part. In his ability to cover his gradations, to express the natural and convincing emotion, and to convey the harsh, inarticulate life embodied in this extraordinary portrait that Eugene O'Neill has drawn, Mr. Huston showed his talent and proved to be the best possible choice for the role." Heyword Broun called Huston excellent, Percy Hammond said he was perfect, and another unidentified critic wrote that he played the old skinflint father to perfection but that it was impossible for anyone who cared about the theatre at all to approve of the play.

Huston had based his characterization on his grandfather, a hard Canadian farmer. He had not liked him, but the grandfather's character served him well for this role. A critic who, in the minority, described the play as a literary masterpiece, described Huston as "a heroic old monument." He gave a detailed description of the scene for which the actor received much praise, in which he sits in the bedroom and talks to his young wife. "He sits on the edge of the bed and recites in his cruel, Jehovan monotone the tale of his work and his wives." When he makes love to his new wife, he "lets fly with all the sensual similes of the 'Song of Songs' and they roll on his tongue on a thick mush of obscenity." Continuing his analysis of Huston's interpretation, he wrote, "He is cruel, greedy, sly, bullying, decent at nothing except building stone fences—and yet, in spite of everything that Mr. O'Neill has to hurl at him, [he is] the man of the play, the giant apologia."

In the Walter Huston file is a long piece by John Corbin written for the *New York Times* in which he analyzed the aspects of the forty-year-old Huston's portrayal of the seventy-five-year-old Cabot. In "Acting in O'Neill," he wrote that Huston could have played the role with "quirky, familiar touches" or with "clever mimicry" but that he "plays the underlying poetry and focuses less on the externals." He felt that Huston was the most successful actor so far to do all that was needed for an O'Neill character. He put his finger on some of the aspects of playwriting that presented a challenge to actors. Noting that Eugene O'Neill doesn't write realism in the usual sense and that the actor has a hard job, he defined the challenge: "The actor has so much actualistic matter on his hands that he must be convincing as realism, but at the same time he must evolve a creation that transcends realism or resemblance." In his opinion Huston was almost the quality "of the writing itself that he interprets. He has the same relation to actuality that Eugene O'Neill's treatment of the material has, the same state of mind and feeling." He, too, praised the bedroom scene with the young wife and noted details of Huston's dance at the party ("wildly, ragingly awry"), and of the "final frustrated moments of the play."

The production was a critical and financial triumph for Huston. The play was sold out every night, the production was moved to a bigger theatre uptown, Huston's salary was increased, and he was paid a percentage of the extra income. He was also given a contract for two films in Hollywood. Because of the content of the play and in response to complaints from the citizenry, New York Mayor James J. Walker appointed a committee to see the play and judge whether or not it was contributing to the delinquency of the public. The mayor himself, a great womanizer, was probably contributing more than any play ever could! (He was famous for having said that no woman was ever ruined by a book.) The committee decided the play was a work of art and should not be closed. The result of all this was an enormous amount of publicity and a greater demand for tickets in New York and on the road. However, O'Neill was angry over the fuss because it drew in audiences looking for risqué material who snickered at anything vaguely suggestive. But he was pleased with the production and grateful to Huston for his performance. He gave him a copy of the play inscribed with his thanks for "collaborating with him." Huston said he was flattered, but couldn't accept the compliment.[38]

Walter Huston was to work with O'Neill one more time, but not very successfully. When O'Neill was casting *The Fountain,* he wished he had a great romantic actor with his father's style and ability. He was hoping (as he so often was) to get John Barrymore for the swashbuckling hero. Then there was an effort to get the English actor Lionel Atwill, but O'Neill wrote to Agnes in July 1925 that he had been acting like a true ham (O'Neill's usual term for condemning actors). He said that he had had lunch with Huston, whom he liked better every time he saw him.[39] He ultimately decided to use him in the new play, but it was not a good decision. Neither Huston's manner nor voice were right for the role. Huston himself said that his performance did not help the play to be successful. He remembered how painful it was for him when Stark Young, so full of praise after *Desire*, came back after the play and sat and sadly watched Huston take off his make-up. When Huston questioned him, he gave the details of the negative review he would write for his column.[40]

While disappointed in the play's reception, O'Neill continued as an admirer of Huston. As the years went by they kept in touch. O'Neill normally felt that making films in Hollywood ruined a stage actor's technique and attitudes. Apparently, Huston and the Barrymores were exceptions. Writing to his agent in 1932, he said he hoped for a revival of *Desire Under the Elms* with Huston, "and that's worth waiting for!"[41] Writing to Theresa Helburn in 1938 he discussed the possibility of using Huston in one of the cycle plays in the future, saying that he and his wife had visited him in the summer and discussed the plays. "He's a fine actor in the right parts, a fine guy, and he has the right spirit."[42] Instead of acting in any other O'Neill play, Huston was in films, made a big stage success with Sinclair Lewis' *Dodsworth* in 1934 and another in the musical *Knickerbocker Holiday*. In this he sang "September Song," which was so popular that later he always sang it in curtain calls regardless of the play. Many theatregoers today know him from the role of the wonderful old codger hunting for gold with Humphrey Bogart in *Treasure of the Sierra Madre*. In 1948 both he and his son, the director, received Academy Awards for the film, the first time a father and son had won together. At his memorial service in 1950, Spencer Tracy fondly remembered Huston's work in O'Neill's plays.

The Huston connection with O'Neill did not end with Walter's death. In his autobiography, John described the importance to him of sitting in all the rehearsals for *Desire Under the Elms*. He was excited by watching the characters come to life, striking sparks, and seeing the play taking on "heroic proportions." He learned all the lines and felt the play had got into his bloodstream. "What I learned there during those weeks of rehearsal would serve me for the rest of my life. Not that I was aware of it at the time. I only knew that I was fascinated."[43] His fascination continued; after the premiere of *The Iceman Cometh,* O'Neill's first production for many years, he got into a shouting match with E. E. Cummings, who did not like the play. Writing in 1980, Huston said, "My feeling then and now is that if any play by any American will endure, it will be *The Iceman Cometh.* To this I might add *Long Day's Journey into Night.*"[44]

Because of John Huston's continuing admiration for O'Neill, he was very excited about the possibility of directing one of his plays. He had just directed *No Exit* in 1946 when Theresa Helburn called from the Theatre Guild to say she wanted to send him a copy of *A Moon for the Misbegotten* to see if he would be interested in directing it. He responded that he didn't have to read it, he wanted to do it. Later he had to call her back to say that Jack Warner wouldn't give him more time off and he had to return to Hollywood. He asked her to tell O'Neill how sorry he was but she said he was sitting there and Huston could tell him himself. So he summoned up his courage and told O'Neill what sitting in on the rehearsals of *Desire Under the Elms* and *The Fountain* had meant to him. O'Neill thanked him and said it meant a great deal to him to hear it.[45] This tribute came at a welcome time for O'Neill: the critics and the public, unlike Huston, had largely rejected *The Iceman Cometh.* It took many more years before John Huston's belief in the play was proved correct.

Strange Interlude is a play filled with ironies, and the production history and the relationship between O'Neill and Lynn Fontanne, the star, is equally ironic. The play became the most talked about theatrical event of its time and gave rise to many jokes about its length and subject matter. The fact that it was so long that it began at five-fifteen, breaking for dinner at seven-thirty and starting again at nine o'clock and ending shortly after eleven o'clock gave opportunity for many widely quoted witticisms. Robert Benchley quipped, "After all it's only an ordinary nine-act play." One of the reviews was headed "Take Before and After Eating." Restaurants in the area of the theatre did a big business: one offered a "Strange Interlude Sandwich" with six layers. Alexander Woolcott was credited as describing the play as "nine scenes and an epicene."

Alfred Lunt, the actor husband of Fontanne, had a sense of humor that could be barbed. He said of the play, the last in which he and his wife did not perform together, "If *Strange Interlude* had had two more acts, I could have sued Lynn for desertion." He generally referred to the play as a "six day bisexual race," mocking both the subject matter of the play and O'Neill's penchant for watching six-day bicycle races in Madison Square Garden. Naturally, news of this got back to O'Neill, who did not find Lunt's quips amusing.[46]

Lynn Fontanne was a highly successful, highly praised actress when she was cast in the role of Nina. Unlike many of the performers described above, she had moved very easily into theatre and into leading roles. At the age of twelve she was taken to audition for the great English actress Ellen Terry, who decided to give her lessons for two years. She was brought from England to America by Laurette Taylor, who served as her mentor for several years. She appeared in leading roles in *The Guardsman* by Ferenc Molnar, Franz Werfel's *Goat Song,* and George Bernard Shaw's *Pygmalion, Arms and the Man,* and *The Doctor's Dilemma.* Her first encounter with O'Neill was not pleasing. George Tyler had brought Lunt from vaudeville to Broadway stardom with the play *Clarence* and he hoped to do the same for Fontanne. He cast her in *Chris Christopherson* but soon realized the role of the woman was not as strong as that of the father and that the play needed a great deal of work. Fontanne, according to her biographer Jared Brown, wrote to Lunt complaining that the play was weak.[47] She must also have known that O'Neill had not been satisfied when she was cast, in part because he believed an American woman was needed for the role. Although the play, not the acting, was blamed for its failure, there were negative criticisms of her Anna, so Fontanne was very displeased with the entire event. Even more annoying must have been the fact that when Tyler did find the right vehicle to bring her to stardom, *Dulcy,* it was somewhat overshadowed by the great success of Pauline Lord in the role of Anna in O'Neill's Pulitzer Prize winning rewrite in the same year.

Fontanne was appearing with Lunt in Shaw's comedy *The Doctor's Dilemma.* It was a tremendous success for the Theatre Guild both in the United States and London. Together they dined with

Shaw, whom they found charming. Brown reports that Fontanne said, "I could have fallen in love with him at once."[48] She was offered the role of Nina written by a playwright she did not find charming. Not only that, she was far from first choice for O'Neill or the Theatre Guild. Their first choice was Katharine Cornell, who said no. O'Neill first suggested Ann Harding, who had been so successful with the Provincetown Players in Glaspell's *Inheritors*. He then agreed that Alice Brady would be good, but she turned down the role of such an unattractive woman, to her unending regret. One by one, other actresses turned down the role and finally the Theatre Guild, feeling a little desperate, tried to get Fontanne to play it. According to Brown, she and Lunt were unimpressed by the script, but Lunt urged her to take it because it would be a big event even if it was a failure. For that reason, apparently, she accepted and he agreed to play in O'Neill's *Marco Millions* at the same time.[49] They were both still appearing in the Shaw play when rehearsals began. O'Neill agreed to the casting but wrote to Agnes that although Fontanne would be adequate, she would be far from the Nina he had created.[50]

When rehearsals began, trouble began. Because of the length of the play Actors' Equity allowed seven weeks of rehearsal. Brown writes that Fontanne found the rehearsals long and tedious and that her dislike of the play increased. She said she respected authors, but that she knew what would "go" and this wouldn't. She asked O'Neill to cut more lines and he felt he had cut enough. So, she said later, without telling anyone, she "cut, cut, cut, and nobody ever realized it." It's doubtful that nobody realized it. Years later she and Lunt still expressed the opinion that the play was no good, even though it was a great hit for her. Lunt said it was "utterly dated, quite unreadable."[51] Nevertheless, the rehearsals, under Philip Moeller's direction, moved well, and O'Neill, possibly in an attempt to patch things up with Fontanne, told her, "You are so exactly right for the part that it might have been written for you."[52]

At this point something very unpleasant occurred: someone in the cast gave the theatre critic for the *World*, Alexander Woolcott, a copy of the play before the opening and he, unethically, wrote a fiercely negative review for *Vanity Fair*, expressing his view that it was the *Abie's Irish Rose* of the psuedo-intelligensia.

Brown says it was probably Fontanne who gave the script to the critic. The Theatre Guild and O'Neill were outraged (possibly at Fontanne as well as Woolcott) and insisted that he be replaced as reviewer for the opening. Ironically, his replacement gave it one of the biggest raves.[53]

Despite her dislike for the play, Fontanne wanted to do her best, being a true professional and a perfectionist. She based her approach on something, as she said many times in interviews, told to her by Ellen Terry. She did not simply think of the words, but of the meaning behind the words. Fontanne was unlike Method actors. She always began by learning all of the text, then rehearsing, and then moving deeper into the role. In her article "Thoughts on Acting" she said that she always rehearsed twelve hours a day, going over the material again at night that had been done in the day. As she did she began to know the character; "I sink deeper and deeper into her, discovering things and traits about her I did not know existed when I began to rehearse. This is a process that continues all during the run of the play, even after it has opened."[54] S. N. Behrman often worked with the Lunts and described with amusement their passion for perfecting scenes through rehearsal. On one occasion they stopped on a busy street to rehearse a scene, forgetting where they were and drawing a crowd of baffled onlookers.[55] During the run of *Strange Interlude,* Noel Coward, the lifelong friend of the Lunts, came to a performance and slightly criticized something in the seventh act. Fontanne close-questioned him and then made him come again to see if she had got it right. Brown says that Coward then told everyone, "I had to sit through the whole boring thing from the beginning. And of course she had the seventh act down perfectly."[56]

The views of the Lunts and their friends about the play were not shared by the public or the critics. The play was an overwhelming hit, running through the hot summer in an un-airconditioned theatre. Critic Dudley Nichols, the replacement for Woolcott, used the phrase "The most important event in the present era of the American theatre." Like most critics, he gave the focus of attention to Fontanne and the play. He said that she was required to give the most an actress can give, "and she gave to the brim at every demand.

She was possessed of an inward power which broke through every restraint as radium shoots its glimmering particles through everything that would contain it." The critic for the *Wall Street News* gave details of her acting, indicating that she passed through moods of "beauty, despair, love, hate, arid and rich tragedy." He said she poured forth a profusion of gifts as "she passes from young womanhood to gray hairs before your eyes. Though the phrase is worn stale with misuse, here is one time when it is possible to say that an actress literally lives the part." Percy Hammond wrote of the difficulty of the part: "Nina's neurotic soul and person [is] madly tossed in a nervous whirlpool of faithfulness and unfidelity." He said that O'Neill explored every corner of her character and that "if he had searched the stage over from Bernhardt to Elsie Fergusson, he could not have found an actress so competent to play Nina Leeds as Miss Fontanne is." He concluded by saying that watching her act, you forget the accomplishments of "all the other First Actresses from Duse to Miss Madge Kennedy." Another critic said the role placed Fontanne among those "whose names are at the top of the rosters of great living players." He, too, noted the difficulty of the role in which she is present in each of the nine long acts. "Her emotional range, her subtlety, her vitality and her lovely presence must have realized the author's character to his entire satisfaction." Several reviewers noted that the characters were the first to be fully developed in a Freudian sense and that the modern theatre had been longing for such a play.

The great success of the play, the fact of its winning the Pulitzer Prize, and the great praise Fontanne received could not overcome her dislike of the play or, seemingly, of O'Neill himself. The longer it ran, the longer she was separated from Alfred Lunt, who was in O'Neill's less successful play *Marco Millions*. Here was another irony: the Theatre Guild initially supposed that Lunt's play would be the big success and that Fontanne's would only bring the organization prestige.

The reverse was true. One of the great disappointments in the history of O'Neill plays is *Marco Millions*. It is a curious mixture of comedy and poignancy, but it would seem possible that a good director with a good cast could create a delightful evening in the theatre. The production directed by Rouben Mamoulian (who had recently been so successful with *Porgy*) is remembered as a major disaster. In fact, it was a modest success. Gilbert Gabriel mentioned it in passing while reviewing *Strange Interlude* and said that while it was not as big a success, it was drawing steadier and larger audiences than anything the Guild had ever done before and that there was talk of adding matinees. For the critics, however, the play was a disappointment. Perhaps expectations were too great: there was a highly successful director, designs by the creative Lee Simonson, and a cast in which the wonderful Alfred Lunt was supported by excellent actors including Morris Carnovsky.

The play opened eleven days before *Strange Interlude*. Before rehearsals began O'Neill had agreed to cuts and alterations in the text, which were made for economic reasons. Although he accepted the changes, he was sorry that he couldn't get a full production of the play as he envisioned it. Brown writes that economic considerations held Mamoulian back, too. The play is a satire on an uninspired and uninspiring businessman, Marco Polo, who thinks only of profit. The director thought it would be fun to have Lunt walk off the stage at the end of the play, up the aisle, and step into a waiting limousine outside. "The effect was intended to suggest that Marco Polo was just another 'tired businessman.'"[57] Although some critics praised the production and Lunt's performance, many felt the whole evening was tiresome or even foolish. Brown writes that even Alexander Woolcott, a great admirer of both Lunt and Fontanne, felt that his performance in the O'Neill play was less effective than his performances in the past. Woolcott wrote that Lunt seemed very tired, and seemed to pause between each speech in his performance: "it was marked by an almost hypnotic weariness, each line of the long role parting from him as if, although he was quite certain what the next might be, he had not quite decided whether to buck up and say it or just to curl up there on the Guild stage and take a good, long nap."[58] Lunt's voice was worn out and Fontanne was so concerned that she objected to him performing in *Volpone*, telling the Theatre Guild she had a letter from a doctor saying his health was in danger.[59]

It is tantalizing to wonder what success the play might have had given a full production with a star who was excited about the play. Following the two productions the Lunts never performed in O'Neill again. The Theatre Guild, however, was to continue with other successful productions of his plays in the future. A major result of the productions was to cause Lunt and Fontanne, or the Lunts, as they were nearly always called, to demand that the Theatre Guild give them contracts in which it was clear that they would always co-star and never perform separately. This continued throughout their career as they performed in *Idiot's Delight* and other great successes. They never again performed apart on the stage and only in 1966 did she appear separately on television in *Anastasia*.

Earle Larimore performed with Fontanne in *Strange Interlude* and was praised for his interpretation of Sam Evans. Like so many actors who never became big stars, his name is nearly forgotten now. He was an actor O'Neill liked very much and who performed in many of his plays. The Lunts liked him, too, and he had performed with success in their production of *The Doctor's Dilemma*. He made his acting debut in 1925. He soon began acting in the prestigious productions of the Theatre Guild, appearing in Behrman's *The Second Man*, Howard's *The Silver Cord* and *Mourning Becomes Electra*, Behrman's *Biography* with the charming Ina Claire, and in O'Neill's *Days Without End*.

Carl Van Vechten is quoted by the Gelbs as saying that Larimore was one of the few actors O'Neill liked "because he wasn't a star."[60] Actually, O'Neill may have liked him because he didn't behave like a star. They became acquainted and got on well during the rehearsals for *Strange Interlude*.

Critics and O'Neill liked Larimore's work in that play. Brooks Atkinson paired him with Fontanne in having the technique appropriate for the play, saying that they showed "admirable distinction and resourcefulness. More than any of the others they have mastered the technique of this strange play; without upsetting the flow of drama they contrive to give their 'asides' a true value. Meanwhile they describe two characters completely. One cannot speak too highly of their skill." Larimore continued to please the critics, especially in *Mourning Becomes Electra* in 1931. Noting that he was an established actor, Robert Garland said that he was "at his skillful best." He was regarded as a modern actor who approached a role, as Brooks Atkinson noted, "from the inside with great resource, elasticity, and understanding." Arthur Pollock wrote, "Earle Larimore is the tortured son, bringing all his fine feeling to the role." Writing about the Theatre Guild years later, Lawrence Langner wrote, "Earle Larimore's Orin was so flawless that you felt Orin in person was appearing on the stage."[61]

The Gelbs quote Selena Royle, the actor's wife, saying of O'Neill, "I never remember his saying anything about Larry to me, but I believe that Larry was his favorite actor. I know he realized that Larry had much the same problem about alcohol that he himself had conquered, but it was not his way to advise or caution. Gene gave Larry several books and bound proofs of his plays, some of which had his corrections written down in longhand, and all of which had affectionate dedications." Because of the affection both Carlotta and Eugene O'Neill had for Larimore, they were very welcoming and gracious when all four met for tea.[62]

These occasions occurred with frequency because Selena Royle was cast opposite her husband in O'Neill's play *Days Without End*. In his clever, topical comedy *Accent on Youth*, Samson Raphaelson portrays a playwright who writes and presents a play that turns out to be a nice success. He remarks, "You know, I never thought that play would be just an ordinary success. I thought it would be a great hit—like an O'Neill play. Or else a terrible disaster—like an O'Neill play."[63] In 1934, *Days Without End* was an example of the latter. Despite fine acting by Larimore (whose wife was less successful), direction by Philip Moeller, and handsome settings by Lee Simonson, the play was a critical failure and only ran as long as necessary for the Theatre Guild subscribers to see it.

Larimore's work with Moeller and the Theatre Guild continued, and in the 1940s he toured with Eva Le Gallienne's company. However, he suffered bad health and turned to playing in soap operas on the radio. His marriage had collapsed, possibly because of his drinking problems. His last work with and for O'Neill came when he was an understudy for *The Iceman Cometh* and performed in it on the road. He later performed in *A Moon for the Misbegotten*, which the Theatre Guild toured but did not bring in to New York.

He died at the early age of forty-eight in 1947. His career was filled with successes in important plays, but many critics felt he reached his height in *Mourning Becomes Electra*. An unidentified critic wrote, "Earle Larimore reaches the highest point in his career in the acting of Orin, a constantly emotional role in which he is entirely free from the falsity of average theatrical neuroticism and alert in conveying the tortured relationships which swirl around him."

The cast of *Mourning Becomes Electra* was excellent throughout and was headed by three superb performers. As Arthur Ruhl wrote in his review, "The burden of playing falls on Miss Nazimova, Miss Alice Brady, and Earle Larimore and they all, Miss Brady in particular, surpass themselves." Casting the roles they played was not very difficult. The Theatre Guild and O'Neill were in agreement on Larimore and Nazimova. O'Neill was hoping to get Ann Harding for Lavinia, having failed to get her for *Strange Interlude*. Although she was unable to play in *Strange Interlude* on Broadway, she had performed the role of Nina on tour. Once again, she was unavailable for the new O'Neill play. The Gelbs quote her as saying that, unable to get a release from films to play the role, "I tried to break my contract—but that proved hopeless, as well. It is the major tragedy of my professional life that I was deprived of that great opportunity."[64] Alice Brady was still regretting the fact that she had turned down the role of Nina because she thought the audience would find the character unsympathetic. The Theatre Guild offered her the role and, to her producer father's delight, she accepted it.

Brady was born in 1892 and made her stage debut in 1909, having studied voice at the Boston Conservatory of Music. Her father was an important Broadway producer who had been a friend of O'Neill's father. O'Neill wrote to Agnes that "She is a good scout but rather a rough neck, a real daughter of her eminent father, Bill."[65] Because of the connection and because of the fact that he admired her acting and that they both shared an enthusiasm for dogs, O'Neill was very friendly toward Brady during rehearsals. He may have also been moved by the circumstances of her career to date. She had looks, talent, and the connections of her famous father, but she didn't seem to have much luck. Many supporters predicted that she would be a star in her next role, but she was in at least a dozen failures. She acted in silent films and by 1923 had been in thirty-two. Her father tried to assist her in becoming a stage success, although he had earlier tried to stop her from becoming an actress by sending her to a convent. In addition to the troubles provided by the weak plays she was in, she had brittle bones and often broke a finger or an arm. After she played Lavinia, Wilella Waldorf wrote a long article surveying her career, beginning by saying, "After a staggering series of negative roles in negative plays, Alice Brady finally found her way into a part." Waldorf said that the announcement that Brady would play the role caused little excitement, but that the opening caused all the critics to praise her, one saying she was "like the young Siddons rising to her opportunity."

Although the rehearsals went smoothly, the role was very difficult for Brady. O'Neill and his wife Carlotta attended all seven weeks of rehearsals. He was constantly working with Philip Moeller to cut and strengthen the script. Therefore, Brady, who had the longest role, was particularly challenged just by learning the words. She was terribly nervous before the opening because she was afraid she might say some of the old lines or leave out some of the new ones. Not surprisingly, she and Nazimova (such different types) did not like each other. That didn't seem to cause problems, but rather to enhance the hatred between their characters in performance.

The play opened on October 27, 1931, at four o'clock so the critics would be able to make their deadlines. Later, the play opened at five o'clock, allowed a dinner break, resumed and played until nearly midnight. Brady was praised for many qualities, but particularly for her voice. Brooks Atkinson wrote, "Miss Brady as Lavinia has one of the longest parts ever written. None of her neurotic dramatics in the past has prepared us for the demoniac splendour of her Lavinia. She speaks in an ominous full voice. Lavinia has recreated Miss Brady into a majestic actress." Percy Hammond spoke of her as "brooding and majestic . . . stark, glacial, vengeful and dominating, even when she displays the mannerisms of a spinster schoolmarm." Arthur Pollock described her as playing with "austere beauty." John Mason Brown said that she gave the kind of performance her admirers had been waiting for so long. "It is controlled. It has the force of the true Electra and it is sustained throughout as a long and severe an actor's test as any player has been called upon to meet. The moments when she stands dressed in black before the black depths of Mr. [Robert Edmond] Jones' doorways are moments that no one can forget who has felt their thrill." In fact, the reviews were the sort that few actresses ever receive in a lifetime, and that Brady had been waiting for through many years and many plays. Arthur Ruhl gave a long description that gives details of the performance, particularly the dominating quality of the actress. He remembered "the stony mask of implacable hatred, the coldly passionate driving force of an unconquerable will. But what a will! What an air of defying gods and men, yielding to no restraining force, earthly or unearthly, whatsoever that would balk her purposes." Again, he noted the importance of her well-trained, beautiful voice, which enabled her to move through the long role with no strain: "Above all, what a voice!—the voice, the cold relentlessness of that pallid mask, the air of clutching all those about her in the steely fingers of her purpose, had that just-rightness which comes only at the rarest intervals in the theatre."

That "just-rightness" characterized the whole performance. O'Neill's play, directed by Philip Moeller, with stunning scene designs by Jones, and with the marvelous cast, created an effect that people would remember years later. As an unidentified critic wrote, "In the moment when Lavinia, in black, stands framed between the white pillars of the House of Mannon, the sunset dying at her feet, the course of passion run—in that moment, playwright, performer, and artist [Jones] came together in a superb conclusion that belongs as completely and solely to the theatre as Mr. O'Neill himself." Brooks Atkinson related the powerful impact of the whole play, but especially the performance of Brady on the mind—the unforgettable quality of it all. He and other critics moved Brady from that position of actress-trying-to-make-it to top-rank star. In his second review of the play he wrote that Brady was the "spearhead of the whole," playing with a force difficult to describe. "To say that it is the best performance she has given is no faint praise, but it is too faint. It is one of the finest performances any contemporary actress has given in any role. At times it is breath taking, at times frightening. I shall never forget one appearance of hers, in black against the blackness of an empty room, white hands, white implacable face."

Unforgettable, indeed. Although Brady went on to other roles on the stage, when she died, she was chiefly remembered for Lavinia. She achieved another great peak in her film career in 1938 when she won the Academy Award for best supporting actress for the film *In Old Chicago*. She was also an excellent comedienne as is clear in her delightful performance as the giddy mother in *My Man Godfrey*. When she was in *Go West Young Man* (1936) with Mae West, the sultry actress found her too much competition, so she cut down Brady's role. Brady did not have long to enjoy her triumphs. She died in 1939 at the age of 46, after thirty years in show business.

Alla Nazimova had an entirely different sort of career. She was born in Yalta, Russia, in 1879. She had extensive training on the violin, studied in Switzerland, and was trained for theatre by Nemerovich-Danchenko and Stanislavsky. After acting in stock companies in Russia, she acted the lead in Ibsen's *Ghosts* in St. Petersburg. She toured to England and Germany and then came to the United States in 1906, performing in Russian. She was such a sensational success that Lee Shubert offered her a weekly salary of $100, English lessons, and twenty percent of the profits for her forthcoming performances in English. She worked with a tutor for three hours a day, six days a week. She captivated audiences with her Hedda Gabler in 1906 and later revived the role. She was obviously capable of playing many different types of characters, but both onstage and in films she was often cast as a vamp. She made a fortune, which she spent on lavish homes and a luxurious lifestyle. Her biographer, Gavin Lambert, quotes her as saying, "When one is a star, one lives like a star."[66] In 1918 she performed in one of the great highlights of the American theatre, an Ibsen season directed by Arthur Hopkins. She played Hedda Gabler, Nora, and, surprisingly, fourteen-year-old Hedwig in *The Wild Duck*. Pauline Lord greatly admired Nazimova in these roles and Nazimova praised Lord for her performance in *Spellbound*. *Theatre Magazine* chose Nazimova for the prestigious Actress of the Year Award for the Ibsen season. She played in more films, some of which Shaw saw, prompting him to suggest that the Theatre Guild cast her as his Saint Joan. But Lawrence Langner was doubtful about the bad habits she had picked up in film acting. He changed his mind after seeing her perform in Chekhov with Eva Le Gallienne's Civic Repertory Company and hired her to act in the Theatre Guild's production of *A Month in the Country.* Lambert says that she was initially disappointed with *Mourning Becomes Electra,* but reread it and decided to accept the role of Christine.[67]

As a young man, O'Neill had been enchanted by Nazimova when he saw her as Hedda Gabler in 1907. He often told people that he had seen it ten times and that this performance of Ibsen had opened his eyes to the possibilities of modern drama. For him, Nazimova had both the qualities he admired in the old school of actors (represented by his father) and the newer actors like Larimore who "acted from the inside," playing the psychological subtleties of the character. Lambert quotes her views about acting: "The theatre is bigger than life. Reality, yes! But *real* reality is dull—it has no technique. It belongs in the kitchen, in the laundry. We must give [the] *illusion* of reality by good acting. Otherwise, stay in the kitchen, stay in the laundry. But tell me, why are so many young actors *afraid* to act?"[68]

Lunching with her before rehearsals began, O'Neill told her how much he had enjoyed her as Hedda. He did not mention the concerns he had expressed in a telegram to Theresa Helburn: "WOULD BE GRAND IF CAN BE DIRECTED TO ACT AS SHE DID IN FIRST IBSEN PRODUCTIONS AND CUT OUT HAM MANNERISMS ACQUIRED LATER." This is often interpreted as another snide crack at actors, but, in fact, as early as 1914 Nazimova was criticized for grimacing and posturing, which disqualified her "for any sort of play in which realism was an important element." By 1920 she was widely criticized for self-parody and overacting.[69]

Under Moeller's direction Nazimova was at her best, which reassured the playwright. During rehearsals he was very cordial and, in fact, acceded to her wishes on many occasions. According to Lambert, after O'Neill had made many cuts during the rehearsals, Nazimova suggested further changes, which he made for the performance (not for the published text). For example, she was jealous of Brady because her role continued after she, as Christine, had killed herself. She managed to upstage Brady at the end of Part Two by persuading O'Neill that she should not be in a dead faint on the floor, but should rise "on one arm, not yet fully conscious, staring before her dazedly," and then call on her lover for help, saying, "Adam! I'm afraid! Adam! . . ."[70]

Nazimova was a very well-educated woman with intelligence as well as charm and beauty. Her performance as Christine was not something that surprised critics, but that reinforced their opinion that she was a great actress capable of performing the great roles. She was famous for her supple and theatrical movement and critics used the term "plastic," making a comparison to a beautiful piece of sculpture. Brooks Atkinson wrote in his first review, "she gives a performance of haunting beauty, rich in variety, plastic, eloquent, and imaginatively transcendent." Arthur Pollock captured the essence of what impressed O'Neill: "Alla Nazimova plays the mother with that plastic intelligence which, mistress of a personality as plastic, makes her a precious actress these days." Robert Garland noted that "Madame Nazimova's accent gets thicker the longer she is in America." Nevertheless, he found her "plastic and glamorous, a theatrical thing to see." John Hutchens wrote, "Alla Nazimova's Christine is a sinister and deeply realized creation, all her fine technical resourcefulness responding flawlessly to the role." Several critics pointed to the challenge of the variety of moods and motivations O'Neill created in Christine, his modern counterpart of Clytemnestra. In his second review, Atkinson wrote that her performance was more varied than Brady's "as the part necessitates [and is] one of high artistry. Hers is a moving, subtle, marvelously complete portrait of the mother-murderess, lover, tortured victim of hatred and remorse, mother who schemes even while she caresses her son." Arthur Ruhl, too, compared the challenges each of the actresses faced with their contrasting roles. He said that Nazimova played a possessive mistress, a reluctant wife, a loving mother to the "more than normal filial quality of her son," and that she did it all with "the virtuosity, the flexible magnetism and persuasiveness of the accomplished artist." Percy Hammond described one of the great theatrical moments of which Nazimova was capable: "Caught in the complicated trap of her destiny she shoots herself after a moment or two of irresistible histrionics. I shall not forget what she did to my emotions last evening as she walked up the steps . . . defeated, desperate, and planning to blow her brains out: the theatre's most subtly effective climax as far as I know." Greta Garbo was so impressed by Nazimova's performance that she came to see it several times. According to Lambert, she "sneaked in and out of the theatre through a side door opened by someone from the Guild's publicity office."[71]

The reviews excited audiences and they poured in to see the lengthy play, willing to pay $6.60, which was $2.20 higher than the next highest ticket price, for the Ziegfeld Follies. O'Neill, the play, the performers—all were the talk of the town. Nazimova was asked to write comments about the play for *The Modern Thinker and Author's Review*. She said that O'Neill's trilogy was hard on the actors, but fascinating because the characters are "mysterious! They are half mask, half character."[72]

Lambert suggests that there was a great deal that was mysterious about Nazimova, perhaps even to herself. As a lesbian, for the latter part of her life, Nazimova was forced to wear a mask, especially in 1930 when "people began to speculate" about her long relationship with a young woman.[73] Her relationships with men and women and her professional choices were often incomprehensible. Although she played some successful stage roles after Christine, notably in *The Good Earth* and *Ghosts,* in the late 1930s she returned to Hollywood where she was no longer the star in the films she made. She was forced to sell her Long Island home and lived in an apartment in the Garden of Alla, her former mansion that was now operated as a hotel. Her fame was almost totally eclipsed. Her goddaughter was Nancy Davis (later Reagan). Seeing Nazimova in the small apartment writing her memoirs, she thought, "How terrible it must be for her after all that fame and glamour." An interview shortly before her death quotes her as saying, "I've reached the heights but it's been a puny success. I could have done so much more."[74] Although she wasted much of her great talent on inferior plays and films, she will always be remembered for her performances in Ibsen and in *Mourning Becomes Electra*.

For O'Neill the play brought the pleasure of a successful production, particularly as far as Larimore's acting was concerned.

He wrote to Dudley Nichols that that second cast for the tour was quite good, though of course not up to Nazimova and Larimore, "whom I think has done the finest work of them all."[75] However, after the production was over O'Neill gave the impression that he had not liked the performances of the two women. The Gelbs quote an interview in which he said, "Alice Brady and Alla Nazimova gave wonderful performances in *Mourning Becomes Electra,* but they did not carry out my conception at all. I saw a different play from the one I thought I had written." Carlotta explained his statement to the Gelbs. She said that as the rehearsals progressed, he became "fascinated by the characterizations of the two women." But she noted that they were not what he had imagined when he created the French and Dutch Christine and the New England Lavinia.[76] Actually, it isn't unusual for a playwright (or a director) to admire an actor's performance without thinking the actor fulfills his/her conception of the role.

An actor who fulfilled O'Neill's idea of a role was, rather surprisingly, George M. Cohan. The announcement that Cohan was to perform for the Theatre Guild was a big shock; that he was to perform in a play by Eugene O'Neill was an even bigger shock. In fact, the whole idea seemed somewhat preposterous. How would the grave and earnest tragic writer put up with the shenanigans and ego of the old actor with old-fashioned outlooks, seemingly wedded to the melodramas and slight farces of the past? As techniques in theatre had changed, Cohan had not. When the lighting designer Abe Feder introduced a new method of stage lighting into rehearsals, Cohan famously declared, "My mother had a spotlight, my father had a spotlight, and *I* will have a spotlight." (This was as often quoted as his curtain speech of thanks using the same phrasing.) An unidentified clipping observed with wonder that Cohan had come into the kingdom of the Emperor Jones, that it would be his first appearance in something he had not at least partially written, and, since he would not sing or dance, it would be a Strange Interlude in his career.

In fact, it was. At the age of fifty-five Cohan had spent most of his life on the stage. As a child he toured in vaudeville with his parents. By the time he was fifteen, he was writing material, and he later became famous in plays he wrote, starred in, and produced with Sam Harris. In fact, he had total control of the casting and the production elements. Famous for his eccentric dancing and his broad comedy, he was a crowd pleaser and became known as the Yankee Doodle Dandy born on the Fourth of July—the title of a famous song he sang in *Little Johnny Jones* in 1904. (That he actually was born on July 3 was finessed.) Throughout the teens and '20s he retired from the theatre about ten times, but some idea for a play always lured him back. In the '20s, however, his plays seemed to find less favor. By the time of *Ah, Wilderness!* he seemed definitely out of critical favor. His biographer, John McCabe, wrote, "If the critics were right and his plays were either stunts or warmed-up melodramas, it might well be that his last retirement should be his last."[77] However, Theresa Helburn of the Theatre Guild sent him *Ah, Wilderness!* to read. In fact, this was no bolt from the blue. The Theatre Guild had wanted to get Cohan to act for some time and had offered him *Marco Millions* before offering it to Lunt (which probably piqued Lunt). Cohan didn't care for that role, however. When he read the new play, he called back to say it was magnificent. One thing that may have influenced him (and the Theatre Guild in offering the role) was the fact that the play is set on the Fourth of July. He was also happy about the billing they offered him: it was the first time the Theatre Guild put an actor's name in lights at the top of the marquee. But as McCabe writes, there was concern about the rehearsal and production process. Cohan, the star, known as the man "who owned Broadway," was to be directed by another person, work with actors he had not cast, and speak lines he had not written and could not rewrite to get bigger laughs for himself.[78]

The public saw him only as a broad comic actor always ready to do an encore, a happy-go-lucky guy, but Don Wilmeth characterizes him as "a complex and lonely man, rarely popular with critics and something of an outcast to his fellow performers when in 1919 he refused to support the establishment of an actors' union."[79] He perceived in O'Neill's play the opportunity to do something of real worth in the theatre. The Cohan file at Lincoln Center contains a surprising article called "The American Way," which he wrote in 1920. In this he said that he had always felt that the play was more important than the actor, "although that is not the popular opinion of me." He said that he had written many plays and stories, "but to my mind they have been negligible as contributions to the American drama—yet some of the worst made a fortune." He believed that American playwriting up to that point had been smothered with tricks. Responding to the current urge to clean up theatre, he said he agreed that offensive plays should be removed—but that he meant plays that offended one's intelligence. He felt that serious playwrights insulted the intelligence by preaching or writing poor literature. He denied the popular maxim that the public doesn't want literature in the theatre, and said that Eugene O'Neill's *Beyond the Horizon* was proof that he was right. Noting that the scene between the two brothers was one of the finest things in the American theatre, he said, "It reads as well as it acts which is the fair test of dramatic literature."

People were amazed that Cohan, "the optimistic yea-sayer" (as McCabe describes him), was a fan of O'Neill's plays. In an article headed "Cohan to Play Guild Lead in O'Neill Comedy," the writer expressed surprise about Cohan's response to the work. Cohan told him that he had "shouted praises" for *Beyond the Horizon* so much that people thought he had a part in it, "So it's a kind of triumph for me to see this guy [O'Neill] become the modern Shakespeare." The article said that Cohan talked banter about everything except the play, over which he "waxed serious . . . almost pious." The actor said, "It's a study in human nature, I guess you would call it a comedy, but it's got a tragic theme—no . . . it's got a serious note in it." Cohan was personally touched by the central relationship between the father and son, according to McCabe, and based the characterization of Nat Miller on his own father, Jerry Cohan, "the warmly stern gentleman of the old school."[80]

His attitude toward *Ah, Wilderness!* must have influenced his demeanor in rehearsals. Apparently, as McCabe describes the process, they were models of order. Cohan took direction, was gracious to the ladies in the cast, sent them flowers like the old-fashioned gentleman he was, sat patiently on an old pile of canvas while scenes were rehearsed in which he didn't appear, and revealed inexhaustible patience. O'Neill liked him because he was Irish, he represented the traditions of his father's time, and he was a thorough professional. Writing later, O'Neill dismissed an actress as a ham who would not "play the game like Cohan."[81] In another letter he expressed concern that the Theatre Guild must be sure to "sew up" Cohan for the road tour.[82]

But it remained to be seen what the critics would make of Cohan in O'Neill. In the event, they thought he was startlingly, surprisingly wonderful when the play opened in 1933. Bernard J. Quinn called it "the presentation that amazed the theatrical world." Gilbert W. Gabriel sounded the motif, writing, "George M. Cohan presents the Guild with the best performance most of us have ever seen him give." Walter Winchell wrote that he triumphed in the role and spoke of the charm, tenderness, and comfort the evening offered." Percy Hammond said that there were few dramas in which one would see subtler acting than that of Cohan, and John Mason Brown said Cohan surpassed himself, giving a performance that was reason enough to see the delightful play.

Edith Isaacs wrote a long article about the play and Cohan's performance for *Theatre Arts*, emphasizing the difference between the "clear line and the sharp active rhythm which have been the familiar marks of his stage personality" and the underplayed, gentle quality of his Nat Miller. He spoke softly, sometimes through his nose or out of the corner of his mouth, "yet his sense of projection is so accurate that, to the last seat in the house, every syllable he speaks comes more clearly, and more beautifully, than most players' shouts." She said that he gave half-gestures and movements, which the audience completed in their minds because they were unconsciously adding their own emphasis to his, "joining him in the acting as in the idea." She said that the role O'Neill created is in fact an easy part to play, "but what Mr. Cohan does to it is a lesson in the art of acting."[83]

People of all different types responded to the play and to Cohan's performance. Alexander Woolcott, no longer reviewing, sent a telegram saying, "THIS IS A BURST OF APPLAUSE FROM AN AGED PLAYGOER WHO WAS DEEPLY MOVED BY YOUR PERFORMANCE TONIGHT." The young J. D. Salinger saw the play and remembered, "He was perfection in it. He'd apparently put his mind to it, as well as everything else he had, and out came the first unstagey acting I think I ever saw on the stage. A real mind working. He was wonderfully clever and talented, too, of course, but he also had a mind, no less than somebody like Paul Scofield has one. Impossible to forget him in that."[84]

Brooks Atkinson gave the performance close analysis, noting the change in acting style: "Mr. Cohan gives the ripest, finest, performance in his career, suggesting, as in the case of Mr. O'Neill [and the comedy] that his past achievements are no touchstone of the qualities he has never exploited." He continued by saying that the term "splendid" was exact, but was not enthusiastic enough for the kindliness and wisdom of the acting. "He is quizzical in the style to which we are all accustomed from him, but the jaunty mannerism and the mugging have disappeared. For the fact is that 'Ah, Wilderness!' has dipped deeper into Mr. Cohan's gifts and personal character than any of the antics he has written for himself. Ironic as it may sound, it has taken Eugene O'Neill to show us how fine an actor George M. Cohan is."

Cohan certainly enjoyed the experience, greeting guests in his dressing room, giving each other "drinking lessons," and generally enjoying life, especially on Saturday nights when he and co-actor Gene Lockhart went out to a saloon to celebrate. His drinking did not bother O'Neill because it was the type his father engaged in—in *Long Day's Journey into Night* James Tyrone defends his drinking, saying that he was never late onstage and never missed a performance. Like O'Neill's father, Cohan saved his drinking until after the performance. Furthermore, he kept in good health by running around the reservoir in Central Park. Apparently, the praise for his acting did not go to his head. When Ward Morehouse wrote about the performance in 1934 he remarked to Cohan that critics were calling him the best American actor since Edwin Booth, but Cohan responded, "Don't let 'em kid you—next year they'll be panning me."

Of course the play was a smash hit when it toured. During the tour in 1934, Cohan was given permission by the Theatre Guild to do something very special. He went to North Brookfield, Massachusetts, which he associated with his boyhood. There, in the town hall he and the rest of the cast (without make-up, settings, costumes, or props) presented the play for Cohan's friends and neighbors. Naturally, this was deeply moving for those who saw it, for the cast, and undoubtedly for O'Neill.

The play touched the hearts of people throughout the country. Although the cast as a whole was excellent, focus tended to be on Cohan. Writing in Richmond, Virginia, a critic said that it was difficult to convert his rich performance into words and phrases, and spoke of his "tenderness, warmth and gentle humor." By the time the play reached Chicago, however, a problem had clearly developed. A few years later, when Cohan was performing in another play, he frankly told reviewer Robert Coleman about a tendency he had in performance. Cohan was performing in a musical and said that he had been writing so long that he had a hard time keeping himself in check: the temptation to ad lib lines of his own was almost overwhelming. Cohan said he didn't mind it so much in *Ah, Wilderness!* because it was a straight play, but that, in fact, he didn't think it was a bad idea: "I always felt it had a tendency to keep the performance fresh and alive." Apparently, Cohan didn't remember that he had often succumbed to the temptation when *Ah, Wilderness!* went on the road. As McCabe says, "He began to add little touches and bits of business which, together with a growing tendency to pause reflectively in reaction to lines spoken to him, stretched the play's original lengthy playing time by half an hour. This was a problem for the Theatre Guild because it added on terrific costs for overtime. Theresa Helburn went back to speak to Cohan about it in Chicago. He told her that in New York it would have been wrong, but that in the heartland, seeing Americans presented onstage, the audiences didn't mind the length.[85] She apparently felt that argument was useless and so he continued in his additions until the play closed in 1935.

Following his success in O'Neill's play Cohan achieved one more great success, playing President Franklin Delano Roosevelt in Kaufman and Hart's musical *I'd Rather Be Right*. When he died in 1942, many long articles were written about his career. Most of them pointed to the surprise of his appearing in O'Neill's play. One obituary noted that he startled the theatre world by accepting the role, then "to the surprise of everyone, except possibly himself and Mr. O'Neill, he turned the role of the small town, philosophizing newspaper publisher into the most subtle acting accomplishment of his life." Another noted that it was remarkable for a song-and-dance man to score a triumph of legitimate acting in a play written by "the darling of the intelligentsia." Despite all of his successes in musicals, despite all the wealth he gained from them, the theatre world and much of the public still remembered him as Nat Miller. An unidentified obituary concluded, "It was as the star of *Ah, Wilderness!* that Mr. Cohan gave his finest performance as a serious actor. Here 'the man who owned Broadway' proved that he could play, with deep understanding and effect, a role far removed from that garish thoroughfare or anything with which he had been previously associated." O'Neill remembered him fondly in 1941 when the Theatre Guild considered a revival of the play. He wrote to Lawrence Langner, who apparently felt O'Neill might justifiably hold a grudge against the actor, "No I don't think Cohan is an all-wrong idea. On the contrary. A revival with him would have real sentimental audience value. Trouble is, he never would know the lines now. It was bad enough for him before."[86] Although O'Neill had been annoyed by Cohan's ad libbing, presumably he forgave it and thought it was partly caused by actual difficulty in remembering the lines. He gave Cohan an elegant copy of *Days Without End* with an inscription that emphasized their friendship.

One more aspect of *Ah, Wilderness!* should be noted. Although most of the critical attention went to Cohan, the young actor, Elisha Cook, Jr. drew praise for his Broadway debut in the role of the young son. He was born in 1903 and had grown up in Chicago where his father was involved in theatre. He became an itinerant actor by his early teens. In *Ah, Wilderness!* he was particularly successful (despite his actual age) in conveying "the tense, nervous, angular speech and motion of youth" in good contrast to Cohan's slow, thoughtful characterization. Several critics called the scene between the two one of the highlights of the play. Cook was much praised for his sensitivity and charm and further successes as a stage actor were anticipated. Instead, he went to the Hollywood where he performed in an almost unbelievable number of films and, later, practically every television show created. When he died at the age of ninety-two in 1995, he was remembered for the O'Neill role and his many movie roles. He was particularly remembered as a sad little man shot down by Jack Palance in *Shane* and as Wilmer, the gunsel, in *The Maltese Falcon*, in which he warns Bogart, "Keep ridin' me, you're gonna be picking iron out of your liver." A far cry from *Ah, Wilderness!*

The failure of *Days Without End* within a few months of the success of *Ah, Wilderness!* was a major blow for all concerned, but particularly for O'Neill and Larimore. Unfortunately, the last play by O'Neill to be performed on Broadway in his lifetime also failed to have great success. Much has been written about the production of *The Iceman Cometh* in 1946. As had happened in the past, the star, James E. Barton, let the production down. Instead of resting at the intermission for the great challenge of the last act, he drank and talked with friends in his dressing room. He had to be prompted so many times that when he once got a long section in without a prompt, he was applauded by the audience. Additionally, Eddie Dowling's direction failed to illuminate all the aspects of the complex play with its shifting moods. The worth of the play (predicted by John Huston) was not revealed until José Quintero's legendary production with Jason Robards in 1956 at the Circle in the Square. Later that year Quintero received permission to direct the American premiere of *Long Day's Journey into Night*.

The interviews that follow give a picture of the work of Quintero, Robards, and others involved in these two productions. However, Fredric March gave such a memorable, definitive performance as James Tyrone that space must be given to it here. As Brooks Atkinson wrote at the time, "The performance is stunning. As the aging actor who stands at the head of the family, Fredric March gives a masterful performance that will stand as a milestone in the acting of an O'Neill play."[87]

March was the type of actor that O'Neill admired. His biographer, Deborah Peterson, titled his biography *Fredric March: Craftsman First, Star Second*. He was a singularly modest man despite the tremendous success he enjoyed and the many honors accorded him. By the time of *Long Day's Journey into Night* he had

had a long career in films and on the stage. He had been in fifty films and had won Academy Awards for *Dr. Jekyll and Mr. Hyde* and *The Best Years of Our Lives.*

Born in 1897, March attended the University of Wisconsin. He played his first big part in 1922 in *The Lawbreaker,* produced by Alice Brady's father, William A. Brady. In 1927 he married actress Florence Eldridge, with whom he usually acted from that time on. He acted on the stage, touring with his wife in Theatre Guild productions in the '20s but then turned to films. He refused to be categorized as a type, like many of the other big stars. A clipping in his file called "March Outlives Screen Average" mentions his success in films and his previous failure to make it big on the stage. He was intending to take up the challenge of stage acting again, saying, "I have never got to where I wanted to in it." He noted wryly that a film actress had made reference to his stage past, asking, "How can you stand all those flops?" He then performed in New York in *Yr. Obedient Husband,* which was another flop, lasting only a few days. March took it in stride, putting ads in all the papers reading "Ooops, sorry." He went on to achieve great success in Wilder's *The Skin of Our Teeth,* and *A Bell for Adano,* Sophie Treadwell's *Hope for a Harvest* with the Theatre Guild, and Lillian Hellman's *The Autumn Garden.*

In interviews before the opening of *Long Day's Journey into Night,* he observed that it had taken him and Eldridge five years to find a play they wanted to perform. The first readings of the play took place at Firefly Farm, the home he and Eldridge shared in New Milford, Connecticut. Initially it had been hoped that Geraldine Page might have played the role of Mary, but March would only perform his role with his wife. The cast got along very well and there was a real feeling of ensemble. So much so, that when Bradford Dillman and Jason Robards left the cast, March and Eldridge were discontent with their replacements. Later, they pulled out of the intended London production because they did not know who would play the sons.

In general, March learned all his lines before rehearsals began. Peterson quotes him as saying, "I think it's almost physically impossible to give a well-rounded performance without knowing it beforehand. To try and rehearse eight hours a day and then go home at night and knock more lines into your head—it just doesn't work. You *know* it first, then try to polish it as you go along."[88] In this instance, he was still working on the lines as the rehearsals went along because it was such a long role. In an effort to develop the character he studied the great romantic actors of the 1890s and early 1900s in terms of their lives and onstage manner.

Peterson interviewed Bradford Dillman, who admired March's performance greatly and who observed him closely during rehearsals. "He always brought not only the vitality, but he brought intelligence. He had a great knack for making choices that were colorful and interesting. He had an element of danger—if I was sitting in the auditorium, I didn't dare take my eyes off him because I didn't know what he might be doing next that I might miss."[89] Although not a Method actor, March tried to become the character he was performing. Peterson quotes him as saying, "To give an adequate performance, an actor must cast off his own identity and become the person he is portraying; that is, at least while onstage. That has been my compelling concern; to lose my own self in the role I am playing."[90]

When the play opened it was obviously a blockbuster hit. The production won for O'Neill the Pulitzer Prize, awarded posthumously. In his book on these awards, John L. Toohey wrote, "There could have been no other decision; *Long Day's Journey into Night* completely overshadowed everything else produced this season (including O'Neill's own *Moon for the Misbegotten,* an artistic and financial failure)."[91] March and Eldridge received *Variety* and New York Drama Critics Poll Awards for their acting, despite the misgivings of some critics that she did not fully exemplify the role of Mary. March received the Tony Award for Best Actor as well as the Drama Critics Circle Award.

Variety wrote, "March gives a virtuoso performance in the painful, complex and exhausting role of the father. It is a masterpiece of 'projected-from-within' emotional acting, skillfully varied and paced and rising to a stunning climax in the final scenes." His success in suggesting the type of romantic actor in the play (an element sometimes missed in later performances of the role) was clear, as Rowland Field wrote: "Fredric March as the swaggering, hectoring father plays with the flamboyance expected of the matinee idol he is portraying." Walter Kerr gave a picture of the details of March's performance: "Fredric March cracks down on the skinflint monarch that O'Neill remembered as his father with majestic authority from the outset. Laughing a bit too much and a bit too hollowly, working off his nerves with a restless cigar, snapping at every insult like a guilty bulldog, he foreshadows the whole sodden fantasia of the midnight to come." Henry Hewes wrote a long, thoughtful article on the production for the *Saturday Review*. In particular he noted March's consistency in a "miraculously sustained portrayal" and his ability to underplay moments that might have tempted a lesser actor to "indulge himself in a virtuoso stunt." He praised Robards for all aspects and commented that he was able to "explode and steal the show." He praised Dillman and Eldridge, but noted times in her performance when he felt something was missing. Like all of the critics, he gave credit to Quintero for the production.[92] Many critics felt that March reached the height of his career with this role and that his success was matched by that of Robards. Richard Watts summed up that feeling, writing, "It seems to me that Fredric March gives the finest and most penetrating performance of his career as the father, but he is no more impressive than Jason Robards, Jr. who demonstrates in the role of the older son that he is an actor of tremendous dynamic skill. All of the promise he showed in *The Iceman Cometh* is here fulfilled."

The play was so successful, and such a source of pride to America as a whole, that it was sent to Paris by the State Department to represent the United States at the International Drama Festival in Paris. The play enjoyed a long run in the United States, which was wonderful, but also exhausting, for the cast. Bradford Dillman told Peterson that he was trained to "give life's blood every night" so that he was utterly exhausted by a performance, but he felt the Marches were not Method actors and didn't feel the same exhaustion.[93] In fact, they did feel the fatigue, as March told an unidentified writer: "Of course you want to be in a hit, but Mrs. March and I did *Long Day's Journey into Night* for sixty-nine weeks, four hours a night."

The total accomplishment of March in this great role is described by Peterson: "March managed to make James Tyrone a dignified, patient figure, even a man of compassion. March lifted him without the audience being aware of it, above the petty disputes and the battle, to the friendly sympathy of the audience at the final curtain. The role brought March not only a challenge, but great personal satisfaction. He remarked, 'I am enjoying it tremendously. It is a most rewarding experience.'"[94]

Although the role undoubtedly marked the high point of his career, it was not the last big success. He played in the film version of *Inherit the Wind* in 1960. In 1963, he and Florence Eldridge took part in a stunning televised program set up by President Kennedy to focus attention on the National Cultural Center in Washington. O'Neill's work was a major part of this celebration. (Robards remarks later in this book that few presidents would have been interested in that.) There were scenes with the cast from *Long Day's Journey into Night*, and Robards and Colleen Dewhurst appeared in scenes from other O'Neill plays. It was a memorable event with orchestras, dances, and other theatrical elements.

March gave his last performance in John Frankenheimer's film of *The Iceman Cometh*, produced by the American Film Theatre. The cast included Robert Ryan as Larry and many other fine actors. Unfortunately, the director's decision to cast Lee Marvin as Hickey instead of the obvious choice of Robards meant the failure of the film. Nevertheless, March is wonderful to see, even as death came near to him, playing the old, tired, partially deaf Harry Hope. In this role, as in so many others, one is aware of the gaze of March. Peterson quotes an article titled "The Eyes of March," which describes the power he had: "They burn from within. They betray a passionate hate, a rather tense love, an inordinate will, a self-consuming pain. He can stare motionlessly at an overstuffed chair, and our spines will crawl with the conflict."[95] Peterson comments that March never became the popular star that Tracy and Gable and Cooper did because he was a craftsman: "he might have settled for superstardom, but instead sought to become a renowned actor. Knowing that in achieving this he must forsake the other, he never regretted his choice."[96] When the theatre at the University of

Wisconsin was named after him, he attended the ceremonies and told the audience that of all his plays *Long Day's Journey into Night* was his favorite.

Many notable directors have contributed to the success of O'Neill's plays on the stage. In the early days of the Provincetown Players it was not always clear who directed the play because of the communal, purposefully amateur quality of the endeavor. Robert Edmond Jones emerged as a major figure in the group and directed a number of the plays. Later, Arthur Hopkins directed important productions for Broadway theatres. When O'Neill became connected with the Theatre Guild, Philip Moeller brought his talents to the plays. After the failure of *The Iceman Cometh* in 1946, José Quintero created a revival of interest in O'Neill's plays beginning in 1956. His important work is discussed in the interviews that follow.

Robert Edmond Jones was a shy man whose photographs often show him looking quite alarmed. Born in 1887, a year before O'Neill, he grew up in New England. Just before World War I he traveled extensively in Europe for a year, returning only because of the war. His sketches of the new approaches to stagecraft, particularly Expressionism, influenced his designs and, subsequently, the American theatre. He is credited with introducing the New Stagecraft to American theatre through his setting for the 1915 Harley Granville Barker production of *The Man Who Married a Dumb Wife*. His knowledge of European theatre methods, particularly at the Deutsches Theatre in Berlin, contributed to the significance of *Continental Stagecraft,* which he wrote with Kenneth Macgowan in 1922. His approach to design was definitely innovative and imaginative. In the early days of the Provincetown Players he designed a costume for an actress/musician that was made of many pieces of vividly colored pieces of silk. These could be rearranged by him, by pinning the pieces together to create the various types of costumes she needed for her work—the only danger being that the pins would fall out, leaving her in a state of embarrassment. In 1915 a group of friends in Provincetown decided to put on two one-act plays in what Edna Kenton described as "a rambling old house by the sea."[97] There was no stage, but "Bobby" arranged to present the first play on the veranda with the audience sitting in the living room, the sea as a setting with two lamps by the wide doors. For the second play the audience turned its chairs around and looked into an alcove where he "had been noiselessly moving with candles and lamps."[98]

Later, Jones would become one of the most famous designers in the world, but he also functioned as a director. He directed some of the early one-acts. Then, when he, O'Neill, and Macgowan founded the Experimental Theatre, he directed O'Neill's *The Fountain, Desire Under the Elms,* and *The Great God Brown.* Later he designed many O'Neill productions working with Philip Moeller as director. He continued to direct occasionally. In 1932, for example, he directed Lillian Gish in a production of *Camille* for the opening of the restored opera house in Central City, Colorado. His approach to theatre was expressed in his book *The Dramatic Imagination.* Rebelling against the detailed realism characteristic of late-nineteenth-century theatre, he wanted to appeal to the imagination of the audience, simplifying staging and settings. He was not only a collaborator and interpreter of O'Neill's work, but a close friend throughout their lives. He died one year after O'Neill. The mutual admiration and close camaraderie is revealed in the letters O'Neill wrote to Bobby. In 1944, O'Neill wrote to him regarding his proposal to revive *The Emperor Jones* with Canada Lee: "I *do* know what you can do with the production, that you will be able to forget all the other productions and make this your imaginative own, as if it were a new play being produced."[99]

Arthur Hopkins was a man who developed a style of directing characterized by Robert Benchley as "the absent treatment." He seemed (as people would later say of Quintero) not to direct at all, but simply to let the actors do what they wanted. In fact, he knew very well how to bring out the best in actors, beginning by working with and developing actors and actresses with great ability and casting them in roles that would enable them to reveal their talents. Born in 1878, he worked as a newspaper reporter, then as a press agent. He worked in the commercial theatre, but chose to present plays that ran counter to the commercial productions of his time. He looked to the future, directing modern, often experimental plays, and using modern methods of staging that he had seen when he studied in Europe. His productions of Shakespeare with settings by Robert Edmond Jones, starring Lionel Barrymore and John Barrymore, were highlights of the theatre in the '20s. He believed in O'Neill's talent and directed *Anna Christie* and *The Hairy Ape* with great success. He then directed Louis Wolheim in another big success, *What Price Glory?*

Hopkins was a part of the commercial theatre, but chose plays on the basis of their artistic possibilities, not the profit factor. He often gambled on unknown playwrights such as Sophie Treadwell, whose Expressionistic play *Machinal* was such a surprising success in 1928. Although he made money on the plays he produced, it was a policy of his never to invest in his own productions. His obituaries retold a famous story about the one time he broke that rule. So certain that a play would be a hit, he put his own money in it, only to see it get worse and worse as rehearsals went on. In the tryout in Philadelphia he actually came to believe that the actors were being bad on purpose because they wanted him to lose his investment. As he sat groaning aloud and swearing during a matinee, a woman turned around and said, "A number of us are enjoying this play and if you aren't why don't your go to the box office and get your money back?" He answered, "I wish to God I could!"

A thoughtful man attuned to mystical elements in life, Hopkins devised an approach to theatre entirely in contrast to the spectacle and trickery that characterized David Belasco and other directors of his time. In *How's Your Second Act?* he set forth his theories on directing, calling his method "Unconscious Projection." He said that there were many actors who said that he had given them no direction and that was what he wanted them to think. "It is always my aim to get a play completely prepared without anyone realizing just how it was done. I want the actors to be unconscious of my supervision. I want whatever direction they require to come to them without their realization. I want them to be unconscious of the movement and the 'business' of the play. I want it all to grow with them so easily that when time for the first performance comes they scarcely realize that anything particular has been done." He wanted the director, designers, and actors to work together to become the "servants of the play": "Each must resist every temptation to score personally. Each must make himself a free, transparent medium through which the whole flows freely and without obstruction."[100] Although he sometimes worked with actors who could not share his views, he found an ideal designer in Robert Edmond Jones. "Jones hopes only for one thing for his settings—that no one will notice them, that they will melt into the play. He is the true artist. He wants nothing for Jones. He wants what is right for the thing we are doing. Given twenty actors with a spirit as fine as his, and I will promise you a reaction such as is now only a dream."[101] At his death in 1950 Hopkins was remembered as one of the most literate, sensitive, innovative directors of the first half of the twentieth century. His direction of *Anna Christie* created a major turning point in the playwright's career. Writing to Hopkins twenty-three years later, O'Neill said that he had often intended to write a long letter to him. His letter concluded, "My deep gratitude for all you did for me. That, believe me, I have never forgotten nor ever can forget. Affectionately."[102]

New Yorker Philip Moeller was born in 1880. He graduated from Columbia University and in 1914 joined the Washington Square Players. He wrote several one-act plays that were produced, including *Helena's Husband,* which became a popular favorite. After World War I when members of the earlier organization established the Theatre Guild, he was a co-founder and became one of the most important directors. Indeed, Lawrence Langner, a great support of O'Neill, felt that Moeller was one of the finest directors in the American theatre. Against the will of a number of the Theatre Guild members, Langner secured the rights for *Strange Interlude,* which Moeller directed. In his review John Mason Brown wrote, "Mr. Moeller has done the most decisive and expert direction of his career, at all times differentiating between the spoken word and the spoken thought, and keeping the pace of each of the nine acts skillfully in hand." Writing to Theresa Helburn, O'Neill asked her to "Tell Phil again how much I enjoyed working with him and how damn grateful I feel for his splendid job on *S. I.*—the most imaginative directing I've ever known. . . . And tell Lynn & the rest of the cast that I hope they're half as satisfied with their work in *S. I.* as I am."[103]

Moeller went on to direct *Dynamo, Mourning Becomes Electra, Ah, Wilderness!,* and *Days Without End.* A sensitive intellectual, he got along well with O'Neill, working with him and Lawrence Langner well up to the last rehearsals on cuts and changes for the plays. As Langner wrote, "Gene attended the theatre regularly and made considerable cuts. Indeed he was usually extremely cooperative in regard to cutting, and once he was in a cutting mood, he cut faster than the director asked in rehearsals."[104] However, when Moeller directed *Dynamo,* O'Neill was not there to work with him and the play was a failure. The playwright took the blame himself, writing to Langner as he was cutting and improving the play for publication, "I should have been there and all I'm doing now would have been done at rehearsals. . . . This is no beef against Phil, of course. I know he did a fine job with what was there—but he couldn't be expected to read my mind and rewrite it." As Langner observed, "After the failure of *Dynamo,* Gene never stayed away from the initial production of any of his plays."[105]

Although they worked well together, Moeller often made good-humored jokes about working with O'Neill. The two often corresponded, O'Neill writing just before *Ah, Wilderness!,* "I know we're going to have a lot of fun doing this play—if we get a cast to work with!—and I know you can direct it as no one else could."[106]

Moeller often came up with unconventional solutions for problems that arose in rehearsals. While directing *Meteor* by S. N. Behrman, he felt a great deal of tension, as did Lunt and Fontanne, because of problems in the writing and rehearsals. Directing a scene with them in which he felt the tension leading to a major storm, he began to sob and cried out that he couldn't stand any more. Langner brought him water to drink, the others helped him to a couch, and Lunt insisted that he be taken to his hotel to rest. As Langner walked with him along the street he asked Moeller how he felt. "'Fine' he said, striding along and smiling happily. 'If I hadn't thrown that fit of hysterics just when I did, some of the actors would have done it a minute later.'"[107] In her introduction to *Directors on Directing,* Helen Krich Chinoy wrote, "Philip Moeller, working as part of the Theatre Guild directorate, staged many of the new American plays of the '20s—those of Elmer Rice, Sidney Howard, S. N. Behrman, and Eugene O'Neill. He placed his urbane, sophisticated theatrical imagination and literary skill at the service of the group expression which he felt to be the major contribution of the Guild's methods of production in the early days."[108] In the '30s Moeller directed some films and then virtually retired from theatre until his death in 1958. His sophisticated touch was missed.

The process of producing plays is complex and fraught with difficulties, as the experiences noted above indicate. Once the plays are performed, successfully or unsuccessfully, legends tend to be passed along as fact, exaggerations are accepted as reality, and praise or blame is assigned, often inaccurately. Many people accept completely the idea that O'Neill refused ever to cut any of his plays, unlike any other director. In fact, he did cut (not always as much as some actors or directors wanted), in contrast to Shaw, for example. Langner was warned by Shaw's lawyer that "Shaw will not permit you to alter as much as one single word in his play."[109] It seems to be in the nature of theatrical production that actors complain about directors and writers and that the directors and writers complain about them. As long ago as the seventeenth century Molière suggested this in his *Impromptu at Versailles,* and the process has gone on ever since. Langner, a playwright himself, offered one explanation for playwrights' discontent with actors: "No author ever succeeds in getting a complete realization of the part he has created, and he blames the actor because the actor is unable to achieve the impossible." He felt that O'Neill's remarks about actors should be taken with a grain of salt.[110] In his work with the Provincetown Players, with Hopkins as producer/director, and with the Theatre Guild, O'Neill formed many friendships and frequently enjoyed the process of rehearsal. He never did attend opening nights and did not care to see the plays once they opened. If he had, on some occasions, he probably would have had the disagreeable experience of seeing business added, lines dropped, and surprising interpretations of lines. George S. Kaufman made it a practice to drop in unexpectedly on plays he had written and directed and once sent a telegram to the cast during a performance: "AM STANDING AT THE BACK OF THE AUDITORIUM. WISH YOU WERE HERE."[111]

Notes

1. Deborah Peterson, *Fredric March: Craftsman First, Star Second* (Westport, CT: Greenwood, 1996), p. 241.
2. Louis Scheaffer, *O'Neill: Son and Playwright* (New York: Paragon House, 1968), p. 134.
3. Arthur and Barbara Gelb, *O'Neill* (New York: Harper and Row, 1962), p. 177.
4. Eugene O'Neill, *Bound East for Cardiff*, in *Complete Plays 1913–1920* ed. Travis Bogard (New York: The Library of America, 1988), p. 198.
5. *Thirst*, in Ibid., p. 51.
6. *Before Breakfast*, in Ibid., p. 395.
7. Unless otherwise noted, the quotations from reviews and articles dealing with each actor or actress are in the file under the performer's name in the Billy Rose collections in the Theatre and Performing Arts Library at Lincoln Center. Many of these are fragments lacking a title, page number, or author.
8. Travis Bogard and Jackson Bryer, eds., *Selected Letters of Eugene O'Neill* (New Haven, CT: Yale University Press, 1988), p. 105.
9. Ibid., p. 109.
10. Ibid., p. 108.
11. John L.Toohey, *The Pulitzer Prize Plays* (New York: Citadel, 1967), p. 46.
12. Erroll Hill, "Charles Gilpin," in *The Cambridge Guide to World Theatre*, ed. Martin Banham (Cambridge, UK: Cambridge University Press, 1988), p. 396.
13. Gelb, p. 448.
14. *Selected Letters*, p. 177.
15. Gelb, p. 450.
16. Hill, p. 396.
17. Scheaffer, p. 37.
18. Martin Duberman, *Paul Robeson* (New York: New Press, 1996), p. 43.
19. Ibid., p. 53.
20. *Selected Letters*, p. 177.
21. Scheaffer, p. 140.
22. Ibid., p. 89.
23. Nelda K. Balch, "Pauline Lord," in *Notable Women in the American Theatre*, eds. Alice M. Robinson, Vera Mowry Roberts, and Milly S. Barranger (Westport, CT: Greenwood Press, 1989), p. 559.
24. Jared Brown, *The Fabulous Lunts* (New York: Athenaeum, 1986), p. 91.
25. *Selected Letters*, p. 121.
26. Balch, p. 559.
27. Brown, p. 93.
28. *Selected Letters*, p. 559.
29. Emily Wortis Leider, *Becoming Mae West* (New York: Farrar, Strous, and Giroux, 1997), p. 123.
30. *Selected Letters*, p. 210.
31. Ibid., p. 558.
32. Ibid., p. 560.
33. John Weld, *September Song* (Baltimore, MD: Scarecrow, 1998), p. 96.
34. Ibid., p. 94.
35. Ibid., p. 95.
36. John Huston, *An Open Book* (New York: Knopf, 1980), p. 32.
37. Ibid.

38. Weld, p. 200.
39. *Selected Letters*, p. 196.
40. Weld, p. 99.
41. *Selected Letters*, p. 395.
42. Ibid., p. 474.
43. Huston, p. 33.
44. Ibid., p. 34.
45. Ibid.
46. Brown, p. 167.
47. Ibid., p. 162.
48. Ibid.
49. Ibid., p. 165.
50. *Selected Letters*, p. 266.
51. Brown, p. 167.
52. Ibid.
53. Ibid.
54. Toby Cole and Helen Krich Chinoy, eds., *Actors on Acting* (New York: Crown, 1970), p. 612.
55. S. N. Behrman, *People in a Diary* (New York: Little, Brown, and Co., 1972), p. 89.
56. Brown, p. 169.
57. Ibid., p. 163.
58. Ibid., p. 164.
59. Ibid.
60. Gelb, p. 650.
61. Lawrence Langner, *The Magic Curtain* (New York: Dutton, 1951), p. 179.
62. Gelb, p. 778.
63. Samuel Raphaelson, *Accent on Youth* (New York: Samuel French, 1935), p. 91.
64. Gelb, p. 747.
65. *Selected Letters*, p. 232.
66. Gavin Lambert, *Nazimova* (New York: Knopf, 1997), p. 170.
67. Ibid., p. 321.
68. Ibid., p. 344.
69. Ibid., p. 192.
70. Ibid., p. 323.
71. Ibid., p. 324.
72. Ibid.
73. Ibid., p. 319.
74. Ibid., p. 389.
75. *Selected Letters*, p. 400.
76. Gelb, p. 748.
77. John McCabe, *George M. Cohan: The Man Who Owned Broadway* (Garden City, NJ: Doubleday, 1973), p. 226.
78. Ibid., p. 74.
79. Don Wilmeth, "George Michael Cohan," in *The Cambridge Guide to World Theatre* (Cambridge, UK: Cambridge University Press, 1988), p. 213.
80. McCabe, p. 227.
81. *Selected Letters*, p. 426.
82. Ibid., p. 430.
83. Edith Isaacs, "Good Plays A-Plenty," *Theatre Arts* (July–Dec. 1933), pp. 908-910.
84. McCabe, p. 228.
85. Ibid., p. 230.
86. *Selected Letters*, p. 519.

87. Brooks Atkinson, "Theatre: Tragic Journey," in the *New York Times* (Nov. 9, 1956).

88. Peterson, p. 217.

89. Ibid., p. 192.

90. Ibid., p. 240.

91. Toohey, p. 290.

92. Henry Hewes, "O'Neill 100 Proof—Not a Blend," *Saturday Review of Literature* (Nov. 24, 1956), p. 30.

93. Peterson, p. 192.

94. Ibid., p. 190.

95. Ibid., p. 219.

96. Ibid., p. 240.

97. Edna Kenton, "The Provincetown Players and the Playwrights' Theatre 1915–1922," *The Eugene O'Neill Review* (Spring/Fall 1997), p. 19.

98. Ibid.

99. *Selected Letters*, p. 551.

100. Arthur Hopkins, *How's Your Second Act?* (New York: Philip Goodman Company, 1918), p. 151.

101. Ibid., p. 93.

102. *Selected Letters*, p. 560.

103. Ibid., p. 291.

104. Langner, p. 283.

105. Ibid., p. 242.

106. *Selected Letters*, p. 421.

107. Langner, p. 245.

108. Toby Cole and Helen Krich Chinoy, eds., *Directors on Directing* (Indianapolis, IN: Bobbs-Merrill, 1963) p. 73.

109. Langner, p. 131.

110. Ibid., p. 237.

111. Langner, p. 232.

2 | James Earl Jones

James Earl Jones was born in Arkabutla, Mississippi, in 1931. He received his B.A. from the University of Michigan in 1953. He received a diploma from the American Theatre Wing and studied with Lee Strasberg. He has received many honorary degrees from universities including his alma mater, Princeton, Yale, and Columbia. His numerous awards, including Obies, Tonys, Golden Globes, the National Medal of Arts, and the John Houseman Award, make too long a list to include in full here, but a few are Tony Awards for *The Great White Hope* and *Fences,* and the Vernon Rice Award and the Drama Desk Award for *Othello.* He also received the latter award for the all-black performance of *The Cherry Orchard,* appearing with Gloria Foster at the Public Theatre. Jones has appeared in several plays by Athol Fugard including *Blood Knot, Master Harold and the Boys,* and *A Lesson From Aloes.* His career in films is extensive, beginning with *Dr. Strangelove* in 1963. Almost everyone knows his voice as Darth Vader in *Star Wars* and as Mufasa in the film of *The Lion King.* His many television appearances on series, specials, and miniseries have drawn praise and many awards. Both his voice and his acting ability have made him one of the most recognized actors in present-day theatre. His great performance as the boxer Jack Jefferson onstage and in the 1970 film *The Great White Hope* (with Jane Alexander) will not be forgotten.

NEW YORK CITY, SEPTEMBER 1999

SHAFER: Now before you played in *The Iceman Cometh* you had been at Arena Stage and then you brought *The Great White Hope* to Broadway. How did it happen that you did *The Iceman Cometh?* How did that come about?

JONES: Do you want to start with my O'Neill beginning?

SHAFER: Oh, yes, please.

JONES: I think I can fit it better in my mind. The key thing to notice, one summer there were picketers on the Boston Commons. The picketers were members of the NAACP. The NAACP was picketing a production called *The Emperor Jones,* because it used the "n" word. That is the ass end of it. We didn't give a shit about what they were doing. I didn't. The word "nigger" is part of our psyche. And I think Dick Gregory once tried to dispel it by writing a book called *Nigger.* And if we say it enough it will go away. Not quite true, but closer than getting all uptight about it. But then I can say that because no one has ever called me nigger. I don't know how I would respond if someone did.

Okay, so that is the ass end of it. The head end of that production, in 1964, was a gathering of young Turks including Dudley Moore, Ben Shacklin was the director, and myself and a bunch of great dancers. One of those earlier heterosexual choreographers and myself and the dancers. The concept that Ben had was to go somewhere new with *The Emperor Jones.* I was bothered from the beginning, and even at the very end, that there were no drum sounds. Dudley used only a piano.

SHAFER: No kidding!

JONES: The whole score was a piano and whatever percussion sounds you could get out of a piano. Which is not drums, but I said, "That's exciting, let's do it." The choreographer had choreographed some of the greatest young dancers into being all those energies in the play, besides Smithers and Jones and Ol' Lynn. Lynn, Jones, Smithers, and the old lady were cast with actors. Tom McDermott played Smithers. But every other unit of energy was a dancer. So they could be rocks at times. They could be trees at times, they could be part of a jungle at times. Once when Jones is trying to escape through the forest, I would escape through massive, beautiful, strong, young dancing arms and legs. But we opened there. Actually, that is all we did. We played in Boston outdoors on the Commons. I was in good shape then. I was in my, more or less, my *Great White Hope* shape so I was presentable in loincloth. And when they hung the Emperor up by his heels you just see him in his drawers. I don't remember any reviews of that production, at the Boston Commons. But, I remember having the feeling, because Kennedy had just been elected, that we had all this young energy. It was like a new order, if you want to use that phrase, of young theatre energy. And in a way, led by Dudley, with his "I will not use drums, I will use piano." It was very exciting to us. We didn't care what the audience thought or what the picketers thought. And that's the end of that story.

Then later we rehearsed that play at the Eugene O'Neill Center, then we took it to Europe. We never played in New York City. Donny McKayle was the choreographer and did something similar. He used his dancers, not as part of the inorganic and the sort of the non-human light, but as the human—the ghost life of the Emperor Jones. He used dancing, the parasols, the auctioneers, and all that sort of thing. He brought it to life with these dancers and then other nights he gave a dance concert. And then we played *The Emperor Jones*. So I did not have to work every night.

SHAFER: Was it a long tour?

JONES: We went all over Europe, yeah, and ended up in Scotland at the Edinburgh Festival. The best performance, the best communication, was had with the audiences in Holland, in Amsterdam, because they understood English as well as Americans did. The Scottish had a little problem with the accents, with mine in particular and being a Southern African American accent. They didn't seem to understand the "snoogers." But otherwise, the Dutch didn't care.

SHAFER: So then after that?

JONES: That was it.

SHAFER: Why didn't it ever play here?

JONES: They didn't want it. I don't know why it didn't play here.

SHAFER: Oh, so then after this time, was it considerably after this time, that *The Iceman Cometh* was performed?

JONES: *The Iceman Cometh* came out of a complex situation. I have a long history with Ted Mann from the Circle in the Square and my father did also with the Circle in the Square. And I think Ted wanted to do an Athol Fugard play. I knew that Ted wanted to do it, but I made the mistake of mentioning it to Lloyd Richards. And so Lloyd made his bid right away and of course, what he offered Athol was the same that he offered August Wilson: a place to work away from New York, an ivory tower. And Athol had to take it. So I thought that I had betrayed Ted in a way. So he and I kept the friendship and we were talking about two other plays. He said, "I am doing O'Neill's *The Iceman Cometh,* you want to think about Hickey?" I said, "I can't get Jason [Robards] out of my mind." Because it was the first piece I saw after my Broadway tour, my grand tour, with my father. He took me to see everything, the ballet, opera, drama, comedy. And then I saw my father play Joe Mott in *The Iceman* at the old Circle in the Square, and I said, "I cannot, and I don't know if anybody can, get Jason out of their mind." And it wasn't just that another actor couldn't do that. But another actor would have to have the quixotic energy that Jason did. Jason created it by tapping his fingers and a lot of really fast talk, salesman type fast-talk. I am lethargic. I am not that kind of temperament. And I said, "I worry, Ted." But I said, "I would consider it if you will give me a chance to do *Of Mice and Men* at your theatre." He said "Okay, it's a deal." And that didn't work out either, because I ended up doing *Mice and Men* with Ed Sherin on Broadway. Okay, back to *The Iceman.*

He gathered a group of young actors; there were no stars. So in a way, Ted became the star. This producer, who was very successful, was going to do his best as a director. He and Joe Papp were the worst directors possible. But they were great producers, and they were always trying to direct and always failed. But Ted was determined to give it one more try and he succeeded.

SHAFER: Yes, good.

JONES: He cast sort of no one who would shine, do star turns on him, but just young actors to do the play.

SHAFER: Do you remember who some of them were?

JONES: Steve McHattie was one of them. Steve played the young kid, that's the first one that comes to mind. Stefan Gierasch played the old man. And when it opened Ted got the hit reviews and it was what he needed, you know. And I wasn't trying to do star turns anyway, because I kept saying to him, "I can't find that temperament in me. So what I do might take the play down, might make the play too heavy temperamentally and maybe emotionally." I think there's an insanity in Hickey and with Jason's kind of quixotic energy you get a flash of that. I think that with that young man on Broadway, Kevin Spacey, you get something similar.

SHAFER: Did you see it?

JONES: Yeah, I loved it. But I couldn't help but compare it with Jason's. I mean Kevin is close enough to Jason's energy. There was something almost amateur about that production contrasted to the one off-Broadway. Something British got into it, the British didn't put it together, didn't quite understand about the play and about America and about American characters. But it worked and Kevin was spectacular. Kevin played it like an avenging angel. Jason played it like a seducer. And I don't know what I played it like; I haven't yet figured it out. You have to ask others! It was not successful for me.

SHAFER: No, I saw some good reviews of it. I saw some that were a little reluctant, but I didn't see any negative. I looked it up.

JONES: Really, I'd stopped reading reviews by then.

SHAFER: No, you are wrong, if I may say so sir. Many of the critics thought you were wonderful.

JONES: I don't read reviews, so I don't know. But I know that it was not successful just from the way it felt. But it is a good play. There I met a great play.

SHAFER: How long did you run it?

JONES: It was a limited time engagement, several months.

SHAFER: And that was all you were playing, it wasn't repertory?

JONES: No.

SHAFER: That was in the new theatre?

JONES: Yes, midtown.

SHAFER: As an experience of playing it, you didn't play the whole play uncut, did you?

JONES: Yeah, oh yeah.

SHAFER: The whole play? There wasn't any cutting? And it was four-and-a-half hours or so every night. So did you do matinees, too?

JONES: Uh huh, as far as I remember, yeah. Yeah, and just like Kevin's, that's a long sit. But the audience didn't seem to mind. I didn't mind sitting there. You get transported.

SHAFER: As far as the character and getting into it, what did you try to do since you didn't feel that it was suited to your nature? What did you do to try and come up with some other alternatives?

JONES: Well, rather then the seducer or the avenging angel, I was somewhat a preacher I guess, somewhat self-righteous and having found the answer, which was kill the one you love, that's the answer. [Laughs.] And then you kill the thing that you love. It was dark and I could not help but play a dark Hickey. The dark both physically and judgmentally, and therefore not as enjoyable as the other interpretations.

SHAFER: Did you think that the comedy at the beginning played, though? There is some comedy there.

JONES: I don't know, I can't even tell a joke.

SHAFER: But you were funny in *Great White Hope.*

JONES: Well, and in *Fences* people were laughing for the better part of that.

SHAFER: Exactly.

JONES: But that's because of the writing. You give me an irony and I can't do an irony. And sometimes it makes you nervous and you laugh. Often, inappropriately, which is a problem for me! No, I didn't look for the comedy in it. I was willing, I think, because I had just had the experience with *The Great White Hope.* And I hadn't learned that you don't bend your character to be entertaining or to be accessible to the audience or to be palatable to the audience. I haven't learned that totally, none of us do. Because we always want the audience to like us. I think I trod lightly, that's the only accommodation I made. I wasn't dooming anybody because after all in O'Neill's world he had a black guy in the play. And the black guy was not running things. He was an important member of that group, but he was not running things. My black guy comes in and he was running things. And I felt, I said, "First of all, Ted, Hickey's a Hoosier, that is not only a Caucasian, but it's a very particular German-background Caucasian, really Aryan American, the Hoosiers." I guess they are a German derived, aren't they? Anyway they have certain almost Calvinistic attitudes about sex and pleasure and playing cards and stuff. So Hickey is working out of a great social depression, social psychic depression and I was able to get in touch with that to some extent, but only like a reformed preacher. A preacher ready to join the devil, rather than God.

SHAFER: Do you remember now who played Joe Mott in that?

JONES: Arthur French. I see him all the time.

SHAFER: To you, was it odd, the business that you say that here's this black man that was part of the group and then you come in?

JONES: No, that was not at all odd. The same thing happened in *Of Mice and Men*. I played Lenny as a black person. I asked when Steinbeck was alive, I said, "Sir, I would like to play your Lenny, but I am black." (I wrote to him.) I mean you rarely, as an actor, get to talk to a live writer who might want to change things. Who might be inclined to change a few words here or there to accommodate a different ethnicity. He said, "Jim, don't change a thing. Lenny if he is black doesn't know he's black. He doesn't know what the word 'nigger' means, he doesn't know any of the social contexts. Just play in the middle of it all." And it worked and in a way, Ted pretty much advised me to do the same thing with Hickey. Play Hickey, do not play a black Hickey. I think that the sort of preacher syndrome was the closest I came to anything ethnic. I tried not to do the huffing and puffing preaching, but that's where I was coming from. My father's father happened to be what we called a "jack-legged preacher," unordained. Men who get the calling and go out preaching without a license. So there is some of that tradition in the family.

SHAFER: Well, I think that this is so wonderfully interesting that your father was in *The Iceman Cometh* and that you were in *The Iceman*

Cometh. I think that's probably not a very likely thing to happen.

JONES: My father and I have a weird professional relationship, that stuff is always happening. [Laughing.] We're always doing something like that—it was nothing unusual.

SHAFER: I think that some people would recognize him from being in the movie *The Sting.*

JONES: That one movie I mention, even with young people, they know, "Oh that's your dad, the one with the mustache," they say, "handsome guy, wasn't he," and I say, "Yes, he was very handsome and a fitting sidekick for and a fitting cause for the revenge theme."

SHAFER: Can I take it back a little further again to this *Emperor Jones* . . . ?

JONES: [Laughing] Which one?

SHAFER: Either one.

JONES: They sort of run together.

SHAFER: One of the things that the audience wouldn't think of is how much work that role is for the actor. The audience just sits there and sees it happening and it's fine, you know, but they don't think about what the actor is doing.

JONES: I almost said that when I mentioned the production in Europe with Donny McKayle, he gave us one night off, one night on. It was a great relief because I would lose weight every night in that role. Because after the first scene, which is a glorious and dramatic scene . . .

SHAFER: You get a wonderful exit line there: "Well, if dey ain't no whole brass band to see me off, I sho' got de drum part of it."

JONES: That's one of the great scenes, I think, in writing. After that he is on the run, and really on the run. I'd run back offstage and tear part of my clothes off and I'd come back and I am on the other side of the stage. And the audience knew this guy is running around like this and that. But there is no other way of doing it, that part should be a movie. The only way to achieve the *Emperor Jones* after the first scene is to go right to the film. Right to the videotape, because there is no way to create it.

SHAFER: About the costume, now that is another part that the audience doesn't think of. You've actually got all of these pieces that are being changed while you are acting.

JONES: Yes, you start out in full regalia uniform and you end up in your drawers. By the way, Paul Robeson probably had done not only the definitive Othello of the Western world, but probably the definitive Emperor Jones. You've seen the movie, I'm sure. He is gorgeous and glorious as a specimen of man and a black man and a man with all those talents and endowments. He brings you a Brutus Jones that you'd like to get to know. [Laughing.]

SHAFER: With your costume, for example, did you actually take something off and put on something else?

JONES: No, the crew backstage would do it, I just ran. They were grabbing things and velcroed things.

SHAFER: It is a very exciting role to play isn't it?

JONES: Well, yeah, but the excitement of the first scene is very different from the excitement of just keeping on like a marathon. Keeping moving, because if you let the audience think about it too much they will start thinking, "Well, where is he now?" In a way, that is why heightening the musical aspect of it, as Dudley did, and heightening the ballet aspect of it, that Dudley's choreographer and Donald McKayle did, that helps. It gives the audience something to focus on. It gives them something that's been stylized.

SHAFER: With the performance that you gave following these things (much later really) of Robeson—is there material in that about O'Neill?

JONES: You know, I don't think we even mentioned *The Emperor Jones* in that. We mentioned O'Neill only in relationship to *All God's Chillun.* We pointed out the irony, I was again in Boston, and again pickets. This time some asshole with Rastafarian hair, *fake,* had picked up the cry that Paul Robeson, Jr., had said that this production is a fraud, you know. This production is a desecration of my father's image. So they had policemen on horses outside the theatre, this is Boston, this is many years ago. And so I walked into the theatre. This man kept following me around and I said, "Are you a member of the cast?" And he said, "No, I'm your man who is carrying a pistol." And I laughed; I just broke out laughing. That happened to Paul Robeson in the theatre downtown [New York] in the production of *All God's Chillun.* There were so many letters and so much agitation going around about the black guy playing opposite a white woman on the stage. To have a black guy on the stage in a hero role was bad enough. O'Neill hired him a bodyguard and Paul said he was the shortest man with the biggest gun he'd ever seen in the business! [Laughs.]

SHAFER: Did you meet Paul Robeson?

JONES: I met him three times, me and my father. I can't say that I knew the man, I just met him. Like a fan, and I certainly was a fan!

SHAFER: Now as you look back at such plays as *All God's Chillun Got Wings* and *Emperor Jones*—those were important opportunities for him as an actor.

JONES: And it brought out one of those ironies, too, that he was on the make. He wanted it; he was hungry for life. He was not a seducer, women came after him, and he didn't chase them. But life, he chased life. He wanted his life. And when the chance came to replace

Gilpin, I think, I don't know what his conscience said to him, but I think he tried to have no problem with that. His career was now moving and if something got pushed aside, okay. It was only later, after London, after he saw how full of holes the whole Western dream was, and he saw Spain with Franco when he went there, then he changed. He was no longer interested in being a millionaire as he had been. He gave it all up. And from Spain on until the day he died. He put himself, in a way, on hold. It's fascinating.

SHAFER: It is, it is indeed. And as you say, women pursued him, people were fascinated by him when he had those opportunities in the two O'Neill plays. I mean all the people described him as beautiful and with the greatest voice of any actor of the time. I am sure people would say that about you now.

JONES: No, my father was a Paul Robeson protégé in a lot of ways, except musically. Neither my father nor I can sing and that's what is remembered more than Paul the activist. Or Paul the one endowed with all the great talents. Thankfully, we can hear on records.

SHAFER: With those two roles, there came a turning point for African American actors in the American theatre. Do you feel that now sometimes people look back and they say that Jones is a stereotype and the play is filled with stereotypes? And that in *All God's Chillun Got Wings,* the guy loses everything, he doesn't come out ahead in any way? I mean people take a negative attitude about these plays.

JONES: That's true, that's still true. It took the longest time for the black guy to ever win the girl. The black guy always ended up dead or lost. So O'Neill gave us the first fully heroic African American character for the stage. And you might say, yes, so the Emperor Jones ends up hanging by his heels. That's not the point. If O'Neill set out to write a straight play about a deposed dictator from a Caribbean island, like Haiti, it might never have been produced. And it sure wouldn't have been a whole lot of fun. So he gave me something that was going to be a whole lot of fun. So he gave you something with a whole lot of fun *and* a great commentary on American capitalist sentiment. Maybe sentiment isn't right. But Brutus Jones was the ultimate capitalist, the ultimate exploiter. And that's not black, that's American. And O'Neill was exploring that, I think, with Brutus Jones.

SHAFER: That's a very interesting viewpoint.

JONES: What's the phrase, "greed is good?" Selfishness, ultimate selfishness. The long green.

SHAFER: Yeah, the long green. And, "I puts my Bible on the shelf," huh? [Both laughing.]

JONES: Yeah, that's what O'Neill was writing about. He wasn't writing about a black guy who overreached himself and failed, ended up on his heels. He was writing about the American spirit.

SHAFER: Wonderful, that's very nice.

JONES: And it was going on in the Caribbean countries, too. We did a lot of stuff down there in the name of money. Hawaii, you know the history of Hawaii, oh God. We were doing that all the time, we were all Brutus Joneses in different colors. Guys down there and in South America are still reeling from our exploitation. And that's what O'Neill is writing about.

SHAFER: So you think that the play holds up?

JONES: I don't know!

SHAFER: But in terms of what he was attempting?

JONES: The NAACP may have cooled off a little bit about the use of the word "nigger," but otherwise the play is not archaic. It is not a play that doesn't work anymore. It is, How does the play work after the first scene?

SHAFER: Can I just ask you, I know you have got to go, have you seen other O'Neill productions that you remember, that you enjoyed?

JONES: I've only seen *The Iceman Cometh*. Both Jason's and Kevin's. I have never seen any other production. And Paul Robeson's movie, *The Emperor Jones*. I remember once trying to, I missed—who's the actor from Charles Playhouse up in Boston, he played *The Hairy Ape?*

SHAFER: Willem Dafoe?

JONES: Yeah, Willem Dafoe. And I think that he must have been a wonderful Hairy Ape, too. I remember trying at a fundraiser with Ted [Mann] to read some scenes out of *The Hairy Ape* and I thought I'd knock this off. But, boy! O'Neill's dialogue is often very difficult, because he over-ethnicizes, he puts in too much accent. And the actor is busy trying to stay on top of that bucking bronco, rather than the dialogue whatever way it comes out. I found that with *Hairy Ape,* I found that dialogue very difficult.

SHAFER: Really, that's very interesting. And Robeson played that role.

JONES: Oh, *Hairy Ape,* no, no, Robeson I don't think he ever played it, did he?

SHAFER: I just read that myself in the *Dictionary of Black Theatre* and I was surprised. It was in 1931.

JONES: Well, he should have, yeah. The Hairy Ape is this stevedore in the hull of this ship, this freighter, and he's the darkest kind of a human being, he's an animal. If Robeson played it, that's good to hear.

SHAFER: So those were the only times that you had anything more to do with O'Neill? At this benefit? So, I guess that in the overall arc of your career, O'Neill hasn't been any central force, but has given you some interesting experiences.

JONES: And also acknowledging that he probably led a whole wave of creativity that went to Miller and Williams, but then opened up a whole road for the avant garde theatre which is of my time. And all the plays of avant garde theatre don't last. I mean Beckett has a few that are worth doing. But they are all experiments and O'Neill started it. Suddenly now, theatre is proletarian. It is not for the Barrymore characters. It's not tea and crumpets, it's not pickled salmon and coffee tables and lace fans. It's about human problem-solving and I think that, because he was more or less a socialist himself, I think that he opened the door to the theatre to being proletarian as it is now. You don't have to have descended from the Barrymores to be an actor, you can just walk off the street and get yourself together and be an actor.

SHAFER: But you descended from an actor.

JONES: Yeah, I did, and a good one, too!

3 | Jane Alexander

Jane Alexander was born in Boston in 1939. She attended Sarah Lawrence College from 1957 to 1959 and the University of Edinburgh from 1959 to 1960. Her career has encompassed acting on stage, television, and film. In 1964-65 she appeared at the Charles Playhouse in Boston. She acted at Arena Stage from 1965 to 1968. She scored a tremendous success in *The Great White Hope* with James Earl Jones and the production moved to Broadway and was then made into a film. She performed two summers, 1971 and 1972, with the Stratford Shakespeare Festival, directed by Michael Kahn. Her many performances on Broadway include *Hamlet, The Heiress, First Monday in October,* and *The Sisters Rosenszweig.* Her career has taken her to all of the major regional theatres, where she has appeared in Ibsen, Shaw, Shakespeare, and O'Neill. In addition to acting she has produced plays, taught, and served on numerous advisory boards that represent her wide interests, ranging from conservation to the promotion of peace. She served as the Chairperson for the National Endowment for the Arts from 1993 to 1997. Her many honorary degrees include Doctor of Fine Arts from Juilliard, Duke University, and Smith College. She won an Emmy for her performance in *Playing for Time* on television. Her outstanding performances in films have earned her four Academy Award nominations, including one for *The Great White Hope.* She won the Tony Award for performing in that play and received Tony nominations for six others including *Honour* in 1998. Her fine acting has won her many other awards including the Obie, and she has also received many awards for public service. Her busy career most recently has involved her performance in the film *The Cider House Rules,* and she has written a book related to her work on the NEA. She is married to director Edwin Sherin.

NEW YORK CITY, JULY 1999

SHAFER: You've told me that your father was involved in acting and that you were very much aware of plays and theatre as you were growing up. Do you remember anything about your first interest in O'Neill? Or what you first saw?

ALEXANDER: I was a *big fan* of Kim Stanley's. Growing up as a teenager I had watched the golden age of television, as they call it. I had followed Kim Stanley whenever she did a TV show. So when she was in *A Touch of the Poet* on Broadway, with Eric Portman and Helen Hayes, I raced to see it. Everyone else was going to see Eric Portman and Helen Hayes, and I was going to Kim Stanley. [Laughing.] God, was she wonderful. Acting the role of Sara, she was just great! I got to play that role later at the Charles Playhouse in Boston.

SHAFER: So you had, obviously, a great theatre sense as you grew up and you had this, I'm sure, idea of some of the roles that you would like to play. What was the first chance that you had to actually act any O'Neill? For example, when you were studying acting?

ALEXANDER: Never did anything that I recall when I was studying. I didn't have a lengthy studying period. I was at Sarah Lawrence for two years. And, took theatre there with regularity but as I remember I was concentrating on *Miss Julie* one year and doing a lot of the plays of Will Leach who taught there then. And then I did a Thornton Wilder at Sarah Lawrence. I don't ever remember doing any O'Neill.

SHAFER: So then, was *Mourning Becomes Electra* the first that you did?

ALEXANDER: No, *Touch of the Poet.*

SHAFER: Ah, tell me about it please.

ALEXANDER: At the Charles Playhouse in Boston, 1964, something like that, I can't remember, maybe earlier! I think it was the early '60s. I am trying to remember if my son was born then because he was born in '64. And that was my first introduction.

SHAFER: Who else was in it? Anybody we would know?

ALEXANDER: Was it George Mitchell? George Mitchell, long since passed away, and his wife, Catherine Squire.

SHAFER: Do you remember anything particular about the experience as far as your development as an actress and what you felt about being in it?

ALEXANDER: I think it was my first great review.

SHAFER: How nice!

ALEXANDER: Yes, Eleanor Hughes, I think that was her name, was writing for *The Boston Herald* then and Elliot Norton was writing for the other paper, *The Globe.* And they both gave me a very fine review.

SHAFER: You know, it's surprising, when I am looking back at the early part of this century, how many actors and actresses that we just assume are wonderful and famous and everything, often found their first success in an O'Neill play and then that was the turning point.

ALEXANDER: That's interesting!

SHAFER: Don't you feel that he writes roles that give actors a real chance to show that they can do it?

ALEXANDER: Well, first of all, I felt that I was eminently suited to O'Neill. I felt I was suited to *Touch of the Poet* because my own background, my father's family, my maiden name's Quigley and Irish is only a couple of generations back. It was very much in my father's looks, black Irish looks . . . my great-grandfather, grandfather . . . and I felt the whole experience of growing up in New England, so I felt very . . . I felt I knew these people surprisingly. Even though I didn't grow up in the kind of environment that O'Neill did, I knew the house, I knew that kind of house. I didn't grow up in it but people I knew did. I knew about living near the seashore. I knew Provincetown, because we summered in Nantucket or the Cape or somewhere. So I felt an affinity there and when I came to do O'Neill I felt comfortable. You know, that is a tribute to O'Neill more then anything. Although, there are some people who have a different kind of ancestry or heritage that don't feel as comfortable as I felt when I did it, because I felt I knew these people.

SHAFER: Well, he had that tremendous feeling about the sea and the water and if you never had that all, I can see how it might seem foreign to you. In fact I was just reading a biography of him and I don't think the writer had that feeling for the sea because he is always remarking on it in a way as if it were kind of odd. Relating it more to the *Count of Monte Cristo,* really, than to the sea itself.

ALEXANDER: All of my life, most of my life, let me put it that way, was spent on the water of one kind or another. And the place we have in Nova Scotia is right on the water and I couldn't be happier. The fog, everything about it is my comfort level. Everybody said, "But it's too cool there," but I said, "No, perfect." So, I think that you're right, O'Neill certainly felt that very, very strongly.

SHAFER: So, naturally, I'm surprised you didn't want to do Ibsen's *Lady from the Sea.*

ALEXANDER: I did.

SHAFER: Did you?

ALEXANDER: Yeah, but Vanessa Redgrave did such a beautiful job.

SHAFER: Ah, there you are. So, anyhow there you were, this young woman with this kind of appropriate background and all of the qualities. You know it's interesting, he felt that was terribly important. He really didn't feel that an actress that wasn't at all Irish or American could act a role in which she was supposed to be Irish or American, no matter how talented.

ALEXANDER: Really? I didn't know that.

SHAFER: No, he felt that was terribly important. So you were Sara and appropriately Irish. Was there anything about the rehearsal process in particular that you remember in terms of bringing out what you wanted to do with the character?

ALEXANDER: I don't remember it very well. George Mitchell did not play Con Melody, somebody else did, but I can't remember who it was. But he and I came to blows almost immediately, but that's in the play. It's a very interesting thing about O'Neill, and I don't know if other actors you've talked to feel this way, but unfortunately he brings out those qualities so strongly and the emotion is so intense, that I found it very difficult to separate from the actors. I mean, we'll discuss *Mourning,* but I had . . . I adored Sada [Thompson] in so many ways, but I would get so irritated with her and that's not like me.

SHAFER: And do you know that in the original one Alice Brady and Nazimova had almost a feud really?

ALEXANDER: That's right.

SHAFER: So, how long did you actually play *A Touch of the Poet?*

ALEXANDER: I would say three to five weeks, you know typical regional theatre at Charles Playhouse.

SHAFER: But, you look back on that as a wonderful experience as an actress, I suppose?

ALEXANDER: Oh yes. Oh, I mean there are a few great roles in my experience. The first one I ever did that was great was Nora in *Plough and the Stars* and that I did at the Edinburgh Festival, predating the Charles Playhouse. But, you know, aside from Shakespeare, some of my great roles have been in O'Neill.

SHAFER: So the next O'Neill is *Mourning Becomes Electra?*

ALEXANDER: Yes.

SHAFER: And how did that happen? How did it all get set up that you were going to play that role and the rest that was all going to occur?

ALEXANDER: Um, Michael Kahn called me.

SHAFER: Did you know him?

ALEXANDER: No, I guess he must have seen me in *Great White Hope*. James Earl and I played that 1968, 1969, then we did the movie. And then I remember getting a call that winter, my agent called me and said, "Michael Kahn wants you to do Lavinia in *Mourning Becomes Electra* at Stratford, Connecticut, this summer." And I had never read it. So I sat down to read it and thought this is incredibly long and so repetitive, it's like a soap opera. I remember turning to Ed [Sherin] (Ed and I were not married then but we were intimate and he was my favorite director), and I turned to him and I said "Ed, you know, this play . . . I don't know." And there was a long pause and he said, "Jane, if you don't do this you're a fucking fool." I was so shocked by his words. First of all, he didn't usually talk like that to me, but the way he said it was so firm, that there was no question. He said "This is one of the great plays, this is one of the great roles, you're going to be working at Stratford with Michael Kahn," blah blah, and he said "fucking fool." So I did it and of course he was absolutely right.

SHAFER: But, of course, he was there directing you in *Major Barbara*. Is that right?

ALEXANDER: But that was the next year. I did *Mourning Becomes Electra* and *Merry Wives of Windsor* the first year.

SHAFER: Michael said that you said that if you were going to do *Mourning Becomes Electra* that you had to have a comedy to play with it. Could you talk a little bit about why that was?

ALEXANDER: Well, I knew enough about myself and I had been through almost two years continuously playing a manic depressive in *Great White Hope,* and one who kills herself at the end. And, unfortunately, I have a very difficult time separating when there are these very deep emotions, as I say, and a playwright is actually able to bring them out in you. You know this about actors, you draw things that are in yourself, but if you are drawing on them on a daily basis like you do in the theatre, they remain up there, in your psyche, for as long as you're doing the play. At least they do to me. It's very hard for me to compartmentalize. So, I knew that if I was going to be playing a murderer, which was Lavinia, people with murderous thoughts, that I needed something to counterbalance that. So at least I had some joyous moments. I always was a little, at that time in particular, I was always a little nervous about my own psyche because I was very, very afraid I was going to go under. Some actors did do that in the past, they just got overwhelmed by the role and ultimately just succumbed.

SHAFER: Gosh, you make me think of that film, *A Double Life,* with Ronald Colman, where he's playing Othello.

ALEXANDER: Oh, I know what you mean, yes.

SHAFER: Well, so then to balance out the O'Neill you had the *Merry Wives of Windsor,* with your natural hairdo.

ALEXANDER: [Laughs.] I think that was a wig!

SHAFER: No, no, natural hairdo I mean in the sense of . . .

ALEXANDER: Afro, yes, yes that's correct.

SHAFER: So that was interesting balancing out for you then. Did Sada Thompson [who played Christine] feel the same way about it?

ALEXANDER: I don't ever remember talking to Sada about it.

SHAFER: Had you known her before?

ALEXANDER: No.

SHAFER: This was the first time you met her.

ALEXANDER: And, as I say, I really adore Sada, I don't want you to think that I don't. It was just something in the roles that made me sometimes irritated with her. But I thought she was brilliant and wonderful and very powerful.

SHAFER: Oh, it was a wonderful, whole evening. I remember it very well.

ALEXANDER: That's good. And I thought Jane Greenwood costumed us beautifully.

SHAFER: She does do wonderful costumes, doesn't she?

ALEXANDER: Yes, the green velvet that she gave us. Now you know that it's on records, don't you?

SHAFER: No, I do not. Please do tell us about it.

ALEXANDER: I think it's a tape recording, the whole thing, the whole play. Now I haven't listened to it because I always get a little nervous and—maybe I haven't listened to it in twenty years, but I just wanted to bring that to your attention.

SHAFER: In the original production, reviews described Lavinia as being ice-cold and very obsessed and driven throughout, almost, one would say, a kind of monotone of mood. I wondered if you could talk about how you feel about, what was your actual attitude towards this woman?

ALEXANDER: Cold is very interesting. I think that, I can't talk about it without talking about Zoë Wanamaker in *Electra* . . .

SHAFER: Do.

ALEXANDER: . . . which I admired extremely, I mean I thought it was wonderful, but I always thought Orestes was the one who had the Furies on him. And, Lavinia is more like Medusa or Lavinia is like, she's Electra, but she's cold, maybe cold with a big ice-cube inside— in here; unable to warm up, unable to get emotional or erratic or anything. Just totally fixated, totally fixated. Something happened that I keep coming back to and trying to figure out what was going on with me. Michael never knew either. It was one little gesture that I had to do when, the lover is dead and the body is lying there I had to take my hoop skirt and put it right over his head.

SHAFER: Huh!

ALEXANDER: I know. And I never knew, I still don't know what it's about. But it was so strong, it was an urge to just stand there covering the top of his head with his dead face obviously looking right up my bloomers, or what have you. Jane always gave us tons of undergarments, which were real. So it wasn't like he was looking at anything really exposed. But I had to do it and I did it and Michael sort of said, "Well, that was a very interesting thing." And I said, "Well, I don't know what that's about, I'll cut it out if you . . ." But he said, "No, no, I love it, keep it!" But, it was that kind of strange, I didn't know ever what I was doing and I still can't describe why I did a lot of it. But I think they were very deep kind of primal urges.

SHAFER: One of the things I felt in your performance that I still remember so well was the change in her character from the beginning to end.

ALEXANDER: After momma dies.

SHAFER: Yes, but also, it seems to me there is a major development in the character from her first act through all of those scenes. What does she go through, what are the different things that she becomes?

ALEXANDER: Well, of course when Christine is killed, when she's gone, it's like a ghost you have to take on a mantle, at least I always felt it seemed natural for Lavinia to do that and to start flirting with Orin. So that's where it started to develop.

SHAFER: Did you think that unconsciously you took on any of Sada Thompson's characteristics when you made the change?

ALEXANDER: I didn't consciously try to do it, but I may have done that. I know, of course, that she does wear green velvet and I wanted my hair to be dressed in a feminine and a sort of an alluring way. That's written into the play, I mean it's all there.

SHAFER: Michael edited himself and he told me that he thinks it's important to have the repetition in the script, not to cut it. Did you find that useful as an actress?

ALEXANDER: Oh, totally. Initially, I could not understand how I could— you know O'Neill writes bluntly. He has Lavinia say things like, "I hate you, I hate you!" It's like, pow! I remember saying to Ed, "There's no subtlety here," and Ed said, "No, that's the point." [Laughing.] And at first I thought, I'll never be at that point but then I was, of course, and Michael was wonderful, he gave us ten weeks of rehearsal.

SHAFER: Did you have ten weeks?!

ALEXANDER: Ten weeks of rehearsal! On that play. Well, it was very, very long, you know. It was four-and-a-half hours. And by the time I started to get to that emotional height, which by the way, probably didn't kick in until probably about the eighth week, then I was *so grateful* for it, so grateful for just *saying* everything right out. O'Neill was brilliant that way, I don't know *any* playwright that I've ever performed that does that. And I think it is such a testament to the depth of what he's writing, of where he's writing from. It's a very, very deep emotional well. And true as all get-out. At first, I didn't believe it was true.

SHAFER: How amazing, hmm?

ALEXANDER: And you have to play it.

SHAFER: You talked a little about the relationship with Christine, which of course is clear, but what about the relationship with the father, Mannon, which Lee Richardson played.

ALEXANDER: Well, Lee and I . . . maybe that was, maybe I'd worked with Lee before that, I don't know but, or maybe it was the first time. We worked many, many times together in the '70s after that and even into the '80s.

SHAFER: He was a very fine actor.

ALEXANDER: Oh, a wonderful actor, wonderful actor. The best Undershaft! Oh my God! But, you know, Lee looked like Grant, one of the great Civil War generals! [Laughing.] He just looked so handsome when he came back and it was easy to adore him, just so easy. But, I remember feeling the jealousy when he went off to be alone with Christine.

SHAFER: Did you get tired of playing the role?

ALEXANDER: Oh no, no, no, no, no, no, no because we were in repertory, it was certainly one of the most satisfying theatre experiences an actor can have, being in repertory. It's just divine. So, you know, I performed at the most four times a week, I would think. It was a marathon when you performed it, but extremely exhilarating because it was so long and Lavinia is on the stage so much.

SHAFER: Yes. That's the great challenge.

ALEXANDER: Not all the time, the playwright, O'Neill gives her some great breaks, but it was enough to redo my whole look.

SHAFER: Did you do anything that was at all different from what you would normally do before you were in the play just because of the length?

ALEXANDER: Yes. This was the other thing, Joe Verner Reed, who you probably remember was the main backer of the Stratford Shakespeare Festival, had kindly given me his house for at least the rehearsal period. And his house was right opposite the theatre, that row of nineteenth-century houses there. And one of them was a lovely white house. But the play was giving me creeps, so the house was giving me creeps at night! [Laughing.] And then I found out that in the 1700s they had hung a witch or something across the street there. Oh, it was . . . I don't know . . . I was starting to hallucinate or . . . I was going nuts. But, why did I bring that up? Did I do anything different? Yes! Ed moved in with me before the end of rehearsal for which I was grateful, because I was really, I was getting kind of goofy, scary, scared. And, he moved in and um, he made sure that I took a nap; that I was thoroughly rested every time before I had to perform that day.

SHAFER: Did you eat ahead? These are rather mundane questions, but people wonder about these kinds of things.

ALEXANDER: No, no. I used to eat with a lot more gusto in the '60s and I could eat and go right on and do a play. But, I think, by then I probably must have started eating around four-thirty or five o'clock for an evening performance. Yes, it's not so good to perform on a full stomach. But you need enough to give you the energy, so I always eat. And I am not a big eater after a performance, so I have to have something substantial.

SHAFER: Well, that's interesting. You remarked to me before we began this, about how much you admire Michael Kahn as a director. What did he do while you were doing this play?

ALEXANDER: I think Michael, and now understand please that I haven't worked with Michael since that time . . .

SHAFER: That was the last time!

ALEXANDER: Yes, we wanted many times to work together, it just didn't work out. But, Michael then, and I am sure he is the same now, is wonderful about just watching. Just letting you have your head for awhile and then maybe just asking a few questions, like "What do you think Lavinia feels about Orin being away for so long?" He's always trying to . . . that is the way, I think that he tries to get you to think about something without telling you anything.

SHAFER: Did he have the movement planned ahead?

ALEXANDER: He had to have a lot of it planned ahead. You have to when you have such a big piece or work. Not all of it. I mean there was always room for maneuvering or changing things if you felt strongly about them. Michael is not didactic, he's . . . I think it's probably what makes him a brilliant teacher—he's trying to draw the best out of you. (Ed has the same quality.) And then by the end of the rehearsal period then he starts to really give you notes that mean something. A very fine director.

SHAFER: And so, you felt, ultimately, I guess, that it was a major event in your career to have been in that production.

ALEXANDER: Oh yes, I always thought it was one of *the* highlights, I mean *The Great White Hope,* I'm talking about on the stage, *Mourning Becomes Electra,* it's hard to come up with others . . . I loved our production of *The Master Builder* and I loved *First Monday in October,* mainly because of Hank Fonda.

SHAFER: It must have been wonderful since he was a friend of your father's, hm?

ALEXANDER: Yeah, *Sisters Rosenszweig* . . . those are a few of what were, for me, highlights.

SHAFER: Now, I have seen that you were in *The Iceman Cometh,* and yet I think . . . well, I don't know what to say, I don't think most people would say "Oh, yes, Jane Alexander was in *The Iceman Cometh.*" When was it and who was in it and how did that come about?

ALEXANDER: That was when I was at Arena Stage and Ed directed the production, I think it was our last year before I went out and did *Great White Hope* on Broadway. So I have a feeling it must have been in the spring of '68. It was a production with the entire company and we had been working together for three years.

SHAFER: You had a wonderful, ensemble feeling there.

ALEXANDER: Oh boy, we hit our stride. By the time we were doing *The Iceman* and we did that in repertory, too, I am trying to remember what it was with, but it was with two other plays, if I recall. And I played Pearl and, you know, there's something— you bathe in O'Neill. You bathe in it, you just, when you're on the stage in that kind of a thing in the bar. You just let time, things, wash over you. There's no rush with O'Neill, that's what I love about it. He takes his time to say something and anybody who thinks about cutting any of these plays radically is, as Ed said to me, a fucking fool. [Laughing.] Because it's in the leisure time, it's in the montage of experience that you find the brilliance. You find it as an actress, actor and you find it, I hope—I think, as an audience member.

SHAFER: Michael says the audience has to work a little bit. That's an interesting idea, I thought, in the sense of not being like a musical or something, where it's just all there.

ALEXANDER: Oh, I think the work is actually . . . I think the audience should prepare themselves as well as an actor does for performance of O'Neill. They should eat early, not drink any alcohol, have a nap and go and see the play, so that they're rested.

SHAFER: Do you know when I walked in to see *The Iceman Cometh* at Long Wharf there was a couple who were clearly a married pair who were subscribers and they had clearly been out having drinks and dinner and all, you know. And the man turned to his wife and said, "What is this, a musical?" I thought, "Well, he has an evening ahead of him!"

ALEXANDER: Whew! That's what I mean, maybe that's what Michael means, too.

SHAFER: I think that he meant that at least, as opposed to just sitting there and watching some idiot sitcom or something, that you've got to have something going on in your mind, too. I saw a German actor who was playing this role in which he had to talk to the audience and he said to the audience "You have to play with me." And I think with O'Neill there is more involvement, in that sense. Well, tell me a little more about playing Pearl. Was it fun? It must have been fun to play a tart.

ALEXANDER: It was a lot of fun, but back in those days in Arena, you know, we did everything, the company. Richard Bauer, Robert Prosky, Robert Foxworth, Frederick O'Neal. Richard McKenzie played Hickey.

SHAFER: How long did you have to rehearse that one?

ALEXANDER: We had about ten weeks, but we were doing other plays, as well, as I recall.

SHAFER: It's interesting to me that at that point in your career you had already played a number of major roles, but you were then playing what is essentially a secondary role, certainly, in this play.

ALEXANDER: But, as members of the company, that's what we all did.

SHAFER: Please talk about that a little bit and how you felt about that. This is one of the glories of repertory system, to me. You see a solid company throughout because you see the stars one night playing roles like Pearl on another night.

ALEXANDER: That's right. Well, we don't have it in this country. It's just the saddest thing, I find. And we couldn't keep it up for very long at Arena either because the Rockefeller and Ford and NEA grants could not meet the budget. It costs more.

SHAFER: And they went to the one play and . . .

ALEXANDER: and jobbing in the actors, for the most part. I mean they kept a few on board. This was a company of over thirty. And, you know, Ed and Zelda had very, very big ideas about a repertory company and conservatory, ultimately, and all the great dreams of the European companies, of German companies. The dreams, but it never came to fruition in this country. And I still remember when Ed came back from a trip to Germany and then he went to Russia. And he came back to tell us all about these repertory companies. And we thought we would become that, of course. So, it was, it was just remarkable to have that experience. And all of us did that. We would play a big role. You would know at the beginning of the season what you were going to play. So you could be preparing for that. And, it worked out wonderfully. I did not enjoy being the spear carrier or one of the crowd, because I don't subscribe to the belief that there are no small parts, there are only small actors. There are small parts and there are thankless parts and I did not want to play them. [Laughing.] But to be a part of the experience of *The Iceman* was something we were all looking forward to. Jim Mackenzie, an actor who went to L.A. a few years later and did a few things on television, was quite a wonderful Hickey. You know, he was, he was not as great as I think Jason was. But he had such a compelling personality, fun, that we couldn't wait for him to come on because he made everything fun and up. And Bobby Foxworth was Parritt.

SHAFER: Oh, how wonderful, he must have been marvelous in that!

ALEXANDER: Oh, it was a great, great production. It was really good.

SHAFER: And you didn't play any other O'Neill. And now, all this time has gone by, ma'am. We are waiting to see you in more O'Neill . . .

ALEXANDER: It wasn't possible to do *Moon for the Misbegotten* because Colleen [Dewhurst] was still so present in the '70s and they had the revival, she was brilliant! I mean I loved Colleen in that play. And *More Stately Mansions* didn't interest me very much.

SHAFER: Were you not attracted to *Anna Christie?*

ALEXANDER: Very much so, but I couldn't get anybody interested and also Liv Ullman did it. Remember Liv did it? And she was wonderful, I thought Liv was terrific in that. And then the other one I wanted to do, of course, was *Long Day's Journey*. But it never worked out because the times I was asked to be Mary Tyrone it was with an actor that I didn't feel was quite right. I think I could still do Mary Tyrone.

SHAFER: Oh, you've got a long time ahead of you.

ALEXANDER: Thank you very much.

SHAFER: Who would you like to do it with, if you had your choice out of all the actors around now?

ALEXANDER: Well, you know I would have, the guy I really adored just left us and that's Richard Kiley. I loved Dick Kiley. And, he and I did *The Heiress* together and then we did *Master Builder* together. And I would have loved to have had him do James Tyrone.

SHAFER: I think that this is something that's got to come about in the future with another actor.

ALEXANDER: The problem is, Yvonne—name the great leading men in that age . . . I mean Dick was a lot older then I was, but somehow we were right together and he could give that image of the great leading man.

SHAFER: Do you not feel that the man has to be able to give a sense that he really was a big matinee idol? It seems to me, and I don't want to be unkind, but I don't see how some of the actors who have played Tyrone could have ever conveyed that sense.

ALEXANDER: There you go. And you got it with Kiley right away. I mean, he looked like one of those great actors. [Laughing.]

SHAFER: Yes, but it has to be more than just looks, doesn't it?

ALEXANDER: Oh yes.

SHAFER: Well, this will be a challenge that I hope will be forthcoming. May I ask you briefly about another thing? Because you keep your eye on the arts in this country, and everybody has been saying for all these years that people just want to go see musicals and *Miss Saigon* and that sort of thing on Broadway. I was just reading that George M. Cohan said in 1920 that people think the American public is not interested in dramatic literature on the stage, but that he believed it was, and the proof was Eugene O'Neill's *Beyond the Horizon*. Now, in recent seasons we've seen a kind of change. Do you think we are going to see more plays like *Death of a Salesman* and *The Iceman Cometh,* which have been so successful? You shake your head no. Heavens, a pessimistic response. Then why were those things so popular?

ALEXANDER: Because there will always be the need for one heavyweight drama production. There's still an audience that will take care of one, but ideally it would be a new play. I mean I think one of the greatest plays of the decade has been, the greatest, has been *Angels in America.* I think, it's filling a gap, that's all. And I do feel that if people like Cherry Jones do *Moon for the Misbegotten,* which she is slated to do, people will go to see that. Certainly the cognoscenti will because I know she'll be brilliant. As long as there is not something else going on that will take it away. Also, there is a whole generation that has gone by in twenty years that doesn't know some of these plays. The great plays will always have an audience, I think. But, I don't see a rash nor do I see them lasting very long. *The Iceman* couldn't really carry much beyond what it did.

SHAFER: It did sell out, though, all the time, that was quite amazing, and at high prices, too.

ALEXANDER: Yes, I know.

SHAFER: Did you get to see it?

ALEXANDER: Sure did.

SHAFER: Oh, tell me what you thought, because you know the play well since you were in it.

ALEXANDER: Summed up, I thought the production was wonderful, brilliant. I really loved it. I thought that Kevin was just off by that much and one thing I didn't see is summed up in one word: ecstasy, he had no ecstasy. And I think that Hickey is in heaven when he comes on because he thinks that he is giving Evelyn *heaven.* So what he did is the right thing. I mean, it's all delusional, but I don't think you come on playing the death of Evelyn. You come on playing the release, "I did it for her!" "I did it for her, I got the power, I got the strength to give her release," so that you have somewhere to go. And then in the end, oh!

SHAFER: It's sort of like Hedda Gabler playing that suicide in the first scene.

ALEXANDER: Yes. Now, I would like to talk for a few minutes about one of the reasons I feel so strongly about Ibsen, because I feel O'Neill is a direct growth from Ibsen. He is the inheritor of Ibsen's emotional strength and relation—understanding relationships. And then I think then after that comes Miller. So that there is almost a through line there and that's why I love Ibsen and O'Neill so much, they are very similar to me. And it's also why I search for a good translation because somehow I want what we have in English in O'Neill, in Ibsen.

SHAFER: That's very interesting, I almost feel like saying "say that again," because so many people pick O'Neill up on what he says in *Long Day's Journey into Night* about not having the poetic ability. And lots of people have just knocked his ability to write dialogue; you obviously feel otherwise about this.

ALEXANDER: The poetry is found in the montage of experience. He is not writing the language of Anouilh or Giraudoux or even Tennessee Williams. He doesn't have that kind of lyricism, nor is he looking for it, nor do I think it was in his soul. I don't think it was in Eugene O'Neill's soul any more then I think it was in Ibsen's and neither one of them, I mean I don't read Norwegian so I don't know. But there's not a lot of poetry, it's not about that! It's about relationships and it's about where one finds oneself in the world at any given time. And the *trap*, trap, everybody is in a trap, and it's trying to find the way out. And I find it just very moving. You know, I think those two fellows understand the human condition.

SHAFER: You've played in both. Could you talk about what it is like when you're onstage in those great scenes and the audience is there?

I mean obviously you get a feeling from the audience at that point, don't you? Or you have a sense of what the audience is getting out of it.

ALEXANDER: That's a really interesting question.

SHAFER: Liviu Ciulei spoke to me about directing *Peer Gynt,* and he said the audience, at some moments, seemed to be breathing as one.

ALEXANDER: I felt that a little bit with *Mourning Becomes Electra,* I think. I couldn't believe that the play would sustain for four-and-a-half hours. I could not believe that, but I knew I was the driving engine and I had a strong sense of that; of moving through something; not tarrying—I do remember somewhere in the third act or something feeling like the audience was asking "Now, what's going to happen?" You know, that's the great thing. Breathing as one is a very good description.

SHAFER: It's been wonderful to talk to you about this. I think that you so clearly have this idea that as an actress you have to find a role that really excites you and that Ibsen and O'Neill are the ones who can do that, is that right?

ALEXANDER: For me. But there are certain plays of theirs that I am not interested in.

SHAFER: Oh, of course.

ALEXANDER: Like *More Stately Mansions* and there's a lot of Ibsen I wasn't terribly drawn to. Well, I have a funny story for you, I think you'll like this. Years ago [laughing] Liv Ullmann and I, who were good friends during the '70s or early '80s, talked about doing *When We Dead Awaken* and finding the right guy to be Rubek. And we also decided she would play one part one night and I would play the other and then we would reverse. So it would be very thrilling for both of us, so we talked about this. And then, she went back to Norway. She was doing something in Norway and she had been over there for about five months or something and we had had no contact. And Alex Cohen, who does this to actresses he knows, sent her a direct telegram saying "Want to do a production of *Ghosts* with you, yes or no?" Now the translation of "ghosts" in Norwegian is like the awakening dead. So she thought it was a production of *When We Dead Awaken*. So she cables her agent back, Robby Lance and says, "Say yes to Cohen." And she said she didn't know it wasn't *When We Dead Awaken* until she arrived in this country.

SHAFER: Isn't that wild! Yes, that is a wonderful story. You and she have both had such an interest in Ibsen and O'Neill.

ALEXANDER: Well, they're the great roles.

4 | Michael Kahn

Michael Kahn was born in New York City. He received a B.A. from Columbia University and has received several honorary degrees from Kean College, University of Southern California, and elsewhere. He was Artistic Director of the American Shakespeare Theatre in Stratford, Connecticut, was the director of the Chautauqua Conservatory Theatre Company, and has directed at many locations throughout the country as well as directing plays for Broadway. He has taught acting at several places including the Circle in the Square and Juilliard. He has served on many committees such as the theatre panel for the National Endowment for the Arts. Although he has a major interest in Shakespeare and has directed almost all of his plays at various festivals and theatres (including the New York Shakespeare Festival), he has directed virtually every type of play. As Producing Director of the McCarter Theatre Company he directed a wide range of plays including *Beyond the Horizon, Mother Courage,* and *A Month in the Country.* His productions on Broadway include *Cat on a Hot Tin Roof, The Death of Bessie Smith,* and *Showboat* (for which he received a Tony nomination in 1983). He is a several-time winner of the Helen Hayes Award, and won the Charles MacArthur Award as best director for *Old Times* in 1973, as well as many other awards. In 1989 he was selected as the Washingtonian of the Year by *Washingtonian Magazine.* His many activities keep him moving back and forth between

Washington and New York City and many other locations as he is the Director of the Drama Division at Juilliard and the Artistic Director of the Shakespeare Theatre in Washington.

NEW YORK CITY, MAY 1999

SHAFER: Michael, you have really directed so many O'Neill plays.

KAHN: Well, I directed *Beyond the Horizon, Mourning Becomes Electra*—twice—and *Ile*. That was in college. It wasn't very good. Have I directed any others? Yes, *A Touch of the Poet*. That was in the Arena Stage with Daniel Travanti.

SHAFER: Many times when there is a revival of an O'Neill play critics and general public will say, "Oh yes, this was a good evening in the theatre. The play wasn't any good but the acting was good." What do you think of that kind of reaction?

KAHN: Well, I think O'Neill is an extraordinary playwright and the thing about O'Neill is that his ambition was so huge in terms of what he wanted to write about, and the cumulative effect of an O'Neill play is quite extraordinary. Sometimes it's clumsy, sometimes it's overwritten, but the very ambition of it and the weight of all of that goes to make an experience that no other American writer ever gives the audience. I certainly don't think that with the productions that I've done people said that the actor saved the play. I think *A Touch of the Poet* is not as good a play as perhaps some of the other plays, although I'd like to have seen the whole cycle that he was going to write but he didn't. He did a lot of wonderful things in *A Touch of the Poet* but I happen to love *Mourning Becomes Electra* and *Strange Interlude*. I mean, *Long Day's Journey into Night* is a masterpiece. It's the greatest autobiographical play written by an American or perhaps by anybody. I guess sometimes people think O'Neill is very heavy, very difficult, but the very denseness, the very weight of it is what makes him very exciting, sort of like climbing a mountain every time you go to see an O'Neill play. And at the end of the evening, I think everyone has had an experience. Getting there requires some work. The thing is that great actors like Colleen Dewhurst and Jason Robards have made great successes in O'Neill plays—and plays that were not successes when they were originally done. But I think any production of *Moon for the Misbegotten* now would probably be a success. It's just that it had not been a success during O'Neill's lifetime and then when Colleen did it for the first time everybody thought, "Oh, it was Colleen." But I also think the world caught up with O'Neill in those cases.

SHAFER: What first attracted you to O'Neill?

KAHN: Oh, because I think he was a very serious, weighted playwright, and I like serious, really complex plays. I wanted to do *Mourning Becomes Electra* for a very long period of time and every year I was at Stratford, Connecticut, at the American Shakespeare Theatre, I wrote to Carlotta O'Neill, asking for the rights to *Mourning Becomes Electra*. It had not been done and I don't think it had been revived since its original production. And it was her play. And I was turned down. She didn't give the rights, she didn't give the rights. I used to send these letters out almost *pro forma* after a while, I never expected to do it. Then the year before she died or two years before she died, all of a sudden her lawyer called me saying, "You could do the play." By that time I never expected to do it and I read it and said, "Oh, my God what have I let myself in for?" Because on the first re-reading I thought, "Do I want to do this now? I did five years ago, do I want to now?" But I felt a responsibility to do it because I announced to do it, so I started working on it, then I realized that this was a wonderful play and I asked if some of it could be edited and the lawyer said yes. I think it was the first time they allowed someone to actually edit. So I worked very hard on editing a bit.

SHAFER: So you did it yourself?

KAHN: Yes, I did it myself. Basically the edits were in Act III, which all the critics had originally said was the least successful act. I felt what had happened was that often O'Neill goes someplace, then he goes backwards, then he goes forwards, and then backwards. Also, in the time that O'Neill was writing, he wrote everything down that any character ever thought, all his contradictory thinking: they think one thing, they take it back, they think of something else and take it back, and I think it was because he didn't think that actors could do any of that. That they had to explain everything that they were doing and feeling. I felt that some of it could actually be done through acting and that it was better to try to make a forward movement of the play and to not have so many retractions. So I made some cuts. And when we did it with Sada Thompson and Jane Alexander as Lavinia and Christine, many of the critics thought that the third act was actually the culmination of what was really a good play.

SHAFER: It was a very exciting evening I remember.

KAHN: I think the cuts helped because they made the story go forward instead of continually turning back on itself, which is something O'Neill does. And since the third act had originally been poorly received, I thought maybe it was all right to do it. I did and I'm glad I did.

SHAFER: That was about 1973 or so. You liked it well enough to do it again?

KAHN: I did it again about two years ago in the same—it's interesting— the same version. I started again from scratch. I went back to the play thinking twenty years later, twenty five years later perhaps I'll think differently. I started working and it turns out that the cuts I made were exactly the same. I don't cut any author's work until I know it by heart, and have worked out all the acting moments.

SHAFER: Did you have any particular changes in your approach to directing it the second time?

KAHN: Oh, I think so. I think I understood Orin better. I think I understood the family relationships in my fifties differently than I did in my early thirties.

SHAFER: This production was in Washington, D.C.?

KAHN: In Washington. It was very, very successful in the Shakespeare Theatre. People were stunned when it was over. Couldn't talk . . . it was very emotional for the audience. A very big success. And O'Neill was called a genius by the critics. Nobody thought it was just the acting.

SHAFER: What about *A Touch of the Poet?*

KAHN: I took over the production for the Artistic Director at Arena Stage because he had another offer for something else he wanted to do. It was pretty much cast and designed and everything when I came in. I had not liked the play at all when I saw its original production with Helen Hayes and Kim Stanley and Eric Portman on Broadway. I didn't like it at all. I thought it was quite boring. So as I began to work on it, I began to understand the play more. I thought it was a small play to be in the big Arena. I wasn't sure it was the right theatre for it, but I enjoyed working on it and I got to like the play better, but I didn't love the play. And I want to do *Strange Interlude*, now, really a great deal—that's what I want to do.

SHAFER: Where would you do that?

KAHN: At the Shakespeare Theatre. Especially if I could edit the play. I believe that O'Neill's work benefits from *some* editing. I think that actually he didn't trust actors. I think with good actors there are things you can cut. I did *Beyond the Horizon* (which I think was the first production since its original production) at the McCarter in my first season there as my first play. I found out about the play because I bought it for $.25 in a tag sale, and I read it and I thought, "Gosh, this is *Long Day's Journey* before he is willing to tell the truth" and I wanted to do it. So I did it and I didn't cut a thing. As a matter of fact, it turns out that what I saw, what I bought, was O'Neill's printed version before the production, and the production had cut some of the stuff that was in the version I read. I left it all in because I thought some of it (because we now knew about *Long*

Day's Journey) was actually more interesting because we knew now about these brothers, we knew something about them. So there were several big speeches which O'Neill had cut out in the original, or his director cut out, which were in this original printing which I left in. After we staged it, we did it for television. It was for Great Performances.

SHAFER: You had a wonderful cast. I remember it quite well.

KAHN: I had the same young people—Maria Tucci, Richard Backus, and Ed Moore—but the parents got grander and it turned out to be John Houseman, and Jimmy Broderick, and Geraldine Fitzgerald [laughs], it got grander. It was pretty good. It was greatly filmed. Out by the O'Neill Center in Connecticut, that's where we filmed it. I remember one day we were sitting on the rocks and luckily a schooner came by—a big clipper ship. I have no idea why! We rushed to get the camera on it, you know. And I thought the young O'Neill must have been out here looking at the ships.

Oh! And I did *Long Day's Journey* in Boston with Jose Ferrer and Kate Reid and Len Cariou. I had a wonderful time. I think Kate Reid was the most wonderful Mary Tyrone I've ever seen. It was interesting for Joe Ferrer to do it because his whole life had been somewhat like James O'Neill's—having been thought of as Cyrano for all those years.

SHAFER: And Len Cariou was Jamie?

KAHN: He was Jamie and Ben Masters was Edmund. Kate Reid, who was an alcoholic, gave the most honest performance of what she knew about herself as an alcoholic that she would never admit in life: she knew of all the lying and the wheedling, and the pretending, and the anger underneath all of it; pretending to be loving. All that stuff that actually she let come out in the theatre and I was amazed. I told her one day, "I know what you're doing and I'm not going to say anything about it. But if you keep doing this, you will have a great success." And she did. The audience stood up every night. One night, one rehearsal, Jose Ferrer did the speech about his life and *The Count of Monte Cristo*—what that play had done to him, and it was so moving. When it was over, I went to Joe and said that it was extraordinary. He said, "I'll never do it that way again." It was too painful and he never did do it that way again. But it was an extraordinary production. That play is a great masterpiece. I loved it. You have to work on that play, but that play does itself. It's just one of the greatest plays ever written.

SHAFER: Do you feel that it is very hard for the actors to perform such long plays, such complex plays as the ones we've been speaking about here? Are they resistant to it?

KAHN: No. You just have to have very good actors. No, I think actors love O'Neill when they get to do it. They feel it's richer. Except for Shakespeare, who's richer than O'Neill? No, I think actors *love* doing O'Neill. I think actors find it difficult to start with because there's a lot to do and a lot to say, but almost all the actors who worked with me on O'Neill thought they were in a major artistic event of their lives. People know that they're working with a genius.

SHAFER: Do you have anything that you particularly remember about working with some actors?

KAHN: Well, I told you what I remembered about Kate and about Joe Ferrer. You have to be very honest to do that. When I was doing *Mourning Becomes Electra* with Jane Alexander, she said, "I have to do a comedy in repertory with this because it's going to be so involving that I'm not going to feel good about myself when I enter the life of this person and I need something to release me when I'm not doing this play." And so she did *Merry Wives of Windsor* with it because the experience is so overwhelming for the audience and for the actor who enters into it. The same thing happened when I did it in Washington with Kelly McGillis, who gave a brilliant performance as Lavinia. And Fran Doran, who is an African American actress who played Christine, was fine because she had the emotional equipment for it. The woman is supposed to be a sort of an outsider from another society, another ethnic background.

Fran went through it and by the end of the second act she was destroyed. After she leaves her lover and then murders her husband. Kelly just found resources in herself (kind of being her father's daughter). You have to go through such emotionally draining scenes, be such a neurotic person to be in those plays, and yet it has the heft of great tragedy so you have a weight of the emotion to support you. What the people do is really awful, you know. Robert Sella, who was in *Side Man*, played Orin brilliantly, too. All the coldness, and the passion underneath the Puritan repression—that struggle between all these things that were going on and keeping a lid on it because it's wrong is really a roller coaster for the actor and you have to have an awful lot of technique to do it. And you have to be very, very honest in order for it not to be overblown and melodramatic. Because it comes from a melodramatic tradition. His father was the king of melodramas. In the theatre of that time emotions were melodramatic. And writing in his time, there's a lot of melodrama in O'Neill. The melodrama is not something you respond to very well right now, but if we can get to the purity of those feelings, and the depth of those feelings, like O'Neill wanted, because he was interested in Greek tragedy, then those plays are very, very acceptable now and resonant now. Now people want in the theatre bigger experiences than television and the Movie of the Week and Problem of the Week. O'Neill provides that and I think that's why people still respond. They may go to the theatre unwillingly thinking, "Oh God, it's going to be a heavy evening," because I heard that a lot in Washington. "Oh, I don't usually like to go to O'Neill, it's so heavy. But this was extraordinary, and I was so moved and transformed. I didn't know four hours had gone by." That's what everybody said: "I had no idea four hours and ten minutes had gone by." The power of O'Neill still gets people. But the audience has to work when they go to a play of O'Neill's.

SHAFER: Do you have any definite plans, or are you just thinking about doing *Strange Interlude*?

KAHN: I want to do it. I can't do it next season. There's someone I'm doing it with that I haven't told yet. [Smiles.] So I can't tell you.

SHAFER: It was very often viewed as a starring vehicle for a woman. Then when they did it in England and brought it over here, Edward Petherbridge was viewed as more of the major figure.

KAHN: I was going to do it at the Roundabout that year and then they asked me to send it to Glenda Jackson who I thought would be miscast. But she's a great actress, so I said, "Fine, if you want to send it to Glenda Jackson go ahead." Then Glenda Jackson took it and did it in England and then brought it here so I never got to do it.

SHAFER: Michael, obviously with *Long Day's Journey* there's an essential realism even though it has a tinge of Expressionism as people don't really speak that way.

KAHN: Well, it's poetry.

SHAFER: Looking at something like *Strange Interlude,* how do you view that in terms of realism?

KAHN: I don't think it should look like a realistic play. I don't think it should be. I don't think *Mourning Becomes Electra* should be. In Washington we had a kind of stylized set. Real things happened, but it was very spare. Doors were twenty-five feet high in the air and it was just all white. The doors were very high like a Greek temple. People just wore just black and green like he suggests. And I made the chorus like a chorus. They actually often spoke facing out toward the audience: the town's people in little spots of light. That was one big thing that I did differently than when I did it the first time when I did those people realistically. This time I thought, "No, they're a chorus. They're a Greek chorus." So they actually came down the circular stage which we had with steps leading down to the orchestra pit so it looked the way O'Neill suggested and they looked out front and said most of their lines out front. So it set up a stylistic thing. And *Strange Interlude* doesn't in any way, shape, or form look realistic. I think that abstracting it makes the play work better, because that's the style.

SHAFER: How long do you suppose that one will run?

KAHN: I don't want it to run more than four hours. But I wouldn't take a dinner break.

SHAFER: We seem to be in a time right now, in New York in any event and I think through the rest of the country, where people are more interested in a return to plays in which, as you suggested, the audience has to work a little bit.

KAHN: Not in a commercial theatre. I think in a noncommercial theatre in many cases "yes." Certainly, in Washington I found that; I've done a four-hour all of *Henry VI* in one evening and both parts of *Henry IV* together in one evening and the O'Neill. If the play is exciting and involves people intellectually and emotionally, and theatrically, audiences are happy. Commercial producers won't do it. It's great that they're doing *The Iceman*. That's great. Because it's so successful and it's doing great at the box office, that might actually encourage some other people to do things like that in New York. I'm going to see it in June, and we just had Kevin Spacey here to talk to the Juilliard students.

SHAFER: Moving back to your Shakespeare Theatre in Washington—the sense of having a place where you can do the kinds of things that you want is an enormously important factor.

KAHN: It's a classical theatre. So plays like that are acceptable. That's what your audience expects. Yes.

SHAFER: And you, of course, you have this wonderful possibility of drawing back to play these great roles a number of actors and actresses that you trained for that kind of theatre—many of them were students at Juilliard?

KAHN: Kelly was, yes, and Robert Sella was, for instance. A while ago, but, yes.

SHAFER: Do you have any plans for doing something by O'Neill here with the Juilliard students?

KAHN: Well, they've done *Beyond the Horizon* here. I'm trying to think of what else they have done. I might do something, but I haven't thought about it. Maybe. They're pretty hard plays for young actors—they're quite a challenge.

SHAFER: As far as I can see, you think to do O'Neill successfully, the director has to have a real comprehension of the play . . .

KAHN: Yes, and the actors have got to have some pretty good life experience.

SHAFER: Could you tell me, what O'Neill you have seen that you liked?

KAHN: Well, I liked *Strange Interlude* with Geraldine Page. I found that whole six hours (with a dinner break) just very extraordinary and important and surprising. That's probably why I want to do the play. That was a long time ago. It was wonderful. I just thought the whole experience was something I'd never seen before. I saw a wonderful production of *Ah, Wilderness!* someplace. I can't remember where. Not this latest one. I think it was at the Long Wharf Theatre and I thoroughly enjoyed it. Such a charming play. *A Moon for the Misbegotten*—Colleen and Jason were really wonderful and I look forward to seeing Cherry Jones doing it next season. I didn't much like *More Stately Mansions* when it was done on Broadway with Ingrid Bergman. Matter of fact, I am not sure that play works at all. I have that book with O'Neill's notes and the other version and all of that, that I found in England. I read it because of *Touch of the Poet*. So, after I did *Touch of the Poet*, I read that long version and I thought, "Wouldn't it be fun to do it?" and I thought, "I don't know, I'm not sure."

SHAFER: I'd like to ask you quickly about *Long Day's Journey into Night*. So many people view it simply as an autobiographical piece.

KAHN: Oh, I think it goes into the realm of art. I mean, *Glass Menagerie* and *Long Day's Journey* are the two greatest plays about families in America and, obviously, both have very strong autobiographical elements but they are transformed into art by the artists. So I don't know if these conversations were ever had or not, and I don't care. I read everything about O'Neill when I did *Long Day's Journey into Night* and now I wouldn't read anything. I'd just do the play. I mean, I'm glad the Gelbs are coming out with even a larger book, but I don't need it any more. I need to just get the play and read the play, and just see what the play says. I think that play, if you don't know anything about O'Neill at all, explains itself. You don't have to know anything about his real life at all to do that play.

SHAFER: Did you play much comedy in it?

KAHN: I think you should find as much comedy in O'Neill as you can! [Laughing.] He was an Irishman after all. There is some comedy. He's a great playwright, after all, so he knew what to do. The audience needs that. I think a couple of laughs in O'Neill are really helpful. I mean Greek tragedies have funny parts, too.

5 | Jason Robards

Jason Robards was born in Chicago in 1922. His father, Jason Robards, Sr., was an actor. Robards did not decide to become an actor at an early age. He spent some years in the navy, then he entered the American Academy of Dramatic Arts in 1946. His first big role came when he was cast as a rather young Hickey in *The Iceman Cometh* in 1956. Following this great success he played in *Long Day's Journey into Night*. He immediately moved into major roles on Broadway and elsewhere, playing in *The Disenchanted, Toys in the Attic, A Thousand Clowns,* and *After the Fall*. He performed in Shakespeare at Stratford, Canada, and elsewhere, playing in *Henry IV, Part I* and *Macbeth*. He came to be closely identified with O'Neill because of the many roles he played, which will be discussed in this chapter. His wide range of abilities led him into productions of such varying plays as Clifford Odets' *The Country Girl*, Harold Pinter's *No Man's Land,* and A. R. Gurney's *Love Letters*. Of course moviegoers have seen him in numerous films beginning in 1959 in *The Journey* and carrying through to his recent performance in *Magnolia*. His many awards include the Obie Award in 1956, the ANTA Award for outstanding contributions to the living theatre in 1959, the Tony Award for Best Dramatic Actor in 1959, an Academy Award as Best Supporting Actor, an Emmy, and others. Robards' work has won him the respect of actors and directors, and a week before the interview Robards was given the Booth Award by the

Players Club in New York City. Kevin Spacey, then performing Hickey at the Brooks Atkinson Theatre, was the host and there were tributes by Christopher Plummer, Barnard Hughes, and others. In 1997 President Clinton presented him with the National Medal of Arts. In December 1999 he was again honored in Washington when President Clinton presented him with the Kennedy Center Honors Award. He is married to Lois O'Connor.

SOUTHPORT, CONNECTICUT, JUNE AND AUGUST 1999

SHAFER: I believe you were introduced to O'Neill in performance as a student.

ROBARDS: At the American Academy right after the war. The Theatre Guild was one of the funders for the Academy, which helped to keep it alive and keep it as a good school. There were still a lot of the old teachers there that my father had—he went there in 1910. They were doing previews of *The Iceman Cometh*. We had about 500 students, maybe more at the Academy then. So they wanted us to come for the previews. We went to see it at the Martin Beck about a week before it opened. There was a dinner break and I went with a couple of buddies and they said, "Let's get out of here" after the first two acts. We were ready to go, but I said, "Well, no, let's see what happens." Because the play was entirely different from when we did it, years later at the Circle [in the Square]. It was like looking at *The Lower Depths* forever—there wasn't anything, comedy or anything, it was just "bluuh." But James Barton was in it and I don't know why, but I was struck by the way that he looked, looked like a death mask almost. There were some very good actors in it, Dudley Digges who was a fabulous actor, E. G. Marshall (who, by the way, later replaced Barton in it), so there were some wonderful performances. But the play, I felt, was not focused right in some strange way. It didn't do what happened when José got hold of it. Eddie Dowling directed it. You know, he was an actor and at one time he was going to play the part of Hickey. You never know in those things when you're playing one part and then they take you off and you're to direct the play—it's very difficult, I imagine; I don't know. But Dowling came back to see me in it and he came to see *Long Day's Journey into Night*. He was very complimentary. But I didn't ask him at that time what went wrong—I didn't feel I had the right to ask him.

SHAFER: Before that time had you seen any other O'Neill or read him?

ROBARDS: Yes, I had read *Strange Interlude* in the navy. We had a ship library and for some reason on this warship there was *some* drama. I remember I read a book of British plays: *The Circle, Mr. Pim Passes By,* a Priestley play, *Dangerous Corner* which I was in years later.

SHAFER: When you got out of the navy you decided to become an actor, but you hadn't wanted to be an actor earlier, had you?

ROBARDS: Not that I know, maybe subconsciously because my father was an actor. I knew that I had to get out of the navy. I'd been in almost seven years. I didn't know what to do, whether to go to college or not, and I was very interested in acting because of these plays. And one guy I knew in the navy did a lot of model work for *Captain Blood* and those movies they made in the thirties. He had worked for Warner Brothers. So we would discuss acting and I think that that and the fact that my father was an actor—so I wrote to my dad and he said I should write to the Academy and he gave me the advice to go there and learn something and not stick around Hollywood. So I did. I wrote, and I went back to New York and auditioned and I went to the Academy. On the G. I. Bill, by the way. Charlie Durning was in that class, Tom Poston and Colleen Dewhurst were just a half a year ahead of me. A year later Grace Kelly went there.

SHAFER: Later, after you had done some acting, the big break came with *The Iceman Cometh.*

ROBARDS: Yes, I did stage managing and acting, and radio just before it went out. But I did get some daytime soap opera. I taught school—

I didn't know anything, but I taught. I staged plays, we had a great time. It was a drama school in the same building as Carnegie Hall was in.

SHAFER: There are so many legends about these legendary productions you were in—people's memories vary. Can you talk about your audition for *The Iceman Cometh?*

ROBARDS: Yes, I can. I had done a play at the Circle called *American Gothic.* This all relates back to my first year in stock. There was a girl in our company named Mary Ann Weller. I came back to the city and I was making the rounds and I came back on my way home and she was tending bar and she said, "I just finished *Dark of the Moon.* Why don't you go over and see this guy Quintero. He's casting now for *The Grass Harp.*" So I ran over there the next day and I got an interview with him. But the role was for the father and I was twenty-five and he said that was not for me and that was the only role open. So I forgot all about it. I never saw him again, it was just that one meeting. Then about six or eight months later he called me up and said, "Listen, I got a play here. I'd like you to play the 'fella.' That was the way he put it, "I'd like you to play the 'fella.'" I jumped out of my skin, because I wasn't doing great, I did some radio once in a while, I was doing other jobs, I worked as a typist-secretary, all that kind of stuff, just to keep alive. And so we did *American Gothic.* It ran for seventy-seven performances and then it went out and after that I didn't hear any more. I went on the road for a year and half with *Stalag 17* as stage manager and understudy. Then later, I was going to a morning radio show and Jimmy Green, who had been an actor with me, was selling newspapers on the corner where I got the subway, a part-time job (by the way, he was in *The Iceman* with me twice), and he said, "Listen, José is casting *The Iceman Cometh.* Why don't you go over and see him?" Well, I dropped everything and ran over there. And he said yeah, that he was thinking of me for the part of Willie Oban. I said, "No, I want to play Hickey." I hadn't read the play again or anything, but I wanted to play Hickey because I remembered Barton's face, I remembered that ghostly face, not his performance so much, but something—maybe it was about O'Neill through what he was meaning in the play. Something about that kind of a person struck me. I don't know why but it did. A guy who thought he loved and found out he really hated—I found that out later. So he said he'd have to ask me to read. He'd never asked me to read, ever. So that night I read the play and the next day I went in. And I read the beginning of that part where he wants to talk and they shut him up—it's a speech about a page and a half. He liked it very much and he said, "All right, now, read some funny part." Some part from the beginning; wanted me to play funny. Wanted to see if I could be funny. So I read some stuff up front, in the early part of the play, where he's joyful. So that was it and he said he'd call me by six. Two minutes of six I was home and he said, "It's yours, you can do it." He had been thinking of an older guy like Howard da Silva or Franchot Tone or somebody. And I was thirty-four or thirty-five and he put me in it.

SHAFER: It's interesting that you say he wanted you to read a funny part. There is a lot of comedy in the play and you played it more than the original production.

ROBARDS: Oh, yeah, the whole first act has great comic pieces of writing, you never heard such laughter—I mean O'Neill built the bubble, he made it *possible* for it to be slowly deflated as the play went on. Because you know the next act, the birthday party, that's supposed to be great, and then a little air is let out here and there, so by the time you get to the third act when he's sending everybody out, it's getting tighter and tenser, and then when it doesn't work, when they're not happy, then in the fourth act when he has to confess. But what it does, it ties everybody in so closely, and it parallels the Parritt/Hickey thing—two guys—and that's how he gets Larry through that relationship—Parritt/Hickey with Parritt as the second violin. José felt it was a symphony, too, you know. And he was right. The themes: instead of becoming repetitious, it becomes almost musical, so you don't say "Jeez, are they ever gonna quit talking, what are they going on and on for? We know their story." But if it's really done right, you don't feel that way. Different things come out. Different themes are played [softly] down, and they're almost extinguished, then they all come back in the end with the tremendous cacaphony of sound when they all sing, except for Larry. But all those elements that were brought out by José were incredible. And we only had about three weeks' rehearsal—it was magic, what happened. And that hot production, and O'Neill had not been done here, that started the whole thing of getting O'Neill going again: it got the Gelbs to write a book, Louis Sheaffer was our PR guy. He was on *The Brooklyn Eagle* and it just closed, so they hired him just to get our name in the paper. And he became completely fascinated—a twelve-year study on O'Neill. It started everybody going on O'Neill. The director Carmen Capalbo told me at José's service, that if it hadn't been for us, he wouldn't have put on *Moon* with Wendy Hiller and Franchot Tone and Cyril Cusack that same year that we did *Long Day's Journey into Night*. He said that started him and made him go to O'Neill. And it wasn't anything we did purposefully, we didn't set out to say "Hey, we're going to . . ." it just happened it was timing, it just hit right.

SHAFER: Everything seemed to be right—the place you put it in . . .

ROBARDS: Oh, that place, that was unbelievable. It was the old Greenwich Village Inn where O'Neill had hung out at times. It was sort of a night club bar and then you went up a couple of steps and it was sort of a night club floor at one time. That's what we used as a theatre with the 200 seats around, entrances either from the bar (from the real bar, not the bar onstage), and then actually from the street, I did all my entrances from the street. And at the end—the exit—I went out into the street in Sheridan Square. It was fabulous. I was sitting out there one night getting ready to go on and Steve McQueen came by and he said, "Listen, what are you doing out here?" He was a struggling actor, and he asked me what I knew about *Stalag 17*. I said that I was in it, on the road with it, I said "They're doing a production of it up in Buffalo, why don't you go see this guy?" And he did, and he got the part. So I always feel good that I got Steve a part. Oh, people would come by and talk to me. [Laughing.]

SHAFER: Yes. And tell me something about that, just to keep on that for a minute, on the old Circle in the Square. When you were outside waiting for your entrances in *The Iceman,* how did you know when to go in?

ROBARDS: Oh, the door there. The set was backed up against the door, I would stand up with my ear to the door.

SHAFER: Oh, nobody came and told you. You had to keep checking on it.

ROBARDS: No, no, nobody came, but I never missed an entrance. And I had an hour, over an hour, before I came on. Now, in the beginning, I sat right behind the flat, which was only about from here to that table. You could hear the show, you know? Then I came in. But after I played it for a while, I didn't want to sit cooped there, and if I felt like it, I could go down around the front of the house, and the audience was already in, and look up at the stage. It was the old Greenwich Village Night Club, where the old Circle was. And you could see how it was going, if it wasn't going well, or if it was going medium, or if the audience wasn't picking up. And I'd always check on it, I don't mean that I would sit outside there forever. I'd keep checking on it and then I'd go out and sit on the steps or get myself set and go in and listen for a minute for the cue to come up and go, go on.

SHAFER: But that would have been awful for many actors—some of them come and sit and meditate alone to get into character.

ROBARDS: No, I don't do all that crap—where did all that come from? It was Lee Strasberg and the lousy method. My father said, "That's not a method actor, that's a methodical actor."

SHAFER: You have said you have to have technique to play these roles. What do you mean when you use the term?

ROBARDS: Years of experience, that's what it is. All it is is getting out there and making an ass of yourself for years and finally you learn something or you get out of the business. And if you get a good part. You can still be lousy in a lousy part. No matter how much dreaming up and interior and all that stuff they do—I don't understand it all.

SHAFER: You seem to be a very intuitive actor, even as Quintero was an intuitive director. Tell me about that gesture you developed in rehearsals.

ROBARDS: Oh, you mean [demonstrates a fast combination of finger snapping, clapping of hands and a gesture]. Yes, I told that at the memorial service for José. Well, we were rehearsing and I had this big speech and I forgot my lines and I did that [makes the gesture]. And he asked, "What's that?" and I said, "Oh, hell, I forgot my lines." But he said, "Forget about that, that's not important. What did you do with your hands?" And I said, "Oh, this?" So, he said, "*Use* that for Hickey. Use that, but use it sparingly." So I did, but sparingly, as he said, and when I sent each of the guys out of the bar, I turned to them and went [makes the gesture], and it was electrifying. You could hear it out in the audience. It's funny how these things come up in rehearsals.

SHAFER: When you were in these plays did you try to find anything out about O'Neill?

ROBARDS: Not at the time, no.

SHAFER: Did Mrs. O'Neill come to see you?

ROBARDS: Yes, she came down and she also had her agent, Jane Rubin, there so there wouldn't be a line cut. But José fooled her a couple of times—not big cuts, he was very judicious. We never cut *Long Day's Journey into Night,* though, we did the full text, all the poems, the full thing.

SHAFER: Did you talk to her about the production?

ROBARDS: No, not at all. She just stuck her head in and out. And then we went to see her and she thanked me for doing it. That was in her apartment at the Lowell Hotel. I went to see her twice there, once when she thanked me for *The Iceman Cometh* and another time when José and I went to get *Hughie*. The first time it was only a short meeting by the way, oh, about half an hour at most. Just to chat, that was all. She went on a lot about O'Neill, calling him a Black Irishman. There was a love/hate thing you could almost feel coming out of her. I'm sure that's a part of all relationships anyway. Yeah. Although, I don't feel that way about my wife.

SHAFER: Then after *The Iceman* she gave you permission to do *Long Day's Journey into Night.*

ROBARDS: Yes, I think Ted Mann and José went there.

SHAFER: It must have been quite exciting when you heard that you could do *Long Day's Journey into Night.* Were you immediately presumed to be Jamie?

ROBARDS: No, it's funny. Leigh Connell, who was one of the partners in the Circle, was actually the one who said to José, "you know you should do *The Iceman.*" José didn't know the play, he hadn't read O'Neill or anything. Then he decided he would do it at the Circle. On opening night of *The Iceman Cometh,* Leigh gave me a book which was the Yale edition of *Long Day's Journey into Night* that had been published. It had been done in Sweden, but it had never been done here and it was a first edition. So he gave it to me, he wrote on the page, "good luck" or something and I read it. They didn't have it at the time. It was just a coincidence—see, all this is a timing coincidence. It was only after we opened *The Iceman Cometh* that the interest was to do *Long Day's Journey into Night.* Then I think I was going to play Edmund, the younger son. José said he wanted Gerry Page, who would have been fabulous in that. Freddie—Fredric—March who was absolutely incredible. Freddie always worked with Florence Eldridge, his wife. So, in order to get Freddie, we had to take Florence. I'm not saying she wasn't good, but often I have thought how great Gerry would have been. Because she could play anything, any age, anything, no matter what age she was. She was an incredible actress. Especially then, she was magic everywhere. And Mary turns into a child at the end anyway. She could look like a crone, she could look like a child, a leading lady—she could do anything, she was one of those people, ephemeral people that can be anything.

Anyway, I was still doing *The Iceman*. I was in it for six months, *I* stayed in it about six months—it stayed open two years. But I only stayed that long because José wanted me to be in *Long Day's Journey*. My wife thought I was going to be Edmund. But one day I was talking to José outside of the Circle, we were on the street just outside the theatre and I said, "You know I don't want to play that, I'm too old for that part. I'd rather play the other guy." Smaller part, but it wasn't a question of smaller. I said, "I think I'd do better in that." He said, "Good, you would. I've got to find a brother." And so he got Brad Dillman.

SHAFER: I think you developed a very close feeling with the whole cast. You went out to the Marchs' house in Connecticut?

ROBARDS: Yes, we all went up there. I think it was in Sharon. They were wonderful, but I had to drive back because I was still in *The Iceman*. The idea [laughing] was that I'd rehearse *Long Day's Journey* in the day and play *The Iceman* at night. But you know, finally, I said to José he was going to have to get somebody else for Hickey. [Laughing.] I mean, I gave him plenty of time.

SHAFER: Looking at the pictures of the productions, I can see that you all look alike, and I think you had a good feeling during rehearsals.

ROBARDS: Yes, we had some pictures taken like Greek coins, four of us in profile, and we all looked like we were a family. You can't imagine what a wonderful thing that was for the play and what a feeling of family we had. It helped a lot. And they were wonderful to work with.

SHAFER: You've said you did the whole play. Was it tiring?

ROBARDS: No, it was exhilarating. O'Neill is exhilarating to play. I mean, sometimes I'd play Jamie and then go to a symposium and do Hickey's big speech. I'd tell Freddie and he'd just laugh.

SHAFER: I know that you said to me that you never found it tiring. But I read an interview with him that he and his wife actually did get tired doing it such a long time night after night like that.

ROBARDS: We did it for two years. I did it for two years, he did it a little over two years. But we had no matinees. Because we couldn't cut because O'Neill wouldn't allow anything cut. Later productions have always been cut because the management wanted to do eight a week and make money. Six a week doesn't make the same money.

SHAFER: Did he find any difficulty learning those lines?

ROBARDS: Yes, yeah he did have a little bit, but when he got them he was fine.

SHAFER: Tell me about the experience of doing *Hughie*.

ROBARDS: Well, we thought we'd do that, but we wanted to get another play to go with it to make it a full evening. It seemed too short, but today people would just do it. So we had to get permission from Mrs. O'Neill. You probably remember this from the memorial service, too. Both José and I liked to hit the bottle in that time, but he told me we had to be very proper and all in order to lunch with her, and not drink during the lunch. So we went to her hotel and were in the dining room and the waiter came to ask if we wanted a drink and we said no. She told the waiter, "You know what I want, a Carlotta Monterey." So he brought it and the meal went along and we noticed that as she was drinking these drinks, she seemed to show a little change. So the next time the waiter came, we said we'd have Carlotta Montereys. Well, the drinks had quite a kick and we had a fine lunch with her. After the memorial somebody sent me a book with drink recipes and there was a Carlotta Monterey with I don't know what all mixed in it. But what we had was really Long Island tea.

SHAFER: What was the run of the play like?

ROBARDS: Jack Dodson and I played it. We had a very short rehearsal period—about ten days. We had sold-out houses for all the previews at the Royale Theatre in 1964. Then someone from the *Times* wrote a piece about it *before* it opened saying it wasn't really good O'Neill, not a full evening, all that. So that affected our ticket sales and we didn't have a long run. But we played it in Los Angeles and San Francisco and had sold-out houses and even broke the house records in L.A.

While we were in San Francisco we performed it and raised money to make part of the mortgage for Dao House—Eugene O'Neill's house in Danville—and we later gave the profits of the run to them as well. While I was in San Francisco, I went over to Berkeley to talk to Travis Bogard's class. Then the class came to see the performance at the theatre. There was a kind of alley you came through when you came out of the theatre that ran between the Geary and the one we were in. When Jack and I came out, the whole ground was covered with rose petals! I said, "What the hell is this?" and Jack said, "I don't know—let's get a drink!" It was the students who had done it.

SHAFER: That's very touching. After that you presented it in a number of other theatres and places, including Donnell Library, plus doing it on television.

ROBARDS: Yes, Jack and I played it off and on for years. It's a wonderful play.

SHAFER: Did you have fun playing Hughie?

ROBARDS: Oh, I loved it. I played it for thirty-two years.

SHAFER: All over didn't you?

ROBARDS: Yes. Thirty-two years, Jack and I played it, off and on, everywhere. And the older we got, the better it was. Funny. We didn't even black up the last time we played it, black the hair, I mean. Lois and others saw it and said it was never better. That was up in Providence at Trinity Rep. We opened the season for them there, to help them out, get 'em some dough in there. Well, we did it a lot for charities, for schools.

SHAFER: *Moon for the Misbegotten* was almost ten years later, wasn't it?

ROBARDS: Yes, José and I would see each other and we'd say, "We've got to get back to the Old Man"—that's what José always called O'Neill. Colleen Dewhurst had done the play twice. At the time of the Kennedy inauguration in Washington, we did a scene from it and I did the speech from *The Iceman*. It was a great occasion and I think I can say that no other president would have been interested in those plays.

SHAFER: There was some class there!

ROBARDS: Yes, he was very interested in theatre. He and Jackie came to see me in *A Thousand Clowns*.

SHAFER: And did he see you in other plays?

ROBARDS: I don't know what else. I know that when I did *The Crack Up* based on F. Scott Fitzgerald material on live television for Channel 13, I heard indirectly from his office that he loved the Fitzgerald thing.

SHAFER: Will you talk some more about *Moon for the Misbegotten?*

ROBARDS: Now, by 1973 José had directed *Moon* twice with Colleen. There was this guy, Marshall Migatz who had a theatre in Lake Forest, just outside of Chicago and he wanted to have this play. I had just been in a car accident and was still in Los Angeles for operations. So they came out with Ed Flanders as Phil Hogan, and

Gordon Davis, who ran the Mark Taper Forum, gave us a very nice rehearsal space to use. We rehearsed it, and then we heard that Migatz was killed. Something went wrong with his car and he pulled over and got out and was hit by a car. My wife, Lois, who was helping us with the show, got on the phone to Lake Forest and arranged it so we could still bring it there.

SHAFER: You must have enjoyed those rehearsals with Colleen and Ed Flanders.

ROBARDS: Yeah, it was a great cast and we took it up to Lake Forest. I didn't really like the play. I called it "Freudian soap" but it was a success and we thought about bringing it into New York. We should have bought the rights, and they weren't expensive, but my agent advised me against it—said it was dead. But then Elliot Martin had the rights. He wanted Jack Lemmon but then he pulled out. And they thought of a production, but not with me. He was thinking of Peter O'Toole or Chris Plummer. Then finally he did get me and Ed Flanders and with Colleen we rehearsed in New York, then opened at the Kennedy Center in Washington. Then we brought it into New York.

SHAFER: Where it was a great success. Did you find it wearing to act?

ROBARDS: You know that's funny. No, I didn't but sometimes I'd say to Colleen, "I'll get through it tonight, but I may not hit all the high points." I mean, you can always get through it and play it all right, but, you know, you get tired. But then, during the production, as it went on, I'd feel this hand on my back, pushing me, and I'd get fired up, and I think that was O'Neill pushing me.

SHAFER: You seem to have this wonderful kinship with his spirit, one might say.

ROBARDS: I think so. But Colleen Dewhurst and I would both get tired. That was a real push. Sometimes we'd start a late matinee, we'd only have an hour between shows. We'd send out for sandwiches, eat 'em and go back out again. Actually, I'd like that better than waiting two or three hours between shows. It's not bad, it's just you do one right after another. *Hughie,* I did twelve a week.

SHAFER: Twelve a week!? Because you had double ones on Sundays?

ROBARDS: Double ones! I'd do three. I'd do a matinee and early evening and a late evening, because it's an hour and fifteen, an hour and twenty, is all.

SHAFER: Did you do anything to keep in shape physically, or just the acting itself did it?

ROBARDS: No, I just did the play, that'll do it. I remember what it was like when I was doing *After the Fall,* Arthur Miller's play. I was onstage four hours; it was all in my mind, the play, so I never left. At the beginning of the play, I had to take two arms to lift Barbara Loden, get her off the bed and lift her up. By the time I was in it about four months, I could pick her up with one hand. She'd say "We're very strong today." Health, is what it was.

SHAFER: Now tell me about being in *A Touch of the Poet* and how you ultimately came to view that character.

ROBARDS: Oh, that's a beautiful play! Chris Plummer gave me a book on the Peninsular Wars because he had just played Wellington. In the play there's a lot about the Battle of Trafalgar. And the theatre in Sweden sent me the play in Swedish and a book in English called *Cornelius Melody.* Well, I never could read the play, but I read the book. I thought that was very nice of them to send it.

That was one of the hardest plays I've ever done. That was really difficult because I was playing a cashiered army officer out of Wellington's army who came to the States and opened a tavern and he was still putting on all the airs of the Peninsula Wars. And he put his uniform on on the anniversary of a battle that he remembered. And he was a drunk. He was a crushed man, he wasn't what he really seemed. He was, it turns out in the play, he was the son of an Irish shabeen keeper from a bar, a place in Ireland, the lowest of the low. And he went to England and then the British army and went through the officer's training and became an officer. And became "veddy, veddy British." He was really something and denied any of his past. And when we see him, he wears the uniform on the anniversary of the battle, he postures, acts grand. But you know somewhere that isn't the man. And the daughter—of course, it's another play about families, the younger generation always rebelling against the older. She does not want him to keep these airs. Also she accuses him about his drinking and the way he treats her mother, who is a very peasant Irish woman. It turns out when he reverts, finally and he is crushed, beaten up and crushed by some of the people in town, everything is broken. Everything is dropped and he becomes low-down, lower than low. And she then realizes that she wants him back the way he was. It's very heartbreaking.

SHAFER: Yes, but as you played it, did you move through various stages of caring, of your attitude about the character?

ROBARDS: No, you got to go moment to moment with it and see how it's working. It's not me, it's the whole cast, everybody. We did a lot of rehearsing, a lot of work trying to solve that thing and it's a very tough play.

SHAFER: I guess this is one of O'Neill's plays in which you could judge that character in different ways and play it a couple of different ways.

ROBARDS: Not really.

SHAFER: No?

ROBARDS: No, no, it was finding how best to get to the depth of the writing was what was hard for me to get to. You know you skip over transitions and things if you don't really know. So we worked all the time about that. And I worked very hard with Geraldine Fitzgerald.

SHAFER: Now did you and she work differently? Was your approach to acting different?

ROBARDS: Not really, it's just that she was . . . Geraldine . . . would make bad choices a lot and actors don't tell other actors that they are making bad choices. And so José had a lot of work. He kept after her a lot, trying to help her so much. And Kathryn Walker was in it and she was wonderful from the beginning—she played my daughter. So our scenes worked. We began working on those and as we played more and more we found the depth—that's the only way you can do it. You keep doing it and doing it and doing it and then finally a light dawns: what O'Neill is saying and where you are going in a particular scene. Of course you have to have the director tell us we were going in the wrong direction or we weren't. He said to me once, "I don't know, I never told you this, I never gave you that direction. But in that scene with Kathryn where you are in the uniform and it's after the party with the old cronies that came around, you're smoking that cigar and being very grand about things. You use that cigar like a stiletto in the scene." I didn't even realize it. But he let me go until I knew it well enough in performance that things began to work. Now if I went overboard and used too much stiletto, that was no good. But I was an experienced enough actor at that point to know exactly what he meant and not to go too far. You know? Those little things that you put in.

SHAFER: You felt, I think you said to me, that you hadn't had quite as much time as you had wanted to have playing the role.

ROBARDS: I only played it about nine months. I would have loved to have played it much longer. Because I felt that I was getting more and more with it, I think just by doing it a lot.

SHAFER: I think you said about this one that you set yourself a little task for yourself each night.

ROBARDS: All I'd say is "I'm going to make it. I'm not going to be brought down by anything." I would go into the production each night and I'd say, "I'm not going to let them get me tonight, bring me down." Of course, the play does that, but I'd say, "I'm not going to let them beat me tonight." And I'd let it happen, you know? And that helped me with the first entrance, the first scenes. And then, as long as I could, I would not fall apart, except certain moments he does, when he's alone on the stage, but he recovers from those very quickly. But O'Neill gives you all that, it's all there, sitting there for you to plumb. That's why this is a great play.

SHAFER: So you would have liked to have played it more . . .

ROBARDS: Well, you know when you are involved that's the playing time, after I played it out of town, in New York, and out of town in a couple of cities before New York. I did the whole thing in about nine months, and then, of course the work in it. You put two or three months before it, it's almost a year you are involved. And now learning it, well that's what I did, I learned it while I was making a movie. I had a cabin in the mountains where we were shooting this movie. The cabin was one room with a couple of sleeping areas, and in fact you could get the phone from any part—just reach out. [Laughing.]

SHAFER: Where was it?

ROBARDS: It's called the Wet Mountain Valley. It was in Westcliffe, Colorado. A town of about a hundred people or something. We were shooting in that valley. And the company was staying fifty-six miles away in, what the hell was that town where the big prison was, big prison. Canon City. But I decided that 112-mile round-trip every day, I just didn't want to do that. I found another guy. Dick Farnsworth found a cabin and I found one. In this sort of little place and you could eat there and a guy had about eight cabins to rent. We rented there, so we were right near the set. We were fifteen minutes from work.

SHAFER: Wonderful.

ROBARDS: But then, I was up there alone, until my wife and kids came out for a while, but I was mostly alone. Anyway, I'd go up there every night and start writing the play out. I had the play with me and I'd write it. I wrote the whole play out.

SHAFER: Really!

ROBARDS: Long hand, like he did.

SHAFER: Yes!

ROBARDS: Then I started learning it. After I wrote it all, well I was on that picture six months, after I wrote the whole play [laughing] *he* wrote the play, I then started learning it. You know, I learned it.

SHAFER: What did you do with that copy?

ROBARDS: Oh, I had a lot of paper, I threw it away. Wrote the whole play, never forget it. Yeah, I threw it away.

SHAFER: So then when you actually started those rehearsals, you knew all the lines?

ROBARDS: No, I didn't know them all, as far as behaving with other people and exchanging. I don't think you can do that. I think if you do that, you . . . I just learned any long stuff. I would never learn dialogue, the back and forth banter and all. That has to take place in rehearsal. But at least I was very familiar with it, that's what I am trying to say. And you know the whole first scene he's terribly hung over, and nobody had to tell me how to play a hangover. I've had too many. I don't need any of that sense of memory, all that crap! You know, it's there. You know? And, you know, he's such a fabulous writer, O'Neill, that it just falls in. Everything falls in for you.

SHAFER: You know, I wanted to ask you, you spoke so fondly of your father and I wondered if he lived long enough to see you in these plays?

ROBARDS: Some. In *The Iceman* and *Long Day's Journey* and *A Thousand Clowns,* yes he did.

SHAFER: That's wonderful, that's very nice, indeed. Do you remember what he thought about *The Iceman* . . .

ROBARDS: No, he saw it only on the television version.

SHAFER: Had he himself done any O'Neill?

ROBARDS: No, he had never done any O'Neill. I remember when I was doing *Long Day's Journey* he had been blind for about eight or nine years when he got cataracts and he got that fixed. And he came back to see *Long Day's Journey* and he saw it, he wore very thick glasses then, they had hard contacts, they didn't have things they have now. And, he felt that there was too much color and too much brightness, it stunned him; the color and seeing again. He asked the next night if he could hear the play, sit in the wings and hear it because he had been used to that and he had attuned his hearing so much. And Freddie said of course and sat him right down on the stage right wings, right near his dressing room.

SHAFER: So what did he say about the play?

ROBARDS: Oh, he loved the play. You know, it was about an actor father, an actor's son, a mother vague and distant, as my mother was. Not on drugs, but distant from the family. You know it was very parallel in a lot of ways. And I am writing about that, though, I don't want to go into that because I'm writing a book, and then it will already be heard a million times. But Freddie March and he had known each other and, in a way, were contemporaries. They're both stage actors and then Freddie went to Hollywood and he was a big star in Hollywood. He was in films and all the way through, but he always came back to the stage. He was always doing plays.

SHAFER: And the relationship you had with Frederic March was so warm as I understand it.

ROBARDS: Yes it was, he was like my father.

SHAFER: I was wondering about that.

ROBARDS: They looked alike; when my dad was young they were very close in looks. They were both very, very handsome men. But my dad didn't really fare well in pictures and he did not go back to the stage until many years later. He should have, I think it would have helped him with his career. Anyway he sort of self-destructed in a way out in Hollywood and that could happen, especially in those days—the transferring to sound, the talkies, and all that. He had a great voice, it wasn't that. Just something strange going on out there for him, for him, not for everybody. But Freddie was a great actor and a sweetheart of a man.

SHAFER: And you had this, as I say, this warmth as you speak of a fatherly relationship that you had. Then this is interesting to me, because that must have given a wonderful complexity to the performance where there is so much love/hate in it.

ROBARDS: Yes, I'm sure it did.

SHAFER: You told me that you would often go out *after* a performance and do something.

ROBARDS: Yes, I did weekly. I did a symposium. I did a lot of stuff on *The Iceman,* I did the monologue. Freddie would always say, "I don't know how you do it." After all, I was young and a turk and he was an older man. You know, he wasn't a young man.

SHAFER: Bradford Dillman said in an interview that he, and he put you in this, too, had been taught that when you act you sweated blood every night. And that he, himself, was exhausted emotionally, but that the Marches who had a different approach weren't.

ROBARDS: No, the Marches were tired, I know, yes.

SHAFER: But you weren't?

ROBARDS: Don't forget that I had been doing *The Iceman* before this, you know I knew how to do it. And I was off a lot. The heavy parts were the mother and the boy.

SHAFER: But you obviously weren't emotionally and ultimately exhausted by it every night.

ROBARDS: No, I think subconsciously it eats away at you, I know that. But what I was, was awake more. I'd stay up all night. Not all night but I would stay up late. I couldn't go to sleep, stay up until three or four in the morning. And, so that was the opposite, I wanted to keep the mood going, keep moving. The play stirred me up, is what it did. I mean that O'Neill wrote it and all you had to do was learn the lines and you can't go wrong with him.

SHAFER: Well, I think some actors do.

ROBARDS: Well, I don't know.

SHAFER: I mean, that's easy for you to say. [Laughing.]

ROBARDS: I never found any problem. I thought it was as easy as walking and looking at a map and saying you turn right at that corner and go up that street, come down that little alley there and you go in. That's how his plays affect me. I think it's very, very precisely laid out, beautifully. Of course, listen, I am not the kind of an actor that's delving into my subconscious and unconscious, I don't believe in all of that crap. Excuse me, but that's something that if you want, go into analysis. It has nothing to do with acting, nobody is interested in *your* problems in the audience. They're not interested in my problems or Freddie's. They are more interested in the play, in the story, in what's going on. They don't give goddamn what we do. That's our business and our problems, if we have them. So whatever came out came out. We had a good director, you have to have somebody who can judge the play and say there is too much there, it's just not that, you know what I mean.

SHAFER: Take that a little further, please. So many people say that José Quintero didn't *do* anything.

ROBARDS: Sure he did! José knew exactly what was going on. Split second by split second. He rehearsed split second by split second. And if necessary, he'd show you how to do it. I noticed that in a couple performances, people were having a tough time with the play and José would do something. He would get up and just sort of do something. And I noticed in a performance that a couple of the actors I saw copied his moves! Which he didn't intend, you don't copy his moves. I mean he would also tell long, long stories about his life and his personal past and how he went about getting into the theatre. When he was an altar boy and when he did this and when he gave up this or that, he would go into long, long personal stories. And for a minute you'd think, "Why is he going on like this?" and then you'd suddenly realize that that was the direction of the play. It can be that way when you have people you can communicate with without having to teach in the rehearsals— he was not a teacher in the rehearsals. He taught, he was a very wonderful teacher. He taught these classes at the universities and at the old Circle he taught a directing class and I think the director Alan Pakula went when he was a very young man to José's class. But that's a different thing, teaching somebody. He didn't teach us, he would set up the situation that was in the play and we'd rehearse it.

SHAFER: How much did he say about the movement?

ROBARDS: Yes, he'd say, "I think you sit too early there." He'd say, "See how long you can go before you sit and then sit at a different point and it may mean more to the scene." He didn't say, "I want you to sit on line so and so, he'd say see how long you can hold it before you sit." That was the opening of *Moon for the Misbegotten* when I come in. And it's true. The minute I sat, if I sat early, then the scene tensions went out differently. He knew all of it. And then he'd say, "I want to change something." About, oh, I would say about a week before we opened in New York. We'd been playing on the road, we just came out of D.C. and we were opening in New York. We had the previews, and about five days before we opened he said, "I want Colleen and you to stay" and we did it. He said, "I want that whole beginning of that scene to be like a pavane on downstage left, not the whole stage, and then we can move to the whole stage." Now, you know, this guy knew what he was talking about, it worked like a charm.

SHAFER: Wonderful.

ROBARDS: We knew. We didn't have to say, "What dance for two?" but he wanted a certain feeling there and it worked. All you have to do is say that to somebody who can pick up anything, who knows anything and you know what he's talking about. That was the kind of directing, and it was never left by chance, anything. Not the smallest moment left by chance. And the notes, everything helped.

SHAFER: You see, I think it denigrates his ability that many people say that he really didn't do that much.

ROBARDS: He did everything. And also he was a master at stage lighting, sets, he knew everything. He and Ben Edwards did plays together. Ben was a great lighting man. José and he would work light, José knew everything. But all the old stuff in the Circle, José lit, impeccably lit. Light keys, when to dim, how he wanted the effects of certain things to be. "I want to burn now. I want to burn that in at the end of the act. I want to burn that in the audience's minds, very brightly, so it would leave a face in your mind when it's dark." He would do all of those kinds of things, fabulous. And he could move a small space into a large space by movement and lighting. It was really incredible.

SHAFER: It must have been! It seems to me that when you were in *Long Day's Journey into Night* you told me that you sometimes had to adjust your performance on account of the time.

ROBARDS: Oh, that was because if we start running over—I think we went at seven and got done at eleven-thirty. That's four-and-a-half hours, because we weren't doing any cuts, including all the poetry, everything was in. What happened was, they said that if we go past eleven-thirty, then we go on Golden Time. It was big money for overtime. That's all. But sometimes it would get slow, we couldn't help it.

SHAFER: And they would say to you to pick it up and go faster?

ROBARDS: They'd say you know the last scene, you can go fast. I'd say, "I don't know, but I can try." [Laughing.] That's a long scene with me and the boy! You speed it up and you could pick up a minute. I didn't know if we were five minutes over and under or what in the beginning. It's a lot of play, that's four hours of play there ahead of you. I remember them saying they wanted me to pick it up. I don't think I ever made it much shorter . . . we might have gone over. All plays are that way, that's why they keep a stopwatch. They'd say, "You know you were two minutes over on the running time tonight, something's wrong." And usually, it is. And you go back and rehearse and find out where things aren't working and why people are taking more time. It isn't all how *you* feel, it's what the play is doing. It isn't "I don't feel like doing this now," or, "I don't understand why I'm doing this"—"Why, why, why?" None of your damn business, that's what the playwright told you to do. And you better—the sooner you get to the point where you know all the lines and can do that, then you can get the timing and then the thing starts to get creative and starts to take on a whole other form. And you discard this selfish, self-aggrandizement stuff that so many people do nowadays. You discard that. Here was a man like Fredric March, a great actor, if it hadn't been for his kindness—well, we couldn't have done the play without him. But he was one of us, like a new actor learning a new thing. He was a wonderful man. And Florence, I loved, too, very much.

SHAFER: It must have been also a kind of a physically demanding thing when you were in *Long Day's Journey into Night* and *Ah, Wilderness!*

in repertory. And it must have been a challenge to play the father in *Long Day's Journey into Night* after having played Jamie in it.

ROBARDS: I kept hearing Freddie's voice. Yes, we played them in repertory. Colleen and I were better in *Ah, Wilderness!* than in *Long Day's Journey*. She was so much stronger than I was. She would have been wonderful in it with George C. Scott. José always wanted me to play it with Julie Harris. We would have been a good pair. But *Ah, Wilderness!* was very good and we always liked it when the schedule had us do *Long Day's Journey* first and then play the comedy—that was a good way to go home that night.

Oh, that was fun. That was fun. At Yale in particular. In New York we didn't stay in rep that long. They got excited about money or something and they pulled out *Ah, Wilderness!* and they only played *Long Day's Journey,* and I think that was a terrible thing to do. Then we had to let the other people go that were not in *Long Day's Journey,* which is only five people. But when we were together, doing it in rep, it was absolutely heaven because there was the same play, opposite sides of the coin. The same summer, 1910, the same family really, only the family he wished he had and then the kind of a kid he wasn't and yet he had wished he had been. And the other one was what really happened, you know, *Long Day's Journey*.

SHAFER: Now this started at Yale, you did both of them there and Arvin directed *Ah, Wilderness!* . . .

ROBARDS: Yeah, Arvin Brown directed *Ah, Wilderness!* and José directed *Long Day's Journey*. And he just had his larynx removed, so it was tough on him. But originally, José and my wife Lois and I got the rights, got them from the O'Neill estate, and we were going to do them out in Minneapolis. We had a meeting out there and were going to that theatre in St. Paul, that fabulous old theatre where Garrison Keiller broadcasts from. We were making a deal for that, but then we got delayed, because he got sick. And we were going to do that on the same set, which is what you should do. Here, we had two different sets. I guess Arvin wanted to do something that José didn't want to. We had Ben Edwards doing José, because we had done so many together. And Arvin had another set designer, she was good, too. The fact is, we used the basic part of the set, but we had to change it a bit. You know, tart it up a bit for the happy time. And also *Ah, Wilderness!* has another set down at the dock, with a boat, where he goes down and his girlfriend goes down and they sit by the water. And also another set in the bar. So maybe it caused a little difficulty, but it shouldn't have. We could have played them, you know, brought a scrim in and played them down in one or whatever. But anyway, we were happy when the matinee was *Long Day's Journey* and the evening was *Ah, Wilderness!* It was such fun to go home. We felt so good coming out of it. We loved *Ah, Wilderness!*—we loved it. Everyone loved that play.

But *Long Day's Journey* was, as usual, a tough play. I played the old man, there, though. And Campbell, Colleen's son, whom I'd known since he was born was the son, Campbell Scott. Colleen, I had known since we were students at the American Academy.

SHAFER: You mentioned, just mentioned, that when you started to play it you always heard Freddie's voice.

ROBARDS: Well, that was in '76, when I first did it. I've done that a number of times. I did it in '76 for the bicentennial, with Zoe Caldwell. University of Michigan, Washington at the Kennedy Center, and Brooklyn Academy. But it was fraught with troubles, that show. José was living in Puerto Rico, could not get the time free to direct it. Roger Stevens, my old friend, ran the Kennedy Center. I've known him for years and he's a great backer of every play that we've all ever done. In fact, he's given the theatre such great things, you know. By making it available, by making the finances available. For everything, any show you think of he's involved in. One of the great men of the theatre. He was doing a production, started in Michigan, which was his alma mater, at the new theatre and he had to go at this certain time. I said, "I'll go and direct it and play in it." Maybe some people can, direct and play in a play like that. But I can't. Because you need to be out there, somebody has to be out there for a sounding board for what's going on up here. Now when I'm on up there with everybody, I don't see what's going on. But I can't, in the middle of acting, suddenly, you know, turn around and start saying something to some actor because I can't really see it out front either. So finally, we got José to come in for about a week, he did get free, helped us out. And then Harold Clurman came in and it was wonderful. José couldn't spend the time at that time, is what happened. His time was taken up. He had to go to Oslo, and this and that. So we got Harold and he did a wonderful job, he pulled us together, so we could get through Washington and Brooklyn, because the company was fraught with troubles. Zoe and I held out, but we were the only ones that could. She and I made it through.

SHAFER: Let me just ask you a few more things just to make things clear. You played it in '76, the bicentennial, then when else did you play it?

ROBARDS: I did a thing for the Mayo Clinic. The first thing I did was a monologue from *The Iceman* for them. We took it all over the country for doctors.

SHAFER: Really!

ROBARDS: Yes, we did it in San Francisco with 14,000 people in the audience. We did a thing on denial and enablement in drinking. And I hadn't really thought of it, while I was doing it as a textbook lesson, but it really was. And that was a very big help. Through that, it became quite a success. Helen Hayes went out and did aging with *Victoria Regina*. Kathy Bates did *'Night Mother*, about suicide. I did *Long Day's Journey* with Teresa Wright and my son Sam. We didn't do the whole play, we did scenes pointing out alcohol and drugs in the family. It's called Insight, this program. But, *Long Day's Journey*, that was interesting that those particular selections were very good. Then I did it for television, excerpts from it again, at Monte Cristo Cottage in New London. Then I did it at Connecticut College for another program on O'Neill, a documentary. I did scenes from it. Then I did this one. But I knew the part because I had heard Freddie every night. But he stuck with me and it's very funny. People that really nail down a part perfectly, you never forget, can't forget ever.

SHAFER: No? That's certainly what so many people said after *The Iceman Cometh* opened recently: that you would always still be in their minds.

ROBARDS: Well, it was not only me. It was the fact that the director for this one didn't know what he was doing. The focus was gone. I felt, God, I wish I had two weeks with these guys. Focus it, so that the audience knows what's going on. But that didn't hurt them any. Everybody kept wanting to see it, so that's that.

SHAFER: Yes, it was certainly very popular. So, in other words, *Long Day's Journey into Night* was at the beginning of your career with O'Neill and continued as a long part of it.

ROBARDS: Yes it did. I went on and on with it, I guess. Because, here again, in *Moon* it's the same character years later, Jamie again. The play about forgiveness of his brother, and understanding of him.

SHAFER: But all those times when you were playing O'Neill, did you not think about doing *Desire Under the Elms*?

ROBARDS: Well, José had wanted me to do that a number of times, but I never wanted to do it. It's too, I don't know what it is, it's too melodramatic for me. I was never fond of that, nor was I fond of *Anna Christie* and Natasha had begged me to do it with Liam. And I hate the play and then I saw them and they were magnificent. And I then thought, "Gee I wish I had done it." [Laughs.] But that's O'Neill—it really works.

6 | Theodore Mann

Theodore Mann was born in Brooklyn in 1924. His education was not in theatre, but was directed toward law, his father's profession. He received his LL.B. from Brooklyn College. His name is most closely associated with the old Circle in the Square Theatre in Greenwich Village and the new Circle in the Square in midtown New York, but he has both produced and directed plays in many other locations. In 1950 he produced *Alice in Wonderland* at the Maverick Theatre in Woodstock, New York. In that same year he began working, together with José Quintero, at the Circle in the Square Theatre where he scored a great success with *Dark of the Moon*. Other productions at the downtown Circle in the Square included *Antigone, Summer and Smoke,* and *The Balcony*. The great success of *The Iceman Cometh,* previously a failure in New York, led to many other productions of O'Neill plays, which are discussed in the following interview. He has worked with many of the finest actors, often providing turning points in their careers. George C. Scott, James Earl Jones, George Segal, and Jason Robards are a few of the actors who worked with him at the Circle in the Square. His work, both as a producer and a director, earned him many awards. Following the production of *The Iceman Cometh* in 1956 the Circle in the Square received the Vernon Rice Award. In 1962 the theatre received the Obie Award for *Six Characters in Search of an Author*. Mann has earned the respect of the profession for his courage in producing or reviving playwrights either unknown or in decline, for his continuing devotion to the plays of O'Neill, and for his vision of what theatre should be.

NEW YORK CITY, JUNE 1999

SHAFER: This theatre, the Circle in the Square, has so many memories for me. One of the most wonderful was the occasion in 1988 when there was a wonderful celebration here, with outstanding actors performing scenes from O'Neill, and a grand party afterwards to celebrate O'Neill's birthday. It seemed to me the most appropriate place in the world to take place, because of your close connection with O'Neill throughout all these years. There have been so many productions of O'Neill here and at the downtown Circle in the Square. I believe when most people think of New York productions of O'Neill, they think of you and Quintero and this theatre. About how many O'Neill plays did you produce or direct?

MANN: Fifteen. More than any other producer in the world.

SHAFER: When you were first starting out, you were studying to be a lawyer and you completed your law studies. When did you first think you might work in the arts?

MANN: I got interested in culture while I was out in Carmel, California. I met a girl that I fell in love with and her mother was a literary lioness. So she had a lot of writers, painters, and sculptors at the house, and I decided because of the way they behaved and the fact that they weren't related to each other, and the way they dressed that I liked this life. I wanted to be in the arts in some way. And at that time, I met Edward Weston, the American photographer, I met Robinson Jeffers, I even met John Steinbeck. I was about nineteen or so and I decided I wanted to do what these people did. I didn't know how or where, but that was in my mind. My father was a lawyer. So, I went to law school because it was expected of me. Graduated and passed the bar. By that time, I had become interested in the theatre. I spent the summer up in Woodstock, N.Y. We had the Loft Theatre, which was the predecessor of the Circle in the Square.

SHAFER: And when did you first become interested in O'Neill?

MANN: Well, after we started Circle in the Square, probably after the second or third year, I would always make a request for an O'Neill play and always got rejected. Mrs. O'Neill was restricting, not permitting, productions. Then in 1956, once again, I went back again to Jane Rubin. She said, "What play do you want to do?" She had called Mrs. O'Neill and got back to me. So we thought we'd have to find one of the abstract ones. We gave her a list of *Lazarus Laughed, All God's Chillun,* and some others. So she called back and said, "Mrs. O'Neill wants to know if you can choose any of O'Neill's plays, which one would you choose?" This was 1956. Ten years earlier the production of *The Iceman Cometh* on Broadway had failed. And we had read it and thought it was a great play. We told her that's the play we wanted. That rang a bell with her, because that was the last play that he had produced in his lifetime on Broadway. There was a lot of angst about that whole production. So, she was thrilled. We went ahead. We had somebody in mind for Hickey, then he dropped out. So we auditioned people for the role and finally chose Jason. José said, "Ah! He's so wonderful, so great, and he's going to play it."

So we had about three weeks to rehearse it. It was such a long play that we had a problem for the opening. It ran four-and-a-half hours and the critics had an early deadline for their reviews, so it was impossible to have a seven o'clock curtain. We invited the critics in at three o'clock in the afternoon. This was in the original Circle in the Square on Sheridan Square, which had been a night club. The windows facing the square had all been painted black. The paint was worn away in lots of places, and after the first act, when the actors came back in darkness, the light was filtering through these glass windows, and it was the first time I ever had this happen: the audience stood up and applauded them. It was a great thrill!

SHAFER: Oh, what a wonderful thing. And that was the first one, but then you did the play again after that?

MANN: I did it again in 1973 with James Earl Jones.

SHAFER: How did you handle the question of Joe Mott's character in that play?

MANN: We didn't deal with it. He was one of the guys of the club. Hickey didn't have any lesser or more regard for him. He loved them all, including Joe. He's not onstage when Joe Mott says all that about "I'm a nigger;" Hickey doesn't hear all that stuff.

SHAFER: That was a very exciting production, too, wasn't it?

MANN: It was wonderful. Jimmy has the energy and the charisma for that character. That's the key to it all. And how quick he is. He's electrifying. You have to believe, by virtue of the persona of the person playing it that everybody loves him.

SHAFER: What were some of the other O'Neill productions that you remember fondly?

MANN: *A Moon for the Misbegotten,* which I did with Salome Jens.

SHAFER: I was lucky enough to see that in Chicago. That was a wonderful production.

MANN: Thank you. I directed that one. In Chicago, we did that at the theatre where Tennessee had done *Glass Menagerie.* That was a great time we had on that one. We toured that all over the country. *Desire Under the Elms* was great with George Scott. His performance was at seven or seven-thirty. He'd come to the theatre about three or four o'clock to put on his old man make-up that was rubber. Rubber to make your skin look old. It gave him protruding arteries and other things, but it demanded great preparation. I remember something happened once during that run. The set had a long runway going down to the stage area and back to the upstage area along one side of the audience. One night, behind him he heard something click —a camera. He whipped around and he went right up to the guy and went, "uhhuum!" like that. That guy did not take another picture. [Laughing.] He also directed *All God's Chillun Got Wings* with Trish Van de Vere.

SHAFER: How do you think that play held up?

MANN: I think it's stagey. There are lots of characters. Sort of like the whole society is depicted. I think it's overloaded. It would be better if it were just centered around the two characters—that's really what the play is. The others become very incidental. That chorus is incidental; I don't think it adds too much.

SHAFER: It's a seemingly realistic play in a way and yet and some other ways it's not at all.

MANN: It is realistic in terms of the incident, but it's not realistic overall. It's in the Expressionistic style, but it's a very Naturalistic drama. Of course, when they first did the play people tried to close the theatre down.

SHAFER: Yes, it was a shocking play in its time. Mary Blair said her obituary would read that she was the actress who kissed Paul Robeson's hand. And she was right!

MANN: We did it in the '70s. There was still a lot of resistance of the play—to the interracial aspect. Definitely.

SHAFER: Gee, that's interesting as it comes so late after some other things like that film, *Guess Who's Coming to Dinner.*

MANN: Well, that was on film. Onstage there hadn't been too much of the interracial element. So our production caused a stir.

SHAFER: This theatre has provided the opportunities for so many actors to create a reputation in O'Neill's plays. Wouldn't you say?

Of course, Jason Robards, but many others such as George Segal who achieved his first big success as Parritt in *The Iceman*.

MANN: Yes. Al Pacino did *Hughie* here. That was a process where I was asking him for about four years to do that play. He must have done at least five different readings of it. And we did a workshop downtown. Two years later he finally said he'd like to stage it and play it. And it was a big success. I've been trying to get him to do some others, but all the other O'Neill plays were getting gobbled up. It's an O'Neill renaissance going on.

SHAFER: There is. You must feel a certain amount of pride, I think.

MANN: I do. I feel that we started that in 1956. Our legendary productions fortified O'Neill. Also, at the time we did *The Iceman*, we resurrected O'Neill's work. It was considered old hat. Too heavy.

SHAFER: Oh yes. When I first started teaching, I was told I shouldn't teach O'Neill because he wasn't any good. It seems to me when people actually see the plays, rather than read them, they actually perceive their quality.

MANN: I think the performance of the play is much more dramatic then the reading of them. Because of the actors and the language. You know a lot of people talk about his language being heavy. I never found that to be so. It's a language of the characters he's writing about. I think O'Neill's plays have tremendous emotion in them, and that comes out in the performance. I think it's very similar to Chekhov in that way. Chekhov, when you read it, is very slight. You say, what's all the fuss here? It's over before it started. What happened? But that all changes when you see the play and begin to understand the subtext in the hands of an experienced director with a good cast.

SHAFER: Is it difficult for the actors to just get into the depths and the subtexts, and learn all the lines, and everything in *The Iceman Cometh*, which is such a long play? It was a problem in the original production.

MANN: The lines are part of the actor's trade, of course, and the subtext is theirs, too. An actor that does not bring subtext to a role is dead onstage. You have to have a life going on. It may not be related to this character, but there's a film of something going on inside that actor that gives him vitality, preferably it would be related to the play. [Laughing.]

SHAFER: I think that is particularly true with some of the characters such as the hotel clerk in *Hughie* who is just thinking most of the time.

MANN: At my suggestion, we used the inner thoughts of the night clerk, and had them spoken out loud by the night clerk, played by Paul Benedict.

SHAFER: Could you talk a little bit about how that worked? Did it change the shape of the play?

MANN: It gave you more substance, because the stage directions, the inner thoughts that O'Neill writes, go totally unnoticed by the audience. They don't know what this man is thinking. There's no way for them to know. I went to see the *Laterna Magika* from Prague with Mrs. O'Neill at Carnegie Hall when I was about to do *A Moon for the Misbegotten* and she said of the voice overs, "That's what Gene would have done if the technology had been there. If it were possible to be done." Back then, it wasn't possible. I think O'Neill would have been very happy with what we did because it gave a very important insight into the play.

SHAFER: How many of your productions did Mrs. O'Neill see?

MANN: She definitely came to see a rehearsal of *The Iceman*. I don't think she ever came to a performance. And similarly, she came very briefly to a rehearsal of *Long Day's Journey into Night*. She summoned us up to her apartment at the Carlyle, this was when we had *The Iceman* on and all this publicity in the papers about *Long Day's Journey*. This was after it was done in Sweden and different people that were going to do it and different producers were saying that they had the rights to do it, somebody else was saying they had the rights to do it. We never tried to get the rights because we were an off-Broadway theatre. So she summoned us up one day. José and I were very nervous when we walked in. She was a little woman. She was wearing a black dress and pearls, black stockings, and black shoes and she was at the far end of the room. We opened the door, walked in, and she stood up and she said "Do you want to present *Long Day's Journey into Night* next season on Broadway?" José and I said, "Uh . . . uh . . . uh . . . uh . . . yes." She said, "Fine, I don't want you to change any of the dialogue and tell me who you would like to act in it." She did not reserve approval for the actors. Then a few weeks later we went back and told her Fredric March and Jason, whom she knew, and she was very happy about it. So that was the total: first there was *The Iceman,* then this was the capper, *Long Day's Journey* was the capper and O'Neill won the Pulitzer Prize posthumously. Oh, that was great.

SHAFER: I think you must have had some very exciting times in your career.

MANN: As they're going by you don't think of them that way. In retrospect they are, you will remember them. As it's happening it's what you are doing. But, of course, that was quite a meeting with her. José and I stumbled out of the apartment that day and we went right down to the bar in the hotel and we normally did not drink during the daytime and we both got drunk. [Laughing.] Because we knew that this was something that was very, very important for us. Because we were given a play, a great play to do on Broadway.

SHAFER: Of course you won various awards for it.

MANN: All kinds, the Drama Desk Award, Antoinette Perry awards. Frederic March, Jason, the play, and José as the director.

SHAFER: That was grand. Did you get to know her any better after that?

MANN: Oh, yes. We had lunch together all the time. She was a very sexy, eighty-some-old lady. She would drink for lunch a Monterey cocktail, which was gin and some little olive or something. In the course of the conversation she would be talking about O'Neill and she would turn and say "I told you, Gene, you can't do that." She would go backwards and have a total recall of the conversation that had been between them. I saw quite a bit of her and I brought my kids to spend time with her. I got to know a lot about her life, her possessions. She had a lot of dear things that were important to her in the apartment. She was, I think, a woman who did a tremendous service to O'Neill because she orchestrated his return. I think the fact that we had a great success with *The Iceman,* of course, would lead her to think of us for *Long Day's Journey into Night.* But she could have got a lot more money, a much more prestigious producer. I think the fact that we were off-Broadway and he had his early successes at the Provincetown was important to her. And also from a dramatic point of view, the fact that these little off-Broadway guys were given this great play.

7 | Arvin Brown

Arvin Brown was born in 1940 in Los Angeles where he now lives and works in film and television. He was educated at Stanford University, the University of Bristol in England, received an M.A. from Harvard, and did postgraduate work at Yale. His several honorary Ph.D. degrees include one from Fairfield University. He was married to the actress Joyce Ebert, whom he directed in many plays while he was the Artistic Director at the Long Wharf Theatre in New Haven. He was also an Associate Director at the Williamstown Theatre Festival. His lecturing and directing have taken him to Salzburg, Bulgaria, Hungary, Shanghai, and elsewhere. The many plays he directed include *American Buffalo* with Al Pacino, for which he received a Tony nomination, *A Day in the Death of Joe Egg* and *All My Sons,* for which he received Tony Awards. He has received many other awards including the George Abbott Lifetime Achievement Award. In 1979 he was selected as one of "50 Faces for America's Future." His connection with the plays of Eugene O'Neill has been a central factor in his directing career.

NEW YORK CITY, MAY 1999.

SHAFER: Could you name the plays by O'Neill with which you have been connected, either as a director or a producer?

BROWN: Let me think. Well, of course, a number of the plays I've done more than once. So, for example, I've done *Long Day's Journey into Night* twice. I've done *Ah, Wilderness!* twice, no, three times onstage and once for television. I've done *The Iceman Cometh*, once in full production and one time as a slightly abridged, rehearsed reading that was rehearsed for three weeks—three and a half weeks, actually. And that was very recent. I just did that last winter with an extraordinary cast. Almost a cast that couldn't be duplicated for a full stage production. I had Al Pacino as Hickey and Harry Dean Stanton as Larry Slade, Bruno Kirby, Michael Jeeter—just an extraordinary cast. This was done in Los Angeles. It was a thrilling experience. Because it was only about text and I had never in my entire life had that experience. I mean we had no obligation to anything beyond the text. I don't believe particularly in staged readings. I find them a kind of anomaly, one never knows how far to go with it. You know, you're going to do a love scene and you're trying to stage a reading, do you make love with scripts in hand?— it's very awkward. So I prefer when I do readings, to do them as readings and assume that people will be able to enter into that imaginative world. So that's basically what we did: just sit around a table for three and a half weeks and analyze the text of the play with that group of superb actors. All of whom began to take fire from each other, just sitting around that way. And to my absolute amazement, although this is once again as much a tribute to O'Neill as it was to us, the reading must have run about three hours and fifteen minutes which is damn long to listen to a reading. And we did it about five or six times to packed houses and without ever having anyone leave. So it was an amazing experience and that was my most recent O'Neill experience. I've produced the sea plays, I didn't myself direct them. What else?

SHAFER: *Desire Under the Elms?*

BROWN: No, I've never done *Desire Under the Elms*. I've seen it several times. And I've never done *More Stately Mansions*. *Moon for the Misbegotten*, I've done, and, most importantly in my memory is *A Touch of the Poet*. I was very moved by that production, I was very happy with it. It starred my wife, Joyce Ebert, and Len Cariou and it was extraordinarily successful. That was at Long Wharf.

SHAFER: It sounds as if for your whole career you've been working off and on with O'Neill.

BROWN: That's right. You know I began with O'Neill at the very beginning. So I think I must have felt that the union between the writer and myself was forged at the very start of even understanding what directing was all about, because the first full-length play I ever did was *Long Day's Journey into Night*. And I tried to keep everybody from finding out that I had never directed a play before. And it was a superb cast: Mildred Dunnock, as Mary, and Frank Langella as Edmund, so I was in the big time very quickly. That was actually my first production at Long Wharf. You asked before we began what my first encounter with O'Neill was. I think, looking back, that I saw a road-show production of *Long Day's Journey into Night* that happened in key cities around the country shortly after the initial Broadway production with Fredric March and Florence Eldridge. An American actress named Faye Bainter and an Irish actor, Anew McMaster, took the play on the road. And I saw it in San Francisco. I don't even remember how old I was, I was pretty young, and I remember knowing, even without knowing that much about the theatre, that that was the greatest play I'd ever seen. It was pure happenstance that I was given that play as my first full-length production, but it felt like there was a reason, that the gods were looking after me. I also felt, when I did it the first time, that I couldn't even presume to touch the play unless I had a sort of inner knowledge that I would be doing it again. Because I felt so inadequate approaching such a masterpiece without any real background. But even the first production was, thank God, for me remarkably successful, and I think it was partly because I did have such an intuitive understanding of the piece. Then five years later I was asked to do it in New York. That was a revisit that was remarkable in my experience because I'd always believed that you could define yourself by your work with great art and that the definition almost of a masterpiece would be something in which you could pour yourself as an interpretive artist with the depth of your experience at whatever point in your life you approached it. So when I did it again five years later, I did a vastly different production with a quite different interpretation from the first time around. The most revolutionary aspect, I think, of the performance the second time was my work with the character of Mary, played by Geraldine Fitzgerald. Partly because of the nature of the actress, and my relationship with her, and the incredible mutual trust that we developed, we took an essentially very explosive approach to the character. I had seen what Fay Bainter did with it, I had read a great deal about what Florence Eldridge did with it, and I myself had worked on a similar interpretation with Mildred Dunnock the first time out, with the mother as a kind of a martyred figure: a waif, fragile, defensive only when she was trying to protect herself against the meanness of James. The second time out I felt very strongly that this was a four-hander, and that the mother did to as good as she got done to, and that there was a lot of aggression and a lot of rage in the woman. That the mechanics of the family were not anywhere near as simple as I had seen them the first time out. And the result of that approach—it was a very dangerous approach at that time, because I honestly believe, and I'm pretty sure I'm right about this, that Mary Tyrone had never been played that way—and people recognized in the character as they came to see the production an alcoholic mother or a disturbed aunt or relatives they had—in other words, there was a kind of immediacy.

SHAFER: There's also a little anger, if you look at it, if you interpret it that way, with her feeling toward the nun who told her not to become a nun. Because if she'd said yes all of the tragedy never would have happened.

BROWN: That's right. And in the years since the play was written with our new understandings of the nature of addiction (even though they weren't as developed when I did the production because we're talking about 1971) nevertheless, Geraldine had researched a great deal, and I had done research about the nature of addiction, and that colored our interpretation. And the thing about the addict, of course, is that the addict blames everyone and everything outside himself or herself. One of the relatively new theories about dealing with addiction that comes out of places like the Betty Ford Center and others has to do with simply letting the addict flounder; letting the addict be responsible for his or her own behavior as a deliberate attempt to remove that whole sense of "it's your fault, it's your fault." Of course what that leads to, as you know, in the family dynamic is enabling, you know, the enabler. So without some of that specific knowledge we, nevertheless, took an approach to the play the second time around that brought us much closer to that kind of thinking.

SHAFER: You know people always talk about the love/hate conflict in this O'Neill play in particular and sometimes take that back to Strindberg and his views of marriage. It seems to me that one of the dangers—you speak of this as being a dangerous approach—is that there could be too much focus on the hate. I must say that sometimes people don't see enough of the love in O'Neill's plays. The love that makes the people stay together. What did you do to focus on the aspect of love?

BROWN: Well, I started from that point of view. I believe in that totally. I think it's a fair criticism and a fair comment, but I also believe that what I'm suggesting in terms of the approach to the mother in a certain sense only emphasizes that love. Because it deals with the real family dynamic as opposed to a fantasy dynamic. I think in a way, that O'Neill when he wrote the play—and I think this is often the case with great art—I think he wrote a greater play than even he realized. And I think that his attempt in writing the play was in a sense to whitewash his mother, because I think he was still in the grip of that kind of deep connection with her memory. But, once again, I think that he was such a great dramatist that the portrait of Mary that he created was not as simple as he perhaps even imagined when he wrote it. I feel that by emphasizing the realities of the family, and of that character you only increase the sense of the love that kept them together. Also, I have to mention the humor. I mean I've always been a great believer in the humor of O'Neill. I've always emphasized that in all my productions. Oddly enough this approach to Mary can lead to more humor than the general approach of the mother as victim because there's an inappropriateness somehow to the behavior of an addict or to the behavior of people trying to cope with an addict that is funny, that is wacky, out of kilter. So some of the humor I think can also come from that and from the self-knowledge of the characters who understand in a funny way the position they're in and are unable to drag themselves out of it. But the self-knowledge can, I think, lead to a certain amount of humor. I think Jamie has a great deal of self-knowledge, I think Edmund develops some self-knowledge and the mother and the father even in their better and more exposed moments have a great deal of self-knowledge. So I don't think we lost the love or the humor.

SHAFER: I'm sure you didn't. I only wish I had seen it because I'm sure you had that unity and balance the play needs.

BROWN: I think so and, thank God for all of us, it was hugely successful, and particularly for Geraldine who dated the revival of her career from that production.

SHAFER: Then she went on to direct it herself.

BROWN: Yes, she then started her long connection with the work of O'Neill from that experience and ended up directing the play several times, once with an all-black cast. So we all joined the O'Neill family.

SHAFER: Tell me about some other experiences you had directing O'Neill.

BROWN: Well, the recent *The Iceman Cometh* was a great experience as well as the first time I directed it in the full production.

SHAFER: Which I enjoyed two times!

BROWN: I was very proud of that show and I think there were individual performances in that show that were quite stunning. None more so than the brilliant character actor Bill Hansen playing Jimmy Tomorrow. Hansen was one of those actors who was so admired by the whole profession and totally unknown outside the profession. He was ill all of his working life; he had a degenerative bone disorder of some kind, which meant that he was in constant pain and yet would never let you know it, would never let an audience know it, but of course it gave a depth to his acting that was just beyond compare. To this day I remember in rehearsing scenes with Bill, not just in *The Iceman* but in other shows I did with Bill, how other actors would congregate and watch the rehearsals just to watch him work and that is a much more rare experience than you think it is. I mean actors have a kind of professionalism about each other's work which they need to have. They sort of leave the privacy and the working process to each individual actor and they don't intrude, but in the case of Bill Hansen they just wanted to be there to watch him work.

SHAFER: And your Hickey was . . .

BROWN: Hickey was an actor named Lee Wallace and he was wonderful. He wasn't, I think anyone's immediate idea of that part. And I think, as with Mary Tyrone, I grew in my understanding of that part. So, when I directed it again, I re-approached it with Pacino, I was so aware of what a different place I was coming from. I think I understood the psychology of the salesman much more than I understood it the first time around. The first time I think I was fascinated by Hickey's business dealings, his personal dealings, but the second time I was aware of what O'Neill was saying about the psychology of the salesman and the metaphor of the salesman. Really, what a dimension that gives *The Iceman Cometh* beyond just the sense of the dead-endedness of the characters and the feeling obviously of the overall metaphor of people hanging onto fantasies and hanging onto dreams as a way of just surviving day-to-day experience. But I think there's also something being said about the nature of the salesman in American life and the way we accept hype, the way we accept ourselves. As you know, by the end of the play, Hickey is so . . . the ultimate fatal dream is his; the ultimate self-deception. And yet that's all part and parcel, I think, of being the salesman. So I think in Miller writing *Death of a Salesman,* whether it was conscious or unconscious, he was affected by O'Neill's groundwork in terms of seeing the salesman as representative of the American dream.

SHAFER: The reviews for the recent production of this play with Kevin Spacey have not made the suggestion that it was worth seeing only because of the cast because the play is old-fashioned and tedious. (That view was expressed in reviews of the recent *Anna Christie.*) Nevertheless, some reviewers said it was too long and the repetition should have been cut. What do you feel about repetition when you work with the actors?

BROWN: I'll tell you exactly how I feel about it. I think O'Neill's longer plays like *The Iceman* and *Long Day's* can be judiciously cut, but I think it's an unbelievably delicate operation and that to make the mistake of believing that the way to cut O'Neill is to cut repetition is, I think, fundamentally the mistake that's often made. I think it is definitely possible to cut O'Neill and I have done it myself. Although in my first production of *Long Day's Journey into Night* I was unable to cut it *at all* because Carlotta was still alive and she was an active force in New Haven which is where I did it, of course. So I had to be very careful. The second time I did make some trims with Geraldine and Robert Ryan and Stacey Keach and Jimmy Naughton. We all worked on that. But it was not a matter of cutting repetition because the repetition of O'Neill has within it a certain kind of rhythm and a kind of poetry that is essential to the O'Neill experience. So that if you try to encounter an O'Neill play without it (as has been done, for example, with that famous Jonathan Miller production where everybody overlapped all the time and everything that was repetitive was cut out) to me all that's achieved is that you make it move faster. That has to do with the 1980s attention span more than it has to do with any really substantial way to approach

O'Neill. I think that part of the repetition is part of his worldview that people do go at each other in recurrent ways, with recurrent grievances. If you eliminate entirely that sense of how people's frustrations become a kind of litany in their lives that is repeated in various ways in various manners, you are eliminating the real sense of what traps these people. And I think you therefore trivialize O'Neill. So that kind of cutting for me is not the answer. You know, I haven't seen Kevin's production. I'm going tonight. I'm very anxious to see it, but I have been struck by the fact that what I have read about the production is unqualifiedly wonderful for him and not unqualifiedly wonderful for the play or for the other actors. And my guess there (and I'll obviously know more tonight) is that I think to me what makes O'Neill so quintessentially American (in spite of his Irish background) is his fascination with deep, specific psychological detail. And I think the only thing that makes *The Iceman* an altogether riveting experience overall rather than as a showcase for Hickey is that every character is detailed. So that you're really creating an almost *pointillistic* canvas and that the absorption of the audience in the experience of O'Neill has to do with that extraordinary character detail as a kind of narrative. Because there isn't the same narrative drive in *The Iceman* that there is in some other O'Neill plays. If you try to go at those characters only from the outside it doesn't work (and mind you I'm not now saying that about this current production, but I have seen other English approaches, not just to *The Iceman* but to other O'Neill), and one of the reasons why I sometimes have trouble with English productions of O'Neill is because the English do tend to approach from the outside. They're wonderful at creating character quirks and surface characteristics, more than they are sometimes at creating the inner life of these characters, and the inner life of the characters is where the ultimate narrative drive of this particular play exists.

SHAFER: In this play we have all of these different people with all the story lines seemingly existing in space in a sense, so as a director it must be very exciting to work with each of them to bring out the inner life, as you put it.

BROWN: Yes, it really is and I think that was what made this recent experience with *The Iceman* so enthralling. All the other obligations of dramaturgy were taken off our shoulders. I didn't stage it, I didn't have to create a certain level of action to keep something moving, I didn't even necessarily have to be overly conscious of certain kinds of dynamics. I was really able to simply put the focus on the kind of character detail we're talking about: inner character detail and character relationships, because the relationships are always fundamental in O'Neill. The characters do not exist in vacuums, but within a very, very clearly defined society. Part of the obligation of the director is to create the society of each play— the bar in *Anna Christie,* the bar in *The Iceman,* the home in *Long Day's Journey into Night,* the home in *Ah, Wilderness!* I mean these are microcosms, all of them, and the microcosms are created on the interplay on the nature of the connections with people, not the isolation of people.

SHAFER: And can we take that a little further and talk about the love in *The Iceman?*

BROWN: Oh, the love in *The Iceman* is supreme because basically what O'Neill is saying about these creatures locked in that bar is that that is their world, that is their life, they have each other. And for Hickey to assume that by destroying that, by violating that and forcing them to go out those bar doors into the real world he will be helping them, and improving their lives, is the ultimate self-deception that I spoke of. It's the lack of the understanding of the love that does connect these people that allows him to make this fatal error, and that lack of understanding on Hickey's part of love is, for me, the central tragedy. Because of course we're talking about in Hickey's character, we're talking about levels of rage and anger that he himself does not understand. His perception of how this death—this murder— occurred, the fact that he has killed his wife, is so self-concealed. It isn't just that he doesn't want to tell the bar what he's done, except in the stages that lead him to his final admission, it's that he doesn't want to tell himself what he's done.

SHAFER: Do you think he really discovers it for the first time when he tells what he said to her?

BROWN: I think that's the turning point of the play, and I think that for him to have to finally confront his own anger and his own rage, automatically gives the lie to everything he's been trying to do with these people in the bar, because he doesn't understand what binds them together—he doesn't understand them as human beings finally. Ultimately, and I think this is what O'Neill is saying, and it's what makes him the great writer that he is, Hickey lacks compassion; in thinking that he has compassion, he lacks it. He does not understand these people and O'Neill, if nothing else, has enormous compassion for all of his characters. So that in creating Hickey, he's creating a force very far outside himself.

SHAFER: Can you talk a little about *Anna Christie?*

BROWN: Yes. Now, I didn't myself direct *Anna Christie,* but we did it at Long Wharf. The difficulties that it presents in relation to *The Iceman* in a funny way have to do with the fact that it isn't quite as long and, therefore not as detailed. I think the trap of *Anna,* and the production that I oversaw didn't quite escape this, is to allow the characters to head more dangerously toward caricature than the characters in *The Iceman*—again its richness is that those characters are so specific, so clearly conceived. I think they are in *Anna* as well, but I think that it takes a greater leap of the imagination to find the depth in these people. It's so easy, for example, with Marthy at the beginning. She's a wonderful character, but she's so often played very broadly, as she was in the movie. You know, Marie Dressler, who was a superb actress, but a broad actress. And her interpretation of that old woman in that famous first scene with Garbo, is delightful to watch, I mean it's wonderful . . .

SHAFER: All that eye rolling.

BROWN: Yeah, and all of that stuff, but it's not real, any more than in a certain way Garbo is real in that first scene, but that has to do with the mystique of Garbo and everything else. Atmosphere is hugely important in that play, people are always fascinated by the sea aspects in O'Neill's works, but I think the danger is that the atmosphere envelopes to the point where the specificity of the characters can sometimes get lost.

SHAFER: That would have been staged three-quarters in the round. Do you like playing O'Neill with the audience so close to the actors?

BROWN: Yeah, I love it! Because I feel in almost every case, and I can't really think of any exceptions in O'Neill of this, that the intimacy that's achieved serves this very specificity that I'm talking about. And therefore allows O'Neill to take on a moment-to-moment life, which is really thrilling. When you work with the grander scale on O'Neill, you can achieve great mythic statements because he writes with that sort of dimension, but I think you lose the "tinyness" of what I'm talking to about it, that's really key to the humor and to the love. So I loved doing O'Neill in the round and three-quarter. In some ways, more than I ever loved doing him in proscenium, and I've had a lot of experience doing him in both. There are problems because O'Neill didn't essentially write for the round or three-quarter, so there are sometimes major concerns with focus that are sometimes hard to solve. For example, with *The Iceman,* you have a situation where people are rooted to those tables. I've always been very concerned about manufacturing stage business for its own sake, I've never believed in it. It's one of the things I find a real turn-off, particularly in the theatre of the last fifteen or twenty years. For me there's far too much aimless racing around the stage. Because theatre people tend to be so panic-stricken about the attention span of their audiences now. There's a reality to that— they're right to be concerned because there's no question but that music video and all the rest has altered the attention span of generations of people. But I still feel that one has to resist that to a certain extent. So I do get concerned about a lot of unmotivated stage movement for its own sake. Therefore, that makes staging something like *The Iceman* in the round very difficult because you definitely want an audience to get an equal sense of every character and if you have one character who sits at a table at the opposite end of the stage from where you're sitting, it becomes something of a concern. But I think those problems are solvable. I found the ways in *The Iceman* to just introduce enough sense of movement and table-hopping without losing the sense that each table represented a world. But because of my feeling about the play—that it's a play about connection, not about isolation—I was able to find a movement pattern. So there are challenges, certainly, to doing O'Neill this way.

SHAFER: And was *Ah, Wilderness!* also staged at Long Wharf?

BROWN: Yes, I did it at Long Wharf, I did it twice in New York, and I did it at Yale—I actually did it four times. Each production that I did of it had two different venues and then there was a television version, so I've actually had five different productions of the play.

SHAFER: It's very funny, isn't it?

BROWN: Oh, I think it's wonderfully funny, I just love the play and I will always love the play and audiences love the play and critics don't. And it says to me everything that's wrong with the state of criticism in America that our critics can't appreciate and understand the delight of that piece of writing. They're so busy drawing the parallels with O'Neill's more serious work. Well, that's fine, I think that's exciting and interesting to do, but it's apples and oranges. I don't think one has to cancel out the other just because *Ah, Wilderness!* isn't *Long Day's Journey into Night*.

SHAFER: It's odd, isn't it? No matter how far back you go in theatre history, you find people dismissing plays, saying, "Oh, it's just a comedy."

BROWN: I know. For me, and it has everything to do with my own tastes, both as an audience member and as an artist in the theatre, or in film and television, my new profession—I love all genres, and I always have, when they're well done. I am a total non-snob about genre. I mean, I think there can be wonderful murder mysteries, I think there can be fabulous comedies, I think there can be great tragedies. Within each form if there is a sense of integrity and purpose and talent, you celebrate it. I have seen thrilling thrillers that were beautifully acted and had a kind of integrity to them. Comedy can be one of the most joyous experiences the theatre has to offer. I found that with *Ah, Wilderness!* every single time I did it. It was a success. It's a successful play, audiences love it. Actors adore it. There isn't a false moment in it. There are näivetés in it, but they're deliberate näivetés and they have partly to do with time and place and there is a fantasy element to the play which the critics have always pointed out. They're absolutely right. I mean it's not a real family and it doesn't have the kind of gritty reality of what O'Neill really knew about family life. But there surely has to be room for the element of fantasy in art as well as the element of reality. I think within terms of *Ah, Wilderness!* itself, if you take that work as a separate work of art and remove it from your knowledge of O'Neill's actual life or what he did with *Long Day's Journey into Night,* it has a complete integrity and a complete worldview within itself. As a result, it has great charm. Is it a play as great as *Long Day's Journey into Night?* No, but what difference does that make? [Laughs.] Some genres are more demanding than others.

SHAFER: It's interesting that so much of the criticism focuses on the parallels with O'Neill's life, almost as if you must first examine his life, then determine the worth of the play. Will you talk a little about *A Touch of the Poet?*

BROWN: I think *A Touch of the Poet* is a great play. That's an interesting example of a play that grew on me through directing it, more than any of the others. I went into *The Iceman Cometh* and *Long Day's Journey into Night* every time with a sense of awe, that no matter what I brought to the table, it wouldn't begin to explore the real dimensions of those works. I went into *Ah, Wilderness!* with a sense that it was a finite world, easily manageable that I understood inside and out and had no trepidations at all about approaching. I went into *A Touch of the Poet* believing that I was dealing with a more flawed piece than any of these others we've talked about with the possible exception of *Anna Christie*. But after having worked on the play, I no longer felt that. It perhaps is flawed in the way that so many great works of art are flawed, but the flaws are totally overwhelmed by the strengths of the writing and the maturity of the writing. There is a sense of pain in *A Touch of the Poet* that I think is equal to the pain in *Long Day's Journey into Night* and O'Neill had the ability to enter into an historical context and fill it with his own contemporary sense of angst and yet not violate the sense of period at all. I think you enter *A Touch of the Poet* and you are convincingly in that nineteenth-century atmosphere. He really had a sense of history and history inflames that play. But I think that his use of history in *A Touch of the Poet* is more effective, at least in my experience, than the same approach in *Mourning Becomes Electra* which I also think is a great work, but ultimately is not, for me, as successful as *A Touch of the Poet*.

SHAFER: As you say, it's a very moving picture because we see tragedy for the three figures, each in a different direction. Who played in it?

BROWN: Len Cariou and Joyce Ebert. Melissa Leo (who later had a huge success on television with a series called *Homicide*) played the girl. This was at Long Wharf, too.

SHAFER: What would you say is the biggest challenge of that play?

BROWN: The biggest challenge in *A Touch of the Poet*, I think, is capturing the love. You need to look for it more deeply than you do in some of the other plays. There is so much about Cornelius, for example, that is antagonizing. He's such a blowhard, he's so hostile, he's got so much anger. He's so vain and lives so much in a fantasy world. There are so many things about the character that render the character unattractive, that are intended to render the character unattractive, that in order to find the oppositions to that you really have to search. You have to search for it in developing the relationships with Sara and Nora and allow the complexity of their feelings toward him to become the audience's feelings toward him.

It's hard to do that partly because Nora and Sara have such different relationships with him. Sara is so much in rebellion and Nora is, if you're not careful, especially for a contemporary audience, kind of the dishrag of a wife who is always being stepped on. But that is, finally, the dynamic that really exists in the play if you look hard enough. I think if you find the kind of strength in Nora and the real love that she feels for Melody and you do the same for Sara, so that her rebellion is coming out of that very same love, hopefully you can transfer some of that feeling they have for him to the audience.

SHAFER: You say it's more difficult to bring forth the love in this play. Is it also more difficult to bring out the comedy?

BROWN: Not quite as difficult as the love, because there is a lot of Irish barroom humor in it and there's a lot of comedy in Sara's vitality and the fact that she won't be put down. You're right—you have to search for it as with all of O'Neill. You can easily allow the grimness of the ultimate direction the play takes to overwhelm it. But I do think the comedy is fairly apparent. But what makes you want to spend three hours with those characters is not always so apparent. As a result, when the play is not done well (and I've seen so many productions of the play), you get a sense of impatience with everybody.

SHAFER: So many times one hears that O'Neill's plays are hard to read—one critic of *The Iceman* now playing said it was an awful play to read but that when you see it onstage, it's wonderful. A common attitude is that the plays aren't good because he tried to do the dialects phonetically and they aren't successful. Do actors find that a problem?

BROWN: No. I mean first of all, let's face it, Yvonne, plays are hard to read. They're not entirely meant to be read, they are blueprints, even the greatest of plays, for what the event will be when they are acted. The things I feel that make O'Neill particularly difficult to read, oddly enough, have less to do with his phonetic spellings and his attempts at dialect and what not, than his overly explicit emotional stage directions—the emotional blueprints of his plays. And generally speaking, actors find that the biggest trap as well. What I have done in working with almost every O'Neill play is insist that my actors virtually block out the emotional indications, the emotional demands of what O'Neill is saying. And I don't do that at all because I feel they are wrong. Ultimately, if you do your work on an O'Neill play correctly, you will, more likely than not, find yourself returning exactly to those stage directions as written. But if you begin there, you're very often blocked. Because what he's writing about, and this is something that makes sense only in the practical terms of being a practitioner in the theatre, but he looks for results in those stage directions and the results are not always helpful in terms of how you get there. It's not necessarily useful for an actor to see in a stage direction a description of hysteria; it's up to the actor to understand what leads up to that, that creates that sense of hysteria. So I feel in reading O'Neill if someone reads O'Neill without understanding the real nature of what those stage directions mean, it's very easy to feel that the work is melodramatic. Because sometimes the emotional stage directions don't feel earned when you read them. Until you actually do the heavy trowelling work that good actors do. And then you realize that they're very real. But they have to be done, again, specifically. They can't be generalized; they have to come from this tremendously specific, clear world that the actor has brought.

I find that difficulty reading O'Neill. I remember once working on a famous moment, working with Geraldine in *Long Day's Journey into Night* and she was having a terrible time with the stage directions of the little scene at the beginning of the third act when she's been talking to the maid. And the men come home from the bar. She wants them to be there, she doesn't want them to be there, she's glad to see them, she's thrilled and happy because they're home, she's furious and in a rage because they're home: it's a tumble of emotions that feel so over-inflated when you read it. Geraldine was having a terrible time with it, she was just not sure how she could get there. So we did a physical exercise that she loves to talk about where I chased her around the stage. I said "Look, just do these lines and I'm going to chase you and I'm literally going to try to catch you and you keep away from me." The physical emotion of trying to escape something, created all the emotions exactly as written, then she understood from that point on. But to try to approach it from the text, from reading it, you think, "How am I going to get there?"

SHAFER: Do you have fun when you rehearse O'Neill? People always emphasize how grim he is.

BROWN: Oh, I love it, I love it! And your question goes back to how much humor I think there is in O'Neill. In fact, one of the great difficulties in doing O'Neill in America for audiences is the expectation of the audience that it is going to be grim, so that they feel very much at first uncomfortable about laughing. When you direct O'Neill, in almost all of the plays, you have to find all of the ways early on, and this is something we talked about very specifically in *Long Day's Journey into Night,* to telegraph to the audience that it's OK to laugh.

SHAFER: Well, he is a great writer, therefore, according to popular perception, he couldn't be funny.

BROWN: Yes, it's a classic, it's an important play. Importance! God help us, save us from importance! No, it's fun to work on O'Neill, partly because there's a lot of humor, partly because there's a lot of love, and partly because it's fun to work on any great work of art when you know that it's there for you, it will support you. You can explore, you can bring your life experience to bear, and you will not feel violated, you will not feel exposed as an artist, because the work embraces you.

SHAFER: And the work allows many different approaches, don't you think?

BROWN: Oh, completely! That was one of the things that fascinated me about José Quintero and watching him work, particularly when we shared the bill, when we did the two productions—he did *Long Day's Journey into Night* and I did *Ah, Wilderness!* with the same cast in repertory. Our approaches couldn't be more different: José Quintero brought to O'Neill a total sense of poetic identification, a sense that his identity was O'Neill's identity, and that O'Neill literally spoke through him in a mystic way. He had a very otherworldly attitude toward O'Neill and I brought to the work a far more pragmatic, earthbound, day-to-day approach. But I think both produced good results because all those levels exist. I mean, yes, there's poetry in O'Neill, yes, there's mist and moonlight and darkness, and all of that, but there's also the sheer mechanics of how a family lives together, how they eat dinner together—his observation of life, I guess that's what fascinates me so much about O'Neill. Not his otherworldliness, but his worldliness.

SHAFER: We've been talking about your productions at Long Wharf and your work in New York. Now you're in California and working in film and television—but you did do the staged reading of *The Iceman*. Do you anticipate more work on O'Neill in the future?

BROWN: Oh, I think so. I'm hoping. I feel O'Neill will always be a part of my life. I'm not even sure there mightn't be some opportunity in the future to combine all of this—to really do some work with O'Neill for the camera, which I would be thrilled to do. You know, there have been some very successful attempts at that. There is also room for reinterpretation of the great classics with the camera.

SHAFER: Do you see a return of interest to high-quality drama in the country now?

BROWN: Well, I'm pretty hopeful in terms of what's gone on this season with the *Salesman* revival and the *Iceman* revival. I wish that it were possible in America to have an American conduit for American work. We seem only to receive American work when we're told by the English or the Irish that it's worth pursuing, which I think goes to the core of what's always been the American inferiority complex which disturbs me and has always created a difficult atmosphere for serious work. But, of course, everyone has been pronouncing the serious theatre dead for so many years. Yet it lives!

8 | Len Cariou

Len Cariou was born in Winnipeg, Canada, in 1939. His career has encompassed musical theatre, Shakespeare, and contemporary plays. He received training at St. Paul's College, the Guthrie Theatre, and the Stratford Shakespeare Festival. He made his professional debut in *Damn Yankees!* at the Winnipeg Rainbow Stage Theatre. He is well remembered for his many roles at the Stratford Shakespeare Festival, including Coriolanus and the leading roles in *Taming of the Shrew* and *The Tempest*. At the American Shakespeare Theatre in Stratford, Connecticut, he played in *Much Ado About Nothing, The Three Sisters,* and *Henry V.* One of his most popular roles was that of Sweeney Todd, for which he won a Tony Award in 1979. Other Broadway performances include *Applause, A Little Night Music,* and *Master Class.* He has also performed extensively in film and on television. His performance in *One Man* won him the Best Actor prize from the Canadian Genie Awards in 1976. He appeared in *Getting Out* in 1994 and *Executive Decision* in 1996. He is familiar to television viewers for his many performances in such productions as *Stolen Dreams, Killer in the Mirror, Witness to the Execution, A Dream Is a Wish Your Heart Makes: The Annette Funicello Story,* and *A Brother's Promise: The Dan Jansen Story* in 1996. He regularly charmed viewers and Jessica as an Irish trickster on *Murder, She Wrote.* He appeared in the television series *Swift Justice.* In addition to acting, he has also directed plays including *The Petrified Forest* and *Death of a Salesman* in Edmonton. His active career keeps him busy in film, television, and theatre.

NEW YORK CITY, NOVEMBER 1999

SHAFER: Mr. Cariou, you have done so many more types of roles than a lot of actors. I've personally seen you in everything from *Coriolanus* to *A Little Night Music*. And how did O'Neill come about in that wide range of plays?

CARIOU: Well, I remember when I was a very young actor, when I had just started out in theatre, I was in my first or second year, I did a play with an actor from New York by the name of Ron Bishop. He said to me, "You should do all of O'Neill's roles. You are one day going to do all of O'Neill." And so when he said that to me, I didn't really know any O'Neill other than the stuff I had read in school and so on *and stuff that I looked at.* And the stuff that I was interested in doing was stuff like *Long Day's Journey,* because I had immediately connected with Edmund and Jamie and I thought that the father was certainly a role that I would one day play.

SHAFER: At about what age do you think this was?

CARIOU: Twenty-two, but I haven't done too much O'Neill. I have only done two or three things. One at the Guthrie, one in Boston, one at the—

SHAFER: At the Long Wharf. Can we take them in order . . . which one came first?

CARIOU: The one at the Guthrie, we adapted the sea plays, you know the early one-acts about the sea. One-act plays and we made them into an evening. We took three or four of the seven plays and a lot of the characters were the same and we tried to string it together in an evening.

SHAFER: Not separate plays? But putting them together?

CARIOU: Yeah, yeah we tried to string them together as a play. With one intermission, was it one? I can't remember if it was one or two. So that we did at the Guthrie and I played the Swede, I played Olsen. And then, I did *Long Day's Journey,* with Joe Ferrer and Kate Reed.

SHAFER: Now how did that happen to come about, where was the venue?

CARIOU: The venue was in Boston, I can't remember the name of the theatre.

SHAFER: Just one of those commercial theatres?

CARIOU: Yeah, they were trying to start a, they were trying to start a company, I can't remember what the name of it is. And they picked the theatre and they presented about four different classics. And *Long Day's* is one of them. They did *Dance of Death* as well.

SHAFER: An interesting combination.

CARIOU: Well, yeah it was, except that I think we did them back to back.

SHAFER: Oh!

CARIOU: I wouldn't have thought as a theatregoer that that would have been much fun!

SHAFER: I can see your point! Well, so Michael Kahn, then, was casting this and he just wanted you for the role, I suppose?

CARIOU: Yeah, we'd worked together. I worked in Stratford, Connecticut, when he was the artistic director. So, yeah, so he had just called me and asked if I would like to do this. And I had never done it and it was just time for me to do Jamie. I had passed the younger role and that was too bad because I would have like to have played it. But I never got to.

SHAFER: Was it a long rehearsal period?

CARIOU: Not particularly long.

SHAFER: Because it's a long play.

CARIOU: I don't think it was, I don't remember a particularly long rehearsal period.

SHAFER: It was good company, wasn't it? Michael seems to look back on it very fondly.

CARIOU: Yes, yeah it was fun. We had a good time.

SHAFER: When you say that it was fun, that always is the kind of thing that is surprising to some people who don't know O'Neill because they tend to think that it wouldn't be fun to be in O'Neill.

CARIOU: Well, I think that that's—I mean I find a lot of actors who say that and I ask them why, they don't really know why. I mean, most of them say that it's so morbid and such a narrow-minded look at what the life is about. But, I disagree. I think that he is very difficult to do, he writes long plays. And I think a lot of people are afraid of doing the work and having to sustain it. Because a lot of it is very grounded in emotion and that tends to be draining and for some people it's easier than others. For some people it is not easy to go to that well and the emotional well dries quickly. And I think that has something to do with people not thinking or believing that it has to come from some kind of their own experience to be emotionally true for them. But, I don't. I am one of those lucky ones, I guess, it doesn't bother. I'm able to go there and find that emotional well. I dug a pretty deep well somewhere along the way because it appeared to me that that was really going to a place you were going to have to call upon the most. So, I tried very hard in my early career to find a way to get to that emotion as quickly as possible. Because I felt that if you were in touch with those characters, not only O'Neill characters, but any of the classical characters, they are very emotionally grounded, most of the subject matter is huge in that sense. In that they are going after pretty big things and, you know, things that are a matter of life and death. There are monumental things happening, especially in the classical theatre, as you know. And that's where I was pretty much growing up was in the classical theatre. While I started out in musical comedy and stuff like that, once I found that classical theatre was being accessible to a modern-day audience, I just went after that. It was the biggest challenge to the actor.

SHAFER: The role of Jamie is a character of great range, isn't it? In that much of the comedy comes from him. And he is also very intense.

CARIOU: Yes, well . . . I don't think Jamie . . . well, he has a little more fun than anybody else in the play.

SHAFER: He gets the comedy out of the scene when he's drunk and fools with the light bulbs.

CARIOU: Oh, yeah.

SHAFER: But he's essentially a very dark figure, it seems to me.

CARIOU: Yes, but it's not that huge of a role.

SHAFER: No, you spend a lot of time offstage in that, don't you? I presume that you enjoyed working with the whole cast. Sometimes this kind of family feeling develops in that play.

CARIOU: Yeah. I am not sure that we actually got there, we really didn't have enough time. But I had known Kate Reid, I had worked with Kate in Canada, and I knew Joe Ferrer, but we had never worked together. And then I didn't really know Edmund, he was new. So then we had about a month to spend on it before we had to put it up. But you do in that because there are only four or five people in the cast and you pretty much spend all of your time together on the stage. Yeah, we tend to get close.

SHAFER: Was there that family resemblance, physically?

CARIOU: No.

SHAFER: I wouldn't have thought.

CARIOU: No, not really. Look at me and Joe Ferrer. I wouldn't expect that I would be a child of his, especially if you had known his own kids.

SHAFER: But it must have been interesting in that there was a parallel to his own life, in that he'd been kind of identified as Cyrano, as Tyrone had been identified as the Count of Monte Cristo.

CARIOU: As Cyrano, yeah, true. True, that was not wasted on him, he knew about that, he talked about that. But, he never did what Tyrone does, though. He didn't go out on the road with it, you know, just doing that exclusively.

SHAFER: So you rehearsed about three or four weeks and then you played in repertory?

CARIOU: No, no we played it straight, a straight run in Boston for probably a month. I don't think it was much longer than that.

SHAFER: Michael Kahn is an interesting person to work with, isn't he?

CARIOU: Umhmm, he is.

SHAFER: Can you talk a little bit about how you worked together on that role? If you remember.

CARIOU: Yeah, right, if I remember, you're right. I think Jamie is pretty much what you see is what you get, I mean obviously there is . . .

when he talks about his father, when they have their arguments about why he is the way he is, and he pretty much blames him. And he has his excuses, you know, being the drunk that he is. But he's pretty much right there on the page, it's not a terribly introspective kind of a role. But, I think, I mean the thing that I remember about working with Michael on anything was the fact that he pretty much left you to your own devices. In the sense that, unless you are so far off the mark that he had to feel that he would step in and say, "Well, you're not anywhere near where I think you should be with what this is about." So, I think . . . what I guess I'm saying is that he allowed me to just kind of do Jamie the way I figured it was. And I think I remember saying, "I mean, is this . . . have I got this totally wrong or is this exactly what this guy is about, is this what this means?" And he'd say, "Oh yeah, I'm sure it is, absolutely."

SHAFER: When you worked with Arvin was the process slightly different for *Touch of the Poet?*

CARIOU: Well, yeah, slightly different, I think. First of all, it's a huge role. It's like Tyrone is in *Long Day's Journey*. The role of Con Melody in *A Touch of the Poet*. Yes, we had a real good time, I have a very good memory of that time.

SHAFER: How long ahead did you know that you'd be doing this? Did you start on the lines ahead?

CARIOU: No.

SHAFER: No?

CARIOU: No, I never do that.

SHAFER: Oh, I am interested to know how you approach it.

CARIOU: I think you have the time, I think it's enough time to learn a play and three, four weeks is plenty of time. I mean that's how I grew up. I grew up working at a theatre where in three weeks you better know the play because you go in front of the audience. So the process is . . . well, I never sit down and learn lines before, before I do a scene or something like that, I mean you can't really do that. Because you have to be with other people and you don't want to walk out knowing your words and other people are standing with a book and trying to figure out where they are going to move. The process doesn't work like that, it just doesn't work. So you don't and I find it, I've done work with people where they've done that and it's most disconcerting to be working with somebody while you have a text in your hand and they know all the words. And I should think that it would drive them nuts because you are not ready to respond in any way, you know, I mean the process is one of taking tiny steps and bigger steps and bigger steps and bigger steps. And I am notorious, I warn directors now when I go into rehearsal, I say, "I am going to have the book in my hand until the technical rehearsal, so I am telling you that now." And they kind of look at me and go . . . what are they going to do? [Shrugs.] I tend to hang on to it as long as I can. Kind of like a Linus blanket.

SHAFER: What do you think is the biggest challenge of that role?

CARIOU: Of Melody? . . . Well, I think you have to be careful about not going too far . . . let me think, what am I trying to say? I don't know, I guess that's not an easy question to answer.

SHAFER: No, it's hard, it's a complicated role and it seems to me, in contrast to Jamie, which is, as you say, is pretty much what he gives you, that there would be a number of ways in which Con Melody could be played.

CARIOU: Oh, yeah, there's a huge back story to Con. There is one for Jamie, too, for that matter, but it is not really as long, for one thing, because Melody is obviously a man in his fifties. So, there's a back story of a lot of stuff that I think he brings and you don't really, as an audience, know what it is that makes the guy go. He's just some kind of, he's a very strange character and you know, his wife treats him like some kind of god. And unfortunately, that just encourages him to be as obtuse and delusional as he can possibly be.

SHAFER: And it's an interesting role isn't it, in that it has the three women with whom he interacts and each one is so very different and so he is obviously different with each one, isn't he?

CARIOU: Yeah, exactly. And it doesn't happen until obviously the end of—but it has the big row, they beat the crap out of him.

SHAFER: Arvin said something about trying to bring out the love that's in the family, despite the superficial antagonism, which you would immediately perceive as antagonism.

CARIOU: Well, I think, yeah. I guess, it manifests itself. It's complicated. He knows what a blowhard fool he can be and he knows that he is a drunk, probably a very useless character. And he is not very pleased about that, and she, of course encourages him and perpetrates the lie. And he, on the one hand, loves her for that and on the other hand, he wants to whack her up the side of the head and say, "Why don't you tell me, why don't you throw me out, what good am I?" And finally, his daughter is the one who finally tries to be the mother's conscience.

SHAFER: That's an interesting way to describe it. What about that relationship between Con and the daughter? When you rehearse those scenes and work them out, what about that relationship, what do you feel is there?

CARIOU: Um, well, I don't know. I think that she is like an extension of the mother in one sense. It's also, I think, there is a danger there of an incestuous relationship, from his point of view.

SHAFER: Would you say this exists for him on a subconscious level?

CARIOU: Yeah. So, the relationship is very complex: she's always kind of throwing things up in his face and he resents it, but he knows that she's probably right and is correct in doing so.

SHAFER: It's a kind of startling scene that he plays with Deborah, isn't it?

CARIOU: Yeah, he's a real delusional fellow.

SHAFER: Do you think that the daughter gets the audience's sympathy?

CARIOU: I don't know that he doesn't, I don't think he does. I think what the daughter is saying about him finally comes through to the audience, whereas they might have given him the benefit of the doubt. But by the end of the scene they . . . they may pity him. I'm not sure they sympathize with him.

SHAFER: Hmm, that's a nice distinction there, I think, yes, that's a very nice distinction. Let me ask you this, you're so busy acting all the time, I don't know how you manage to do it all. But, you haven't fulfilled what you are supposed to do, you were supposed to play all the O'Neill roles.

CARIOU: No, I haven't, you're right. I wanted very much to be in *The Iceman.*

SHAFER: Well, you have plenty of time for that.

CARIOU: Oh yeah, oh sure. But, I wanted to do this one that they just did with Kevin Spacey.

SHAFER: And you had conversations about this?

CARIOU: I talked to the director about this, yeah.

SHAFER: And which one, which one role would you have liked to play?

CARIOU: Well, there are one or two that I could've played. I would have played Harry Hope or Larry Slade.

SHAFER: Larry would be a great role for you.

CARIOU: Well . . . yeah.

SHAFER: But it didn't work out because of timing or something else?

CARIOU: It just didn't. They decided to use the English.

SHAFER: Ah, ha, I see. But initially there was more thought about using more Americans in it, was there?

CARIOU: I doubt it. I think they just thought . . . They ended up using Americans, obviously, but I don't think they really had any intention of ever using one for the roles that I was interested in. I think they probably wanted to use people he had done it with in England, because I don't think, and I may be all wet about this, but I don't think they had the same amount of rehearsal time. Simply because Spacey knew it and didn't want to spend that much time on rehearsal.

SHAFER: Sure, of course it would have been easier indeed. So as you look ahead, you still would like to play some of the other O'Neill roles, wouldn't you? You've been Jamie, is it time to do Tyrone?

CARIOU: Oh yeah, well that's a guy I should play all right. I'll do that someday. In fact I was offered the chance to do that last year, but I wasn't able to do it.

SHAFER: I would have thought that people would have been asking you to do the role.

CARIOU: Yes, but not at the right time.

SHAFER: Well, there is all this talk about him still being attractive and sometimes you see it played by somebody who is really past the point, it seems to me. But you still have a lot of time, so I hope to see you in it. That would be very nice. I'm just sad that I missed you in the other two ones because I've seen you in other things in Canada and here and, of course on television and things, too. Are there any other roles that you would like to do?

CARIOU: I wouldn't mind doing *Moon for the Misbegotten.*

SHAFER: I was just thinking that that would be such a nice role for you and interesting because you played Jamie in the earlier one. Do you find it harder to get back to do things for the stage because you have so many other opportunities now?

CARIOU: Well, I think it's a matter of my own choice on my part. Primarily, because I spent so much time working in the theatre and have decided in the last ten years to really concentrate a little bit more on working in film and television. But, I am a theatre animal, I am really someone who loves working onstage and I love that rapport that happens between an audience and an actor.

SHAFER: In both the Guthrie and the Long Wharf, you were three quarters round, I guess, one would say.

CARIOU: Well, the Guthrie is a true thrust. The Long Wharf is not a true thrust, I mean it is a thrust, it kind of looks more like in the round.

SHAFER: It is, isn't it? Did you like that closeness?

CARIOU: The intimacy of the place is not bad at all. It's a good space.

SHAFER: Joyce Ebert, of course, was a very accomplished actress, so it must have been interesting to interact with her in the rehearsal and the performance.

CARIOU: Yeah, it was the first time we had ever worked together and we had fun working together. Yeah, we enjoyed it.

SHAFER: Arvin's fun in rehearsal, isn't he?

CARIOU: Yeah, he's fun. He's pretty loose.

SHAFER: May I ask you, and I know that you are tired after recording for Audio Book all afternoon, but let me just ask you a couple of things. What have you seen of O'Neill onstage that you like?

CARIOU: Onstage, not a hell of a lot. I've liked, I loved the film . . .

SHAFER: Of *The Iceman?*

CARIOU: *The Iceman,* yeah.

SHAFER: Did you? With Lee Marvin? I mean, Robert Ryan, of course, and Fredric March were wonderful in it.

CARIOU: Sensational. It almost killed Jason that he didn't get to do Hickey in the film.

SHAFER: That would have made a really sensational film.

CARIOU: Yes, I think it would have.

SHAFER: Was that a role that attracted you, by the way, Hickey?

CARIOU: Yeah. That's still possible.

SHAFER: And that would be, I think, very exciting. Did you actually see it here?

CARIOU: No, I didn't.

SHAFER: When you were younger did you see any O'Neill that impressed you?

CARIOU: I didn't see a lot of O'Neill when I was younger. I did see *A Moon for the Misbegotten* with Colleen and Jason here. Let me think of what else I saw. Not a lot.

SHAFER: I don't see how you would have time to. You've had such a busy career.

CARIOU: Well, I'm not a real big theatregoer. I'm a bad audience. I don't—you know, it's kind of a bus man's holiday to go to the theatre.

SHAFER: Well, as you look at the future I am hoping that you are anticipating doing something more with O'Neill onstage that we can all see.

CARIOU: Well, as Tony Guthrie used to say [very British], "Make me an offer!"

SHAFER: [Laughs.] Fine, okay.

9 | Teresa Wright

Teresa Wright was born in 1918 in Maplewood, New Jersey, where she graduated from Columbia High School. Her teachers there encouraged her interest in theatre and helped her to her first job, appearing as Blossom in *Susan and God* at the Wharf Theatre in Provincetown in 1938. Shortly after followed the roles of Emily in *Our Town* (after understudying Dorothy McGuire and playing Rebecca on tour) and Mary in *Life With Father*. She gained further stage experience in summer stock and various theatres throughout the country. For a number of years she lived in Hollywood, appearing first as Alexandra in *The Little Foxes* (1941), for which she received an Academy Award nomination. She was also nominated for her performance in *Pride of the Yankees* and won the award for *Mrs. Miniver* in 1942. When she returned to the New York stage in 1957, she played Cora Flood in *Dark at the Top of the Stairs*. She toured as Mary in *Mary, Mary* and appeared at many regional theatres including the Long Wharf Theatre, the Paper Mill Playhouse, and the Westport Country Playhouse. Her television appearances are too numerous to list. She was nominated for Emmy Awards for her performances in *The Miracle Worker* and *The Margaret Bourke-White Story*. Her active career continues as she moves between various media. She is fondly remembered for her role in Hitchcock's *Shadow of a Doubt,* playing Joseph Cotton's niece, and has been much in demand as a speaker during the recent centennial celebrations of Hitchcock's work.

NEW YORK CITY, JULY 1999

SHAFER: You remarked that this interview is a little odd for you because you haven't really done much O'Neill.

WRIGHT: I haven't, no. And it's a little odd for your first one to jump in doing *Long Day's Journey*.

SHAFER: Did you have much time to prepare?

WRIGHT: The truth is that when you are doing a Broadway show and you know way ahead of time, there are quite a lot of things you can do. Such as, really break the spine of the lines before you begin and so on. And you study and talk about the costumes and think about what the person would look like and all of that sort of thing. There are a lot of things that you can do. But when you do it at a regional theatre and there isn't much time, or in summer theatre it's sometimes a little harder.

 The other O'Neill was the *Ah, Wilderness!*—the opposite side. So I did the two, I did the tough one first.

SHAFER: Let me ask you. Just make this point then, about your comment, "for Broadway you can do this, but for regional you just haven't got the time for . . ."

WRIGHT: Well, as a rule, sometimes you do, but when you don't have time you have to sort of learn by doing, that kind of thing. And if it's short and you just found you are going to do it, then you are going to have to do it in rehearsal. I find that the script, the playwright, and the character teach me what I want to know about the role, and I don't make up my mind ahead of time about who she is or what she does or so on. But I learn and sometimes as I am learning the lines and so on, I may be kind of in the dark about why she's doing this. But the more I do it and begin to say the lines, I begin to feel the part and I begin to think with her mind. And then, I have her thoughts so I know what she is feeling. And I feel that, people always ask me my approach, and it sounds overly simple to say, "I am learning from the script and from the character," but I do. And, to me, it's the only place I would get any real security about who she is and what she's doing because the playwright has said this is who she is and this is what she is doing. He's told me what she's thinking and with his telling me and me feeling it, bringing whatever I have in my life of trouble, or whatever, to her feelings in this situation, that's the way I approach any role.

SHAFER: You know, that's marvelous. Now before we actually move in to talking about O'Neill I would like to know something more about your career. It's usual in Britain for actors to move back and forth between film and stage, but less usual here. In this country it tends to be that somebody makes a success, let's say Bradford Dillman, in *Long Day's Journey into Night,* and then moves out to Hollywood and never comes back to the stage. You managed to balance it. Would you give an overview of how you started and how all these things came about?

WRIGHT: Well, from the time I was a little girl, very little, I just loved to act and I would sing songs and act out the songs wherever I was. I didn't have much of a home life as a little child. I lived with a lot of different people. My mother was a troubled person and I would be with her a little bit and then I would be with somebody else, friends of my father or relatives of his. And then I would be back with my mother and then I would be in some school someplace in New York, like a kindergarten or something, and then out of that and into another apartment. Anyway, the good part of a childhood like that, you are constantly thrown into a new setting and a new family and everybody has their own ways of doing things and their own rules. It would go from one extreme to the other and you just adjust because you have to. And I realized, as an adult, how very much it shaped me into wanting to act. Because acting and making believe are ways of escaping from whatever is troubling. And so you do a lot of daydreaming. You know, I spent a lot of time in these classrooms where I didn't know anybody and I didn't know what they were talking about because I had just come in and so I was looking out the window and daydreaming. So, I was never a good student. I got better when I was in one environment, going to very good schools in New Jersey—South Orange and then Maplewood. There was a very fine high school in Maplewood called Columbia High School. And there for the first time, I got, in a way, in the theatre by public speaking. And say, I'd give a book report and I would kind of get away with dramatizing it and so they thought, "She really understood that book!" [Laughing.] Because I would deliver it. And those teachers knew I was interested in theatre, so they took me (two teachers there) took me to see the first live thing I ever saw, which was *Cornelia Otis Skinner and Her One Woman Show.* And that was the first theatre I ever saw.

SHAFER: No kidding! Do you know she encouraged so many actresses with that, it's in my book on American women playwrights.

WRIGHT: Isn't that amazing! And at Columbia High School, where this was, this wonderful teacher was head of the dramatic society. So I worked with her and we loved each other. So we put on very good productions and that was my introduction to theatre as such. And as such, from there I went to see some plays, eventually. When I could get the five cents to go to a movie, I would see Helen Hayes in something. And I would listen to her on the radio. Anyway, I spent a whole year wanting to see her in *Victoria Regina.* That's the first play that I ever saw and I hate to say it, but I think that it's the only time I've ever used a young man in my life. And that was because he wanted to take me to Coney Island. But before he knew what happened, we were going to *Victoria Regina* instead. So there we were, I was in seventh heaven and he was sitting in the first row of the balcony looking at this play about a queen and not knowing anything. And thinking, "God, it must be great at the beach today." Later the kids would all go together and take the train. So I saw a few things. I saw Katharine Cornell in *Wingless Victory,* I think, and something else. And there was another teacher there, a public speaking teacher, who was going to be building sets at the Wharf Theatre in Provincetown. And he got me a working scholarship there for the summer. And that's my real introduction into theatre because it was run by two people from Carnegie Tech. Edith Skinner was a wonderful public speaking teacher and she was head of the Speech Department or Drama Department at Carnegie Tech. So there were a lot of young people who came with her from Carnegie Tech who were older than I was.

SHAFER: Not the same theatre where O'Neill's plays were first put on, but isn't it interesting that you first worked in Provincetown?

WRIGHT: I think so. It was on a pier. So anyway, from there, that first summer I met wonderful professionals—these kids came and the professional actors. Blanche Ring was one and Sally Rand.

SHAFER: Sally Rand!? The fan dancer?

WRIGHT: Yes, Sally Rand. And Sally did *White Cargo*. The one where she says, "I am Tondeleyo." She would come in with little sparklers on her face and in her sarongs and say [deep voice] "I am Tondeleyo!" But the funny thing is that she was very intent on doing away with that image. So she did this play, but for her curtain call they had to wait until she got into this long blue gown and a big picture hat and that's how she took her curtain call. It was like she wanted everyone to know that she was really a lady. It was a wonderful story. But anyway, Doro Merande was very important in my life, because she was a character woman and worked almost every season in something. And she said you can always come to New York if you want. When she went back to New York she got her job in *Our Town*. So, I guess I wrote to her to say how happy I was about the play and she said you must come backstage to see me if you ever come see the play. I didn't get there until it had been running a long time, but I went back. But it turned out that Martha Scott was going to go to California to do the film of *Our Town* and they were looking for an understudy because her understudy was going to be playing the part. Her understudy was Dorothy McGuire, who is still my great friend. So that was my real entree into the theatre business. All because my public speaking teacher in high school got me the working scholarship. Doro Merande got me the chance to read for the stage manager and the stage manager wanted me to read for Jed Harris. Well, I spent about two months, maybe more, waiting to read for Jed Harris, a very eccentric man, as you know.

SHAFER: Oh, yes!

WRIGHT: They would call me and tell me that they think he is going to be here tonight and I would rush down there on the subway from 94th Street where I shared a room with a girl. I would go there and wait and wait and wait and he wouldn't come, wouldn't come, wouldn't come. Then one night, it was after the hurricane season, the hurricane of '38, and I went down, had a terrible cold and felt awful. So I went down and sure enough, he was there. And he was there reading this thing with somebody else and I was sitting there very nervous. And Frank Craven, the lead, had this sweet dresser, a black man, who consoled me 'cause I was just shaking and nervous. So I did get to read for Jed Harris and I got the job. So that was my entree into theatre in New York, understudying Dorothy. So I went off on tour with that show. We were supposed to go on a rather long tour, but by the time I got to Chicago something happened, maybe Frank Craven was tired of doing it or something. The tour stopped in Chicago and I came back to New York. Dorothy went on to do another play and most of the actors in the original production went to other jobs and most of us, understudies, got to play it again with Eddie Dowling.

SHAFER: So, then, from this point on you went out to Hollywood and did films?

WRIGHT: No, first I did this play and I got seen by people and that was when I really got to know Thornton Wilder and his sister Isabel. They gave me clothes for my doll, Emily (because I was playing Emily), a part of my doll collection. For me, it was my family. I took them wherever I went. So that went well and so on and at least I was known and had an agent. So then came the fall and I read for Mary in *Life With Father*. I read for it about five different times.

Because she was supposed to be a blonde and then they finally decided that they'd do it with a dark-haired girl. So that was mine, then I was in the theatre and then I was in that for a year and a half. Then supposedly Lillian Hellman saw me in that and told Goldwyn about me for *Little Foxes* because William Wyler was going to be doing *Little Foxes*. I was free to go under contract and that is when I went out to do the *Little Foxes*. So then I got married and had my family and then I worked and I didn't work and I worked and I didn't work and then, finally I was divorced and I'd left Goldwyn and I was out there doing mostly live television. And I met Bob Anderson out there through friends of mine and I came back to do a play with Elia Kazan called *Dark at the Top of Stairs* and then after that Bob and I were married and I came back here and was in theatre again.

SHAFER: Now, obviously, you have these two O'Neill experiences that come after this and as you said, oddly, *Long Day's Journey,* the big challenge, came first at the Hartford Stage Company where I had the pleasure of seeing you.

WRIGHT: Well I must say, that I really at first almost went mad in that because it is an awful lot in a short time without a long, long schedule of working on it and the lines and getting to know the character. I was working with a wonderful actor, Bob Pastene and a very good director. One of the things that I discovered, purely a technical thing, that because of the drugs affecting the character's mind, I found that I was very disoriented and I couldn't seem to concentrate on anything. And then, suddenly, I realized that I was bringing in this drug thing in with me. And I thought, "I've got to forget about that until I get everything else settled. I have to know the lines and know where I am going and I have to know who I am talking to and so on. And then I can get into the haze of the drugs." But it is amazing how you have to learn it, but if I were going to do another part like that at another time, I'd know that. But I had to learn that myself.

SHAFER: How long did you have to rehearse it?

WRIGHT: Not very long. We had a very short time, not long enough for *Long Day's Journey*, really, but it was adequate. And I loved doing it.

SHAFER: You didn't know these people before you did it, did you? Bob Pastene and Tom Atkins and John Glover?

WRIGHT: Oh no, but I learned to love them all.

SHAFER: Oh good, that was just what I was going to ask you, if you were able in that time to develop a family feeling?

WRIGHT: Oh yes, of course in rehearsal you do it and playing it you do and they were so good. They were so good, I loved them. I still follow John Glover—I feel like his mother.

SHAFER: He certainly looked like the young O'Neill. Did you read about O'Neill's family, did you talk about it?

WRIGHT: Oh yes, not at the time, not when I was doing it. I knew whatever I knew from one thing or another, from general knowledge. But I think I probably read while I was doing it, but not before.

SHAFER: This would have been about 1972?

WRIGHT: Something like that.

SHAFER: And, how did you find the experience, in addition to learning from the script itself, as you say. As a rehearsal process was there anything in particular you remember about it?

WRIGHT: No, it was just that the more we all knew the more we became a family, and then, you know we just reacted as family members as well as actors. But I just loved doing that play and I loved Santo Loquasto's set. There was something about that whole set that had a wonderful aura. And the costumes.

SHAFER: This was before he was so well known, wasn't it?

WRIGHT: I guess it might have been, though he was very busy then. I have a lovely sketch that he gave me of my lovely gown with the lace.

SHAFER: It seems to me that many people have an attitude about O'Neill that his plays are full of animosity and grimness and there's no comedy.

WRIGHT: Well, his comedy is amazing and I think that when you have comedy in the middle of such tragedy it is welcomed by you and by the audience because it needs it. You know, it's great, it's comedy that I love and I think it is very important in that play and he does do it, whether it's technical or he is taking it from life. And again, I think he is taking it from life, because in his own life, obviously, you know, there must have been horrendous times and sad moments and funny moments. But they all have that Irish humor, you know. It's got to escape. That's that Irish glumness that can come over and the blackness and sadness, all the orneriness, all the things that are deeply Irish. My grandmother was Mary Kelly and her family was from Dublin. She wore all her clothes at once, layer on layer. She always carried this bag which was full of every card and note her sons had ever sent her. I never saw her being angry or anything except if she would get to go on a bus and somebody would go to help her and she would say, "Take your hand off my bag!" [Irish accent] And she was really, I mean, she'd be fierce and that was the only time that I could see her being fierce, other than that she could be very funny.

SHAFER: She had a strong Irish accent?

WRIGHT: Oh yes, she did. It was New York/Irish, you know.

SHAFER: Did you play with the idea of having any Irish accent yourself as Mary?

WRIGHT: It seems to me that I thought about it, but I thought because she went to a convent for an education that she would not have.

SHAFER: Let me take you back to another point, which also grows out of this story of your grandmother here. The picture that I have (as you know I loved seeing the play, it's always still in my mind), and I always remember the comedy and I remember how funny Tom Atkins was up there on the rocking chair with the lights when he was drunk. The photograph I used in a book shows you embracing Bob Pastene and you are bending down and he is in a chair. And it looks like a couple in love. It just says that these are people who love each other and you are laughing. To me, it was a wonderful picture to have from the play because it seems to me to show the kind of love that this grandmother of yours had for her sons. Could you talk about that element of the play?

WRIGHT: Well, I think one of the saddest things about the play is that they really did love each other, these parents. And in a way, they were killing each other. She with her drugs and he with his stinginess. And, of course, she blamed her drug habit on his stinginess and it was a love/hate relationship. But the love was very strong. I mean she had adored him. When her father took her to see him in his play, she loved him from that moment. It was that kind of love. But then, actually, I think the physical love and the closeness that they had was very, very important to her. I mean, she obviously didn't have her mother around much so her love was for her father and she transferred that to this man who was a friend of her father's, but a glamorous friend of her father's. And she loved him from that aspect, a young girl's awe in love. And then finally, in marrying him, I think she had a very physical, warm love for him. And then with the first child I am sure there was a great happiness, but then there was the death of the other one. So there is all of that, she loved her child, but blamed him for the death. And then blamed herself and blamed her husband for being stingy and not getting a better doctor and all that, that kind of thing. And, so you see, she is obviously capable of this deep ability to hurt. And she does, she uses it on him when she is in her drugged state. And you can see that this resentment is very deep in her that she is capable of that awful Irish turning on somebody and making them suffer, as well as capable of great suffering herself. But it is interesting, it's amazing how a writer like that could be so mixed up when he went through so many things himself and was shy and bitter and yet, had had times of happiness and fun with his brother whom he loved. I mean, they loved each other very much, and yet, they were not good to each other in ways. But it's the complications of love that are really so well drawn in this play.

SHAFER: And now, Santo Loquasto did the costumes as you said. There is a lot in the first act about her being plump.

WRIGHT: Yes, he was kidding her. But probably, she did get to be plump after her children.

SHAFER: Well, when she had been on the drugs she was thin because she didn't eat, but now she is not on the drugs so she is eating and she's gained a little weight.

WRIGHT: And he's happy to see that. I think she would get too thin when she was on drugs.

SHAFER: I remember you had a very pretty costume on in that and you looked quite healthy, certainly not fat, but pleasingly full. I recently saw a production with a Mary who was actually skinny!

WRIGHT: Well, that's certainly all wrong.

SHAFER: Would you like to talk about the woman's role you played in *Ah, Wilderness!*?

WRIGHT: Yes, and it is amazing, how O'Neill could do that play and then years later wanting to see another side of the family and doing this. It's just like, you know, two sides of a photograph, the negative and the positive. Except the positive is the dark side and the other is the light side. *Ah, Wilderness!* is amazing with the quality of fun and the mother being sweet and the father being gentle . . .

SHAFER: How did that role come up?

WRIGHT: I was working with Arvin Brown in a production at the Long Wharf, where I was just doing a very small thing. Well, originally Arvin had asked me if I would play the mother, but Bob and I had just been separated and I was emotionally upset and just did not feel up to doing the mother. So then Arvin said, "I'd like to take you out of this play and I'd like you to play the mother." And I thought about it and I said, "I don't think I can now," and I suggested Geraldine [Fitzgerald] and she was wonderful. She was wonderful in it. Then we did it later and he asked me to play the mother in that, too. But in that case I said no for another reason. I felt that mother is a very good, good mother, but Geraldine has a way of saying things like, "You're a bad and horrid boy," or whatever it is and it comes out funny. Geraldine says everything with kind of a smile. And it takes the curse off being too prim and righteous about it. And I was right, she was lovely in it. One of my things about Geraldine is that line she says, "It's so hot, it's so hot!" And most of us would say [sighing] "It's so hot, it's so hot." And Geraldine would say "It's so HOT!" And I think that only Geraldine can say, "It's so hot" with a smile like that. That's Geraldine's look on life. She just has a very up thing. So she can play a mother who's a very good, good mother who is sweet and nice and not have to be oppressively nice. So I loved doing it with her.

But it was, it is interesting, getting back to O'Neill. Probably one side he made blacker then it was and the others made whiter than it was or gayer than it was. But it is interesting how he was capable of it because you wouldn't think that a man who wrote *Long Day's Journey* would be capable of those really funny scenes, funny scenes between the young people. And he was terribly funny, so he really did have that Irish humor. It wasn't always the sarcastic humor, it was really funny, funny, light.

SHAFER: So you played Aunt Lily in this comedy.

WRIGHT: Yes, at the Circle in the Square. But Arvin directed the Long Wharf company at the Circle.

SHAFER: To my mind one of the things that O'Neill does in a play is really give the actors something wonderful to do, whether it's the lead or not.

WRIGHT: Yes, yes he does. Everything.

SHAFER: And I feel that even in the smaller roles in *The Iceman Cometh,* each one of those has a scene . . .

WRIGHT: Oh, they're marvelous . . .

SHAFER: Each one has a scene to play. There's something all of the time.

WRIGHT: Absolutely, I loved Aunt Lily, I loved playing her. I think it's a wonderful role.

SHAFER: And who was your Uncle Sid?

WRIGHT: Johnny. Johnny Braden.

SHAFER: Oh, John Braden, he's wonderful! I love John Braden!

WRIGHT: Yes, he's so good. He was so good. I loved working with him, he's just darling. I saw them recently at the Long Wharf for the memorial for Joyce Ebert.

SHAFER: Oh how wonderful! Yes, he was a very hilarious man. Aunt Lily is a very complex character, isn't she? On the one hand she seems to love him and yet, and yet she won't marry him.

WRIGHT: She loves him but he drinks. She hates liquor, she hates drunks. She loves this man and his sweetness and he's dear and if he could only stay sober she'd love to be married to him. But she can't tolerate drunkenness, which is something I understand, having lived with it some of the time.

SHAFER: So, for her, it isn't just out of some puritanical belief, "Oh, people shouldn't drink!"—it goes beyond that, doesn't it?

WRIGHT: It did in my case, I think I had no idea who Aunt Lily had known or knew that might make her feel that way, or whether it was puritanical or whether it was that she hated drinking, I don't know. Or that because he became unattractive as most drunks do. And if people are repelled by drunks then it would be very hard to be married to one. Some people could say, "Oh well, he's fine when he is not drinking, you know, and he's a good man." But I can't imagine anyone really completely forgiving a drunk. The behavior of drunk people just isn't attractive, it's destructive. And I think that it's the destruction that stopped her. I think that Lily would have loved to have a family, she would have loved to have children and to be around someone who is destructive would be difficult.

SHAFER: And she loves the home, doesn't she?

WRIGHT: Oh yes, and she loves the home and the children and she's been kind of like a surrogate mother to her niece and nephews. So she loves that role and is at home with that role, she would love to be married. But now it's later on in her life and she might not have children anyway. But I don't think that she wants to settle for a man who's going to be out drinking.

SHAFER: It's interesting, if you look at that pair, and then look at *The Iceman Cometh,* you see that situation, don't you? Where she kept on forgiving him, which is finally what ended up destroying him.

WRIGHT: That's right, yes, he couldn't take it anymore, that's true. That's true and it would have done the same thing to Uncle Sid. Because a person resents having to be forgiven. So finally it becomes the other person's fault.

SHAFER: Yes, yes because of course he can very readily say, and there is a conversation in the play, isn't there, that maybe the reason he drinks is because she won't marry him.

WRIGHT: The same thing, I'm sure, O'Neill saw that in his family with his mother's addiction to drugs, his own addiction to liquor and his brother's addiction to liquor and his father's sometime use of liquor. So that he shares that guilt with him and knows well with guilt, that you blame the person you're victimizing while you're drinking. We tend to blame them.

SHAFER: So you had these two very fine experiences acting and . . . and was there anything that you remember about working with Arvin in the rehearsal process that helped as far as bringing the play along?

WRIGHT: Well, Arvin is always a very loving, loving director. He loves the characters and he enjoys your—whatever anybody is bringing to them, you know, and he enjoys seeing them come to life. He's probably done many plays more than one time, as Michael Kahn does, you know. And I think that is probably very interesting then, to see what other people/other actors would bring, too. And I would imagine, sometimes, they find, "I wish they would do so-and-so the way so-and-so did." And you stop and eventually they'd probably just learn to go with whatever the person is giving.

SHAFER: But I mean, this is an interesting point, isn't it? I think that many people who don't know about acting, assume that you read the play and here the playwright has said to you what this person is supposed to do. Could you talk about what an actress ACTUALLY does. I mean, you don't really . . .

WRIGHT: I was going to say, I might read what the playwright says this person does and you might read it, but we'll come out with slightly different versions of what the person said. Each one of us believes that this is what he said and this actress or character is going to do the same and this is the way they're doing it. Another person will see it slightly different. If it's vastly different then it is up to the director to decide whether he wants that vast difference or what. But that is what makes theatre interesting, I think. I mean, I love going to shows with different people doing the parts.

SHAFER: May I ask you further, because I know that you are a theatregoer as well as an actress, could you tell me about some of the performances of O'Neill that you saw and that you remember?

WRIGHT: Yeah, well *Touch of the Poet,* I did love *Touch of the Poet.* You know I would love to see Bob Pastene do the father in *Touch of the Poet.* He is a marvelous actor.

SHAFER: Yes!

WRIGHT: And I have only really worked with him on that one play.

SHAFER: You saw it with Eric Portman and Helen Hayes, I suppose?

WRIGHT: Yes, I think so.

SHAFER: Somebody told me he was difficult to understand in the role.

WRIGHT: I can't remember, I don't think that I thought that. But I was a great admirer, I just adored Helen Hayes as a kid and on and on, you know? Having gotten to see that play from the first row in the balcony instead of going to Coney Island and I went right on loving her. I'd seen her in films, she was my idol when I was in school. I used to have her picture on my dressing table, I don't know what happened to it. It was signed by her.

SHAFER: Can you remember any others that you saw? I know that part of the time you were in Hollywood so you wouldn't have seen everything that was done. Did you see the original production of *Long Day's Journey into Night?*

WRIGHT: Yes I did. Yes. The one with Fredric March and Florence Eldridge. Yes and they were very good friends of mine. I'd been in *Best Years of Our Lives* already and by that time Bob and I lived in Connecticut and we saw a lot of each other there. They were very good friends and they came to see me in *Long Day's Journey.*

SHAFER: Oh, how nice!

WRIGHT: They drove to Hartford to see it.

SHAFER: Oh, that's lovely!

WRIGHT: Yeah, they were darling. She was dear.

SHAFER: And did you see *The Iceman Cometh* with Jason Robards?

WRIGHT: Yes, yes I did. He's marvelous.

SHAFER: Yes.

WRIGHT: And I loved it!

SHAFER: He told me something interesting about that time, he had to make his entrances from sitting on a bench outside the theatre. And, obviously, you know, he couldn't be getting into character out there because people were coming by to talk to him.

WRIGHT: Oh, God, awful! Why was that? Why was that?

SHAFER: Because the theatre didn't have any offstage space. You know what it was, that little theatre.

WRIGHT: Which theatre was that?

SHAFER: That Circle in the Square downtown. Now I was just wondering, as an actress yourself, before *Long Day's Journey into Night,* and during and you know, what is your approach to getting yourself into character or going onstage? I mean, a lot of people have different attitudes about it.

WRIGHT: I don't have a lot of preparation. Until I get there, by myself backstage I begin to think of it and, you know, and then I just kind of walk on. But I don't do a lot of backstage, I mean walking back and forth kind of preparation thing. It's more interior. But, let's see if there's anything else I wanted to tell you about it . . . no. I think, as I said, one of the big memories of that production was how long it took me (when I say how long I mean maybe several days) of not realizing that I couldn't bring the drugged state right away, I had to have all the other foundations firm. Because if you're thinking in that hazy mind you can't, you can't do movements, you can't write down notes, you can't think of what you're doing, you can't think ahead of where we are or what we're doing. So, it is amazing, you feel like playing a part if you were drunk, which must be an absolute terror.

SHAFER: Oh goodness, yes, yes. It is interesting, in a sense, that you are saying, that the role began to take you over.

WRIGHT: Yeah, it does because that kind of haze is mostly just awful to get out of. And if you allow it to come over, and it's funny how long it took me to think, "Well for god's sake, of course you can't think. You've got to get rid of that until this is so solid and then let it come in again." It's amazing, it's like a secret weapon!

SHAFER: Yes, yes. Did you ever have anything funny or odd that happened in rehearsals?

WRIGHT: Well, no but in the other one, *Ah, Wilderness!,* one of those great horrible theatrical moments that I will never, never forget. Whoever designed those costumes designed the most beautiful gown that I wore in one scene. It was a sheer, a voile or something, a printed voile. So that, without its petticoats, it was very sheer. We had this table setting scene, it was lovely the work with Geraldine just going back and forth. And we were chatting away and we had it all worked out. I loved scenes where we had a lot of props, setting the table and busy and full of talk, and so on. And it was fun and it was great, but there was this great big tray, you know, full of dishware. Well, Laurence Olivier was in the audience and I can't remember whether I knew he was out there or not, Geraldine knew and she told me, but I don't know if she said it before or after. I think after, because I think I would have probably just fainted right then if I had known then. Because in the scene, we're doing the setting of the table, a petticoat or something had gone out to be fixed or something and came back and the girl dressed me. And I don't know if it was a new girl or if she was in a hurry for some reason, somehow. Anyway, I get out onstage and suddenly I feel that my petticoat is going. And, I am trying to think if there is any moment where I get off long enough to fix it or something and there wasn't. And here was this scene coming up, setting the table, and I am going around, if you can imagine such a thing, trying to hold the skirt. And all of the sudden there's the thing with the tray and the stuff and never, never stopping a minute talking. And somehow, God knows, I don't know, there must be special angels that come watch over you in these circumstances, I got through it. But I thought I would die. And certainly, my energy, every bit of energy I had went into keeping this petticoat on! So God knows what the scene sounded like. But I was in absolute terror until I could get away. And I don't know if Geraldine knew, but it was not soon enough to be of any help with the dishes. But anyway, when it was over I found out that Olivier was out there, he was a friend of hers and he was coming backstage and he came back. I just wanted to die!

SHAFER: Oh, he had to come that night! Were there any other O'Neill roles that you wished you could have played or that you thought about?

WRIGHT: No, I . . . there's one I like emotionally but I wouldn't be right for it physically and Colleen was perfect for it. I am trying to think of its name, but it's the girl that is the tomboy and is very big for her age.

SHAFER: *A Moon for the Misbegotten.*

WRIGHT: Yeah, *Moon for the Misbegotten.* Now *Touch of the Poet,* I could do and would have liked to have done, but I preferred the two roles I played.

FOSTER: At the Goodman. The head of the school did her doctoral dissertation on O'Neill.

SHAFER: And who was that?

FOSTER: Dr. Bella Itkin.

SHAFER: Isn't that marvelous!

FOSTER: So, O'Neill had been a part of my early learning environment.

SHAFER: How did this happen to come about, you being in *Long Day's Journey into Night?*

FOSTER: Geraldine Fitzgerald and the head of the theatre facility, the Richard Allen Center headed by Faith O'Brien. They came up with the idea to do *Long Day's Journey,* came by my house and they engaged in this conversation, so they approached me with it. I was quite surprised they were going to do it at City Corp. We were going to rehearse at the Richard Allen Center, which was right around the corner from where I live. This was not a play that I would have expected that I would have been asked to do, that character. I guess because of the way in which she has been portrayed in other productions, very much the victim. And this was not Geraldine Fitzgerald's thought, her vision of the piece. She had done it in five different productions and I understand they had been absolutely excellent in that role. And her thought was that Mary Tyrone designed a way of escaping her environment, that household. Her husband was a failed actor who turns to his own vision of himself doing this role, this one role, over and over and over again. And missing out on the opportunity to be the great rounded actor he could have been had he not gone for the money, the security—he became a very unhappy drunk. Her son, her older son, a falling-down drunk and her younger son . . .

SHAFER: And who played that?

FOSTER: Al Freeman. Yes. And the younger son, Peter Francis James, with the expectation for his not recovering and going to a sanitarium, which is as close to a state hospital you can get. Nowadays, he would go to a facility where he would get the specialized and individual care. Again, the father being an old penny-pincher. This is a household that is the antithesis of what she grew up in. She came out of a convent-like environment and to be thrown in with show biz, which is what her husband was after, had to be a blow to her spirit.

SHAFER: Can we go a little bit further on the production itself? They came and asked you to play the role and at the same time were they negotiating with the other actors, Earle Hyman and all?

FOSTER: No, I asked for Earle Hyman, for Al Freeman and for Peter Francis James. Those were the people whom I felt, given her vision of the piece, those were the people I felt that I would like to work with.

SHAFER: And you had acted with them before, all of them?

FOSTER: I had worked with all three of them before. So I knew their work and I knew their styles and I knew that we would be compatible in an acting style.

SHAFER: You know, I had the pleasure of seeing you in *The Cherry Orchard* and Earle Hyman was, of course, in that.

FOSTER: Yes, he was. And he also was in *Agamemnon,* that we did out at the Delacorte. And Al Freeman I had worked in *A Raisin in the Sun* many years ago but subsequently in something else, but we had always been friends. And Peter Francis just seemed to be so perfect for Edmund. And Geraldine was amenable to that.

SHAFER: Was the intention to have a long run with it?

FOSTER: [Laughing.] Well, I think people always go into a play thinking they are going to have a run.

SHAFER: I think it's the location that was rather surprising.

FOSTER: Oh no, I think that was scheduled just for a particular period. And *Long Day's* did not have a history of long runs like some of these plays that run for five or ten years. It wasn't being done anywhere professionally in the United States at the time that we were doing it. It wasn't until after we did it that subsequently we saw where regional theatres were going to do *Long Day's Journey* and somebody else was going to do *Long Day's Journey* and Jack Lemmon was coming to New York to do *Long Day's Journey*. It was kind of like we revived *Long Day's Journey into Night* because we respected the author and the play and felt very strongly about it. So we did our rehearsal at the Richard Allen Center, engaged the City Corp for a brief run and at that time, I think, that's when Geraldine and Hayes were looking for a producer where they could move it. And Joe Papp took it sight unseen because he knew all of our work. He had worked with all of us. And of course, he knew the play. So it was just say sight unseen, bring it on down.

SHAFER: That's great.

FOSTER: And it was just wonderful, but that's how Joe worked, you know. He was such a positive force.

SHAFER: How long was the rehearsal period, do you remember?

FOSTER: I don't recall it requiring any more time than other plays did. And generally, that was anywhere between four to five weeks, depending on whether you consider previews and technical rehearsals.

SHAFER: In that rehearsal period, was there anything in particular that you remember? Any time that you did something and there was a breakthrough, or that Geraldine and you worked together on then?

FOSTER: Well, one thing that was very interesting about our particular working situation. We didn't deal with the arthritis almost until opening. Geraldine didn't feel that that was the area of concentration, since this was an escape, since her condition, her reason for deciding to use drugs beyond their recommended usage was to escape this environment, because she could not cope with the environment in which she lived. It was not the arthritis that made her addicted to drugs. It was the absence of a pleasant environment in which to live. So we had to deal with that. The hands, the use of the hands in a deformed manner, did not come about . . . well, I know we were in costume and Geraldine said, "You have to do something about this." Because I remember discussing it with her, I had a friend, at the time, he had rheumatoid arthritis and I had seen the way the hands had been affected. There were periods of pain and then other periods where everything seemed fine. So I had discussed this with Geraldine, but as I said we were concentrating in a different area. But she supported this approach with the fact that once Tyrone and the older son were gone, Mary cleaned up her act. She went back to the sisters and got rid of her drug addiction. But not until they were out of her life.

SHAFER: That's a very interesting approach. Was there anything else about the rehearsal process, about, for example, how you interacted about the husband and the sons?

FOSTER: Nothing that I could specifically point to. I know that the older son was able to deal, on a head-to-head basis, that was the character of Al Freeman in this play. He had great trepidation about playing my son. We were, you know, about the same age and we were also friends and I had to convince him that because of their relationship it wasn't a nurturing kind of affair. She fought with him. She saw too much of her husband in him. So Al was perfect, I mean he was just perfect.

SHAFER: He's an actor with a great deal of power, but he also has a lot of charm, doesn't he?

FOSTER: Yes, uh huh. He was just wonderful, just all of them were. Well, this was a production to which actors came back four and five times. I mean I thought it was just—it was absolutely satisfying in the sense that many of these actors had never seen a production of the play before. There were others who had seen productions so they were able to evaluate on a comparative basis. But those who had not seen it before were just extraordinarily responsive. And as I say the word, actors, when they came, some came in groups, some came with friends. And to come and to see that production—it's a long show.

SHAFER: How much did you cut it, by the way?

FOSTER: I don't think we did. I don't recall that being an issue.

SHAFER: You've mentioned other performances and the success of this production as a whole. Sometimes the husband has been played by actors who don't have any quality of a great nineteenth-century matinee idol. But Earle Hyman was able to give that quality.

FOSTER: Oh yes! Yes! I mean, he knew, he had that style. And yes, there are actors, I gather, who forget that period and the declamatory style of acting. And that, of course, is a very important element in that character. And yes, he very much presented that.

SHAFER: So when you moved then from the original space to work with Joe Papp did you have the same company?

FOSTER: Same company.

SHAFER: Same company, and did he come to see it? I presume he talked to you about it sometime, didn't he?

FOSTER: I am sure he saw it. I don't recall any specific conversation with Joe about that production other than he wanted it there and he extended the run because the response was so great.

SHAFER: Wonderful.

FOSTER: And I'm sure that he, you know, he came and talked with us as he always does with the productions that go on there.

SHAFER: This must have been a very nice experience for Geraldine Fitzgerald, I think, to engage in this and have such a success with it.

FOSTER: I would think so. I know that she was very thrilled and moved . . .

SHAFER: Had you worked with her before?

FOSTER: No, I didn't, I had never met her before.

SHAFER: You didn't even know her?

FOSTER: No. However she arrived at deciding that she wanted to ask me to play this role, I don't know, but it didn't come from any history of knowing each other.

SHAFER: As a director, had she worked with you in any way that was different than you had ever done before?

FOSTER: No. In fact, I do believe that the whole rehearsal period was . . . she was very much an editor in a sense that she stayed glued to the script. So she must have been listening as opposed to watching. This was for a long period of time. I recall that there was some concern about whether she was observing the action/ reaction of what's going on between and among the characters. Because her concentration seemed to be on the written page.

SHAFER: It must have been of some interest that she had played the role so often and you had not. Did you have any different points of view?

FOSTER: Well no, she had never played it this way. That was the interesting approach that she had with my theatre work. She had played it, like I said, in five different productions, but she always felt that this was intentional on Mary's part. And she supported it with her later history, cleaning up her act when the source of her frustration was removed. And I had no problem seeing Mary in this light. She was very much in control.

SHAFER: You would feel that gives a stronger sense of what you felt was more appropriate.

FOSTER: Absolutely, absolutely. She's more determined. She is in control of removing herself from this unpleasantness.

SHAFER: Did it give a kind of different effect, do you think, to the last scene then?

FOSTER: No, the last scene, she's out of it then. I think that is the experience: that is when you see her totally enveloped in the drug. There's no halfway point, it didn't happen in one of the other scenes. The night before she had been heard, moving around and what have you. But you see her the next day and she is more composed. Here you see her in the midst of her drug-induced state. So I don't know that it was that different than any other actor would have played it other than other choices we made. But she is in a drug-induced state.

SHAFER: Now, you mentioned that you were in costume when this question about the arthritis came up. What was your costume actually like?

FOSTER: I don't recall, but it was very comfortable and very appropriate and less frilly.

SHAFER: Less frilly?

FOSTER: Much less frilly than what I have since seen in terms of pictures, you know, the much more elaborate dresses. I was very, very comfortable in the costumes that we agreed upon. A long skirt and blouse and a dress and a nightgown, you know. So, I do know that I subsequently saw a film version with Katherine Hepburn, and she's in this gown, you know in the lace and what have you. But no, we didn't go in that direction.

SHAFER: That's interesting.

FOSTER: And I found it very, very comfortable to work in.

SHAFER: Did you find the part wearing? Were you tired at the end?

FOSTER: Oh, at that time, I don't think I ever got tired. This was a few years back and I loved so working on the play and with the actors and at the Public Theatre, that I can't imagine that I was ever tired.

SHAFER: That's great.

FOSTER: It isn't until later years, you know, that you begin to feel it.

SHAFER: Classes of acting and literature courses dealing with O'Neill plays always interested me—I should mention to you that I played Mary when I was in the University of California. Since that time I have talked with many students and professors who think that O'Neill is dull. One of the reasons that I wanted to do this book was because I think actors find O'Neill's plays exciting. Did you find it so?

FOSTER: I certainly wouldn't think of it as dull. But then you have people who think Chekhov is dull! [Laughing.]

SHAFER: Well that's true.

FOSTER: You know, I think that this is where the actor frequently goes to the subtext and brings to the dialogue, the colors that are necessary to produce the language and to communicate the play-wright's intent and emotion to the audience.

SHAFER: You didn't happen to see the play on television last week, did you?

FOSTER: No, I only came in for a bit of the end. But I think the play is perfect for that medium.

SHAFER: I didn't feel at the beginning that they were playing the subtext very much.

FOSTER: I was too late—I didn't see the top part of the show.

SHAFER: The top part is where you have quite a challenge, isn't it? You have to, on the one hand, be kind of fitting into the circumstances. On the other hand, your mind is on that room upstairs with the drugs. And yet it can't seem to be too obvious . . .

FOSTER: No, I think those were choices that we made as to what the immediacy was, how long a period can one comfortably be away from the drug. When she goes upstairs, she goes upstairs to do what she has to do. At other times, she is functioning. So those are the choices that are made and I'm sure they are made between the actor and the director.

SHAFER: With a rich play like that there are obviously a number of different choices which can be made. May I turn to a slightly different direction. When you acted in *The Cherry Orchard* and when you acted in this play, despite the success of both of them, there were people who questioned the validity of a black cast in these and other plays written with white actors in mind. I'm curious to know if you followed any of that aftermath of the so-called debate between August Wilson and Robert Brustein, in which the question came up about color-blind casting and interracial casting? Some people seem to be so very in favor of those approaches and some other people are very much against. You've had the opportunity to play this terrific range of roles, and I was just curious to hear what you have to say about that.

FOSTER: I was very much aware of the debate, in fact, I went to the Town Hall session they had. And it's a reflection of how this society functions in many ways. I think I understand now that August Wilson's concern had much to do with plays that were written about African Americans and our history being produced on a wider scale and also being directed by knowledgeable people. Because there is a great deal of concern about directors who are not knowledgeable about our history imposing what they think they know drawn from television or drawn from one African American whom they've encountered for a brief period of time. I think his concern in that area is that it's—well, you know it's one thing to have a recipe, another thing to have a cook. So there were many elements that brought him to his way of thinking. On the other hand, I gather you have these institutions that are run by others. They have their directors on staff or engage them. Frequently they come to the theatre to direct the play with little knowledge of certain material, then they're gone. And it leads to the question of, How valuable, then, is the material in terms of educating a public, engaging a public? Yes, you can entertain them, engage, but what kind of truth is coming forth? Could their vision possibly be compatible with the writer's? It comes up, the question comes up, you know, in many ways. On the other hand, since the African Americans have been exposed their entire lives to the culture of white America; been taught it, worked in it, lived in it, that is not foreign territory . . . never has been. But the reverse is not true, it is not true to date.

SHAFER: Now, what this would suggest, then, is that for an African American to be in an O'Neill play which is not about African Americans presents no problem, is that right?

FOSTER: It presents no problem: even the situation of a failed actor, alcoholism, those are not foreign subjects to the African American or any other person. That's why it is considered a universal work because it speaks to people of different cultures. If you don't want other people to play them, then don't call it a universal work! [Laughing.] *A Raisin in the Sun* is considered a universal work because people of other cultures can play that situation, Irish, Chinese, you name it. *Raisin in the Sun* has been done all over the world. It speaks to different cultures when they are in that level. Recently, I did this, played the Momma in the play, and Asian people have come back to say how involved they were because it was so similar to their family situation. So, great works have to be played by everyone because it goes beyond the thing of color. We thought of it as a play, a black family in that situation, there was nothing foreign about it. There was nothing foreign about a black actor failing, having a drinking problem, having a disappointing life, living with a woman who takes drugs. There was nothing foreign about a woman being raised in a convent-like situation. *I* went to boarding school. I went to boarding school because there was no home at the time. There's nothing foreign about being in a sheltered life. There's just nothing foreign about that play.

SHAFER: Now, I have two things, two things further on this one to ask, if I may, and one is, do you read the critics?

FOSTER: Not until afterwards.

SHAFER: After it's over, after the production is over?

FOSTER: No, if we are into a run sometimes after a month or so, I am able to deal with that. Once I am comfortable that our play is functioning as we expected it to, then at some point I read them.

SHAFER: Well, I know that they were very positive about your production of *Long Day's Journey into Night.*

FOSTER: I don't recall. I recall that there was some criticism, there are some critics that just do not want any environment with other cultures in it. You know, they think this is specifically for, I guess, anybody other than people of color. The critics' prejudices are so blatant and they are so hurtful and they are so harmful to a theatrical community.

SHAFER: I know that there are some critics, too, when you were in *The Cherry Orchard,* who said, "Why are these people black, why Russians who are black?" What can you say? It's the same thing, I suppose.

FOSTER: It is, yes it is. You see, they are dealing with their visual prejudices. They just can't get past their history. As most recently said by someone, no one ever knows of a Dane playing *Hamlet.* But as long as the skin is white, then it seems to be acceptable.

And that is unacceptable if that is a language and that is a history that is being taught to us. If that is being held up as the great learning tool, the great teaching tool, the great storyteller and you choose a profession that requires your use of it, then you can't have somebody saying that you can't use it.

SHAFER: Good, good.

FOSTER: I have a hard time with that kind of thing and I have a hard time with the masking of prejudices and bigotry.

SHAFER: Yes, I am certain that the criticism seems to be on some other ground . . .

FOSTER: Yes, it is . . .

SHAFER: But it really comes down to that.

FOSTER: So, I don't trust until I am so familiar with the critic's history that I can read it and know that there is some integrity in the criticism. Nine times out of ten the critic does not know the character as well as the actor in the play.

SHAFER: That's true, too.

FOSTER: And unless they've had access to the director or to an actor in the production where they talk about what they hope to be able to do, what they hope the vision is and what they have worked on, then the critic doesn't know. Frequently, productions have access to the media and interviews are given. And I feel this is an instruction manual to the critics, "This is what you are going to see now!" [Laughing.] Or at least, "Look for this, this is what we hope to do." But that's frequently done with productions that have access to the papers and what not.

SHAFER: We've been talking here about a number of different aspects because this is a very rich subject, this production, which was historically significant in the American theatre, of course. It seems to me, that one of the questions one might fairly ask is because of this casting, did the audience draw in more black Americans for this play who might not otherwise have seen it?

FOSTER: Oh, absolutely! There are people who came who might not ever have seen a production of *Long Day's Journey*, because they did not know it would speak to them. I've come to the theatre time after time and quite frequently the material does not speak to various cultures. I wish that productions could touch more on universal themes of material rather than being so limited. I think that would engage audiences, provide a variety. I do know that regional theatres work towards having at least one black actor working. It's pitiful!

SHAFER: Yes, it is. I know a lot of actors going around playing in August Wilson plays have told me that people think they are doing them such a great favor to hire them to come and be in an August Wilson play, but they all want them to come in Black History month.

FOSTER: Uh, hmm. Yeah, it becomes the one show that a theatre, I guess, does so that they can qualify for the grants and so that they can speak to the needs of perhaps some members of the community. Or, perhaps, speak to their own need to be more diverse, given whatever circumstances they're working on. It is a complex issue and I do know that it can be improved upon. But all of this stuff starts at the top. All of it does. It does not start with the actor, it starts at the top.

SHAFER: So that was interesting, that in the case of this production of *Long Day's Journey into Night,* the decision was just simply made that this was going to be the one to do it and they just did.

FOSTER: That's right, I mean that's it. Uh, huh!

SHAFER: And it was a big success.

FOSTER: Yes it was, yes it was. And it was a rewarding experience for those of us who worked in it and for those who saw it. I still get comments about that production and how proud people were and how much they were involved in it, and that they never would have believed that they could have been. And just on and on and on. These are things that the critics don't hear, they are so locked up into their little boxes of prejudices.

SHAFER: Now, your career, which continues at a great rate, has spread over these wonderful classics of various kinds. I know that you have had so many high points it's probably difficult to pick any out and say, "Oh, this one was better then that." But I wondered, did this play have a kind of special meaning for you?

FOSTER: There was the pleasure of doing O'Neill and working with a company of actors that I respected and doing it at a theatre that I absolutely loved. But other than that it wasn't different. Usually whatever I am working on I love the most. Sometimes that proved, at least once or twice, not to be true. But I invest everything in whatever it is that I am working on and coming off of the show, the excitement rides high if there is more that I have to look for. And I just finished doing *Raisin in the Sun,* and it was done in such a short period of time, it was really summer stock, you know, and there's more work I want to do on it and I can't wait to go further with my vision of Lena Younger. I always knew that someday I would play this character and I have kind of come full circle in the sense that the first time I played it, I played Ruth. So I always knew that I would play Lena later, you know, later in my life and in my career. And, I love her, but I've got some work I'd like to . . .

SHAFER: That's very interesting. It works that way for some actors who first play Jamie in *Long Day's Journey* and know that some day they will play James Tyrone. In fact I just talked to Len Cariou about that. This is the only O'Neill you played, I believe. Was there any other O'Neill that you ever think that you might like to try or to play Mary again?

FOSTER: You know, so frequently things come to me. They don't ask choices, and we don't sit down and I say, "Oh, I want to play this part and I want to play that." It has been more that someone else, a director, a producer, a writer, would see me as such and such. So, you know, that's just not something I really think about.

11| Edward Petherbridge

Edward Petherbridge was born in Bradford, Yorkshire, in 1936. He was trained at the Northern Theatre School, Bradford. He also studied mime with Claude Chagrin. His first stage appearance was in 1956 at the Ludlow Festival as Gaveston in *Edward II*. His first London appearance was at the open air theatre in Regent's Park in 1962, playing Demetrius in *A Midsummer Night's Dream*. Since that time he has become a major actor with a wide range of roles from Euripides to Feydeau. In addition to acting he has presented mime workshops and directed, particularly for the Actors' Company of which he is a founding member. In 1976 he toured Australia and New Zealand with the Royal Shakespeare Company (RSC). He has been praised for both tragic and comic parts, including the Cardinal in *The Duchess of Malfi* at the National Theatre in London and Mirabell in *The Way of the World*, which delighted New York audiences in 1974. He also performed the role of Marsden in New York in *Strange Interlude* (having won the Olivier Award for the role in London) and received a Tony nomination. He was so effective in the role that much of the focus of the play shifted to his character. He is also well remembered for his role as Newman Neggs in *Nicholas Nickleby* in London and New York. He has acted frequently with the RSC. At the time of this interview he was touring with the company, performing at Brooklyn Academy of Music (BAM) in Beckett's *Krapp's Last Tape* (which sold out months before the presentations) and playing the ghost in *Hamlet*. This interview took place between the two performances, while machines tore up the street outside the theatre.

BROOKLYN, NEW YORK, MAY 1998

SHAFER: I'm chiefly interested in asking you about your experience as an actor in *Strange Interlude*. I thought I might begin by asking how it happened that this play, which is so rarely presented, was done and whether you or someone else had a particular interest in it.

PETHERBRIDGE: I don't think I know. I had never read it myself, but I was approached by the director and the management who were doing it, and asked if I would like to play Marsden. And I do remember thinking that I didn't want to play the part, that I would have preferred to play the doctor. But Keith Haggert, God, was that Keith Haggert?, said there was a film of this and, who's the big star?

SHAFER: Clark Gable.

PETHERBRIDGE: Yes, and he told me Clark Gable was the big star and he played Marsden. I said, "I don't believe you." He said, "It's true." Well, of course he was lying. He thought that I would fall for the fact that a great, glamorous leading part was played by Clark Gable, but I wasn't so stupid. Anyway, I just felt that it was just a piece of casting that was a little bit obvious, and I didn't want to be cast to type. And I think I thought probably the character was a bit of a wimp. Anyway, he begged me to reconsider this and I thought, "Well, maybe it's quite a good part." Then we began to rehearse it and after two or three days there was some awful trouble about the boy who appears as about ten years old, then grown up, just about to marry. Keith Haggert had had the idea that he wanted to cast somebody, a young man who would play both and Glenda Jackson thought this was a terrible idea. We all had a sort of unofficial Sunday reading before the Monday official beginning when this boy was going to be there. She felt that he was being foisted upon her. There was an awful lot of trouble about whether or not he was going to do this and I thought that he was a perfectly nice guy and it seemed a way out, but, of course, not very naturalistic, or realistic. Or do I mean naturalistic?

SHAFER: Either one.

PETHERBRIDGE: We were then invited to have opinions about this, discuss it, you know. The poor boy was either in the room or sent out, I can't remember. I finally said, "Look. Don't let us pretend we're in some sort of democratic situation here where all opinions are equal. I don't have anything in my contract which says casting approval, I don't know if anybody else has, but if anyone has that, then they should exercise it on their own, and get on with it." Meanwhile, I rang my agent and said, "I really can't bear the atmosphere of these rehearsals." Odd that we should have this construction work on the road outside here which our readers won't appreciate, but we have to suffer, because those rehearsals were somewhere in Kingsway where they seemed to be trying to undermine the foundations with drills and things. And it was also quite cold, I remember, and there were some gas heaters suspended from the ceiling in this old church hall which made a sort of terrible hissing noise. And the acoustic was terrible. And I thought, "Well, this is five hours, we've got five weeks [face in his hands], five weeks to rehearse five hours and I haven't heard a word of dialogue yet, and I'll never learn it and I'm having such a terrible time." So I remember one lunch time, going to the pub, for a drink, I'm afraid. [Laughing.] I went with a bunch of the other actors and I remember saying, "Excuse me, I think I'll ring my agent." And I said, "You have to get me out of this." So he said, "Oh, don't be hasty. Leave it for a week." I said, "I can't leave it for a week, by which time they'll feel even less like replacing me." Anyway I don't quite know what happened, it's a long time ago. Somehow or another, I stayed on.

SHAFER: Did it get any better?

PETHERBRIDGE: We moved to another, quieter rehearsal room some-where. Somehow I managed to learn this incredibly long, I thought rather turgid, play. We rehearsed in a huge drill hall which was freezing cold and we had portable oil heaters, I remember, which were put at each corner of the marked-out area of the stage to kind of radiate warmth on us in this huge frozen waste. And I remember thinking at this point, "This is the dullest, most turgid, long-winded domestic drama I've ever had anything to do with and I wish to God I'd never said I'd be in it." And then we went two places. I think we played Croyden, which is the sort of Brooklyn of London. Actually, there isn't really an equivalent to Brooklyn, but it's out of town and you might as well be playing on the moon really (so it isn't like Brooklyn at all), for all the feedback one gets. And a terrible auditorium like a huge shoe box and the audience is not known for its comic response. Not that we were expecting any laughs and certainly we didn't get any. Then we went to Nottingham which is a beautiful old theatre which has one thing in common with the Brooklyn Academy of Music and that is that Sarah Bernhardt played there. Of course, she played most places. And D. H. Lawrence (while we're thinking about literary figures, since we're doing this in the name of O'Neill), D. H. Lawrence saw her there. Indeed, he put an episode about seeing her there in, I think, *Sons and Lovers*. 1913, this was. When *he* saw it, I hasten to add. So, I always feel rather romantic about that theatre, thinking of him seeing her there, and it had a *profound* effect on him. I know I digress, but she was playing in *La Dame aux Camélias* by Dumas, and was (now let me think, I used to know all this by heart), she was about sixty-four. And he thought she was just the most wonderful creature, like some gazelle, a wild animal, actually, but incredibly graceful and passionate. Although he referred to the play as a "dime show," curious American phrase, nevertheless, she worked the magic and touched him enormously. Well, I didn't know about our "dime show," maybe I thought it was worth a few dollars, but Nottingham is *also* not known for its comedic response and I can tell you I just played *Twelfth Night* there not very long ago, playing Malvolio, and I can't say that that was a particularly happy experience—in that particular town. Everywhere else it was.

However, in one of these dates a friend of mine came from London, if not a friend, at least an acquaintance—he's now a rather important director. He came around afterwards and I said, "Fancy you being here," and he said, "Edward, this is the best thing I've seen you do for years." I said, "Really? You amaze me." And he said, "It's extraordinary." I said, "Do you mean it's the best play I've been in, or the best performance?" He said, "Probably both." Anyway that was the first chink of light, not that I particularly respected his opinion, generally. But I mean, if a dog wags its tail at an actor, the actor, as you know, always takes notice. This was better than the dog.

SHAFER: What happened next?

PETHERBRIDGE: Then we went into London with it and we did some previews. I have kept mentioning comedy, haven't I? I gather that when it was first done and Lynn Fontanne played Glenda Jackson's part (Glenda Jackson, by the way, is my member of Parliament now, so things have moved on rather). I had to carry her offstage—she falls asleep famously on the novelist's knee and I have to rise with this comatose character from this sitting position and get to the door with her. So I know the full weight of Glenda's political persuasions and everything else. Well, now, where were we?

SHAFER: You were starting to discuss comedy . . .

PETHERBRIDGE: Oh yes. Lynn Fontanne, apparently kept saying to O'Neill, "You realize that this will get a laugh" [laughing] because he was very concerned that nothing should get a laugh.

SHAFER: That may have been her perception of him.

PETHERBRIDGE: Yes. Whether she got laughs or not I don't know. In fact, I do remember speaking to—who was the grand old man who was together with Orson Welles . . .

SHAFER: John Houseman.

PETHERBRIDGE: I met him around about that time. I don't think he saw our production but he was in England with a production of *Awake and Sing!* and he said he'd seen *Strange Interlude*, he was one of the few people still alive who'd seen it originally when it was done on Broadway and he said, "Oh, sure, it got laughs as I remember." And that was the amazing thing. Of course, audiences are very corrupting things for actors. I think once you discover that something you've rehearsed . . . now I have to be careful here because there's nothing unserious about comedy, we all know that comedy is a serious business. I mean it's a serious craft, but it's also as seriously intended as anything else. I mean you can make as serious a point through comedy as you can through tragedy or you can through any other kind of dramatic form. But it was interesting to find that some of the behavior of the character struck the audience as funny—a modern, contemporary English audience. Then when you find that out, you start to play it as a comedy, naturally, and that is the point where some possible corruption can come in and you can begin to slightly distort the material and say, "How about this folks? This is a rather cunning way for me to deliver the line, don't you think?" So one has to preserve a certain amount of innocence, I think, and I hope one did.

Now the man who wrote *Bent*, Martin Sherman—American writer, but rather an Anglophile—he was around in London at the time, and he said that he'd seen a production of the play years before, off-Broadway, I think it was, with the Actors' Studio. I think Lee Strasberg directed. He said that it was very earnest and turgid and long and didn't strike him as very good and he thought we'd maybe kind of rescued the play because of the British sense of irony. He said there was a whole chunk of American drama that needs to be rescued in this way, that maybe had been played wrongly and therefore evaluated wrongly for years. I reminded him about saying this to me about ten years later and he looked at me as if I'd made it all up. He said, "I wouldn't ever say that now." So it was clearly something he felt at the time; maybe American acting moved on or he moved on—somebody had moved on, anyway.

But certainly I do feel the comedic element, whatever O'Neill felt about it, I do feel that there was a curious energy released in the playing and in the audience in the sense of these rather flawed characters, and this flawed and foolish behavior, and the way they took themselves sometimes very seriously, and, of course, all these thoughts that they speak aloud to create a kind of double sensitivity.

SHAFER: Did you find that an interesting process?

PETHERBRIDGE: Well, I kept saying that O'Neill seems to have set European and, therefore, American drama back several decades because in the realistic or naturalistic tradition writers began to find that they didn't have to turn to the audience and say, "Ah, little does she know that I am (ahem) her real father" or whatever, in the tradition of melodrama. Shakespeare, of course, got round the way of telling the audience what the character thought by soliloquies and, indeed, asides. But this was not quite in that Shakespearean convention at all because it was, as you will remember, there was much more of it—it was as if Hamlet had been continually turning aside in the closet scene to let us know how he felt right in the heat of the drama. And it seemed to me to be a bit of a clumsy device when I was in the circle of gas or oil fires. But there was a moment, I do remember now when I think about it, I was probably sitting very near to where D. H. Lawrence would have been sitting in Nottingham, and Glenda was sitting very near to where Sarah Bernhardt would have been *standing* (this is pre-wooden leg period, you understand) and hearing Glenda do some of the stuff—I can see it now—in the last scene, she was doing a long soliloquy of her part. I hadn't rated Glenda very much in the part, she'd been quite difficult to rehearse with. I suddenly realized that what she was doing vocally was very spellbinding— the words were spellbinding and her delivery was spellbinding, musically; extraordinarily enticing to listen to. I think the binding of the spell is the way to put it. And so it was gradually that one realized that these apparently *odd* devices that he used, and, let's face it, fairly melodramatic, schematic situations, the three men and the one woman and the symbolism that goes through: God, the mother and all that—on every level symbolically from the soap opera point of view, nevertheless, were effective in performance.

And somebody said, oh, it was Anna Massey who has an American connection . . .

SHAFER: Yes, I like her very much . . .

PETHERBRIDGE: And she said, "I have to say I adored it and my video machine isn't working at home, and I missed 'Dynasty' [we used to call it 'Dinasty'] which I'm very keen on. However, *this* is 'Dynasty' shot through with poetry. So it was worth it." And there is that soap opera element. But it got to be wonderful fun to perform the play. Of course, I'd been quite misguided to think that I ought to be looking after my image of sort of romantic virility, of trying to get away from playing dithering character parts because it was a perfect part for many aspects of my . . . gifts and probably the nicest of the characterizations in the play.

SHAFER: Yes. Certainly the most amusing. And I must tell you that a friend of mine, who is no great fan of O'Neill, said that he remembered waiting for the parts when you came in.

PETHERBRIDGE: Nobody can say that O'Neill wasn't a comic writer when he wrote that buildup for Marsden's entrance at the boat race and you know that he's been getting drunk and you think, "Oh, now we're going to see Marsden drunk," or even if you don't think it you suddenly do and this man with all his restraint and constraint and all these tortured emotions he occasionally lets the audience know about, carefully edited, and the kind of self-loathing as well, and the fear of life that he despairs about and all that, and then he's suddenly there as if he'd grown a pair of ludicrous wings. I don't remember exactly . . . I don't remember a single line from all that, but I do remember the Universal Television version of that, we have it on video, and out of curiosity I had a peep at it, maybe two or three years ago and I do remember laughing out loud at that scene.

SHAFER: [Laughing.] Really!

PETHERBRIDGE: Yes, and thinking, "You didn't do that so badly." Not only that, but it's always such a surprise to find that . . . it's sometimes a surprise to be taken by, stopped by your own timing. You think, "Oh! That was pretty good." [Laughing.] But it's not just that, it was that I realized what a fine piece of comic character revelation that was. And how *bold*, too, because there's the woman, Nina, having her great crisis about her Gordon, and the father in the background, well, he's not the father, of course, he's having a great heart-stopping excitement, which is what it actually ends up being, about his boy winning that race which actually kills him, that's all going on, the boat race is going on, and the girl is crying to her boy, too, and the two women and this terrible rivalry, Nina's love for her son. And it's like a fugue, or perhaps that's wrong, but it's a musical piece for at least four different themes, interweaving, and all the characters' different levels of passion. You are feeling pain for Nina, you are being comically released by Marsden, and then you have to put up with the sudden death of that character you really rather sympathized with all the way through, who'd been that sweet boy who married her. And there's the doctor, too, who has his own soliloquies during that part of it.

SHAFER: May I ask you what you ultimately thought about Marsden as a person?

PETHERBRIDGE: As a person. Well, it's a long time ago and I'm surprised I remember as much as I do.

SHAFER: You said you initially thought of him as a wimp and you were not attracted to playing the role.

PETHERBRIDGE: These are all the wrong reasons, sort of showbiz, vanity reasons. I have to say that I consider myself to be quite a good judge of plays and parts when I read them and I think that I've seldom made judgments that have been proved very wrong. But in this case I think I was way off the mark when I read the play. When I say I'm a good judge of plays, I'm only going on the evidence of what's turned out to be the case in practice. I mean one occasionally finds there is more in a role, or less. But here I was kind of wrong—it's now hard to remember what I thought, but I do remember the rehearsal process was not a particularly happy one for some reason.

SHAFER: As you got to perform places in which the audience had more of a response to the comedy, did you start to enjoy playing it then? I mean it's a very long role, in a very long evening.

PETHERBRIDGE: Well, I used to think I spent far too much time in the dressing room, but I hadn't played a ghost then—at least I didn't have to do any quick changes. Oh, except I did, of course. My hair wasn't quite as white as it is now. It probably went white during the rehearsal period for this. I used to have to wear a kind of toupee arrangement and my own hair at the back, because if you don't wear your own hair in that period, no wig will ever be short enough. So I had to put some sort of brown gel stuff on my own hair. People wondered how I actually did get from sort of brownish hair to very, very gray, but it was through, first of all, having this toupee and then taking the toupee off and having a slightly higher forehead, and a bit of gray in the hair, and then shampooing it in the interval or something like that.

SHAFER: It's very kind of you to take the time for this interview when you are performing in a very short while, and now people are starting to come in to do various things. May I just ask you one more thing? I have enjoyed your performances in many plays and look forward to more, but particularly more O'Neill. Are there any plays which would interest you?

PETHERBRIDGE: I don't know. I hadn't really thought about it. What plays would you suggest?

SHAFER: I would certainly think of *A Touch of the Poet,* but I would love to see you in *Long Day's Journey into Night.*

PETHERBRIDGE: What part? . . . Oh, I see, I suppose it would have to be the father. But I don't think I would be particularly suited to that role.

SHAFER: Why not? You have the appropriate qualities, especially the voice and appearance.

PETHERBRIDGE: Of course I said I wasn't particularly keen on Marsden and then it worked out well. Perhaps somebody should try me.

SHAFER: I hope somebody will.

12| Fritz Weaver

Fritz Weaver was born in Pittsburgh in 1926. He began acting at the Barter Theatre in Virginia in 1951 and swiftly moved to major roles, which he has continued to play. He appeared off-Broadway in many plays including *The Doctor's Dilemma* and *The Way of the World*. His many Broadway roles have won him a significant number of awards including the Tony Award, the Drama Desk Award, the Outer Critics Circle, and the Clarence Derwent Award for *The White Devil* in 1959. The range of plays in which he has acted extend from Alan Ayckbourne's *Absurd Person Singular* to *King Lear*. He was closely connected with the Phoenix Theatre under the direction of Stuart Vaughan and their work together is well remembered by theatregoers. He appeared in numerous plays by Shakespeare at the American Shakespeare Theatre in Connecticut with Michael Kahn for several seasons. He starred in Arthur Miller's *The Crucible* and *The Price*. His work in film includes *Marathon Man* and *Fail-Safe*. His television work includes guest appearances, leading roles, and miniseries, including *Holocaust*. He recently delighted audiences as the unhappy rich man in Jean Anouilh's *Ring Around the Moon* on Broadway and appeared at Lincoln Center in A. R. Gurney's *Ancestral Voices*. He is married to actress/acting teacher Rochelle Oliver and lives in Manhattan. He is perhaps particularly remembered as the tragic school teacher in *Child's Play* (for which he won a Tony Award) and a cunning Sherlock Holmes in *Baker Street*.

NEW YORK CITY, MAY 1999

SHAFER: Your career has encompassed so many great roles. I think many actors in America have long careers but don't get the opportunity to play great roles. You've played Hamlet, Macbeth, Peer Gynt, and other wonderful roles. You have played in O'Neill, and I wonder if you can just talk about what roles of O'Neill you have played.

WEAVER: Well, the first role I played was the role in *The Great God Brown,* with our mutual friend Stuart Vaughan directing. That was my introduction to acting in O'Neill, although I went through a period where I read the entire canon of his work , and I thought to myself, "I want to do all of these roles." And I still to this day, regret the fact that the early plays of O'Neill are more or less ignored.

SHAFER: Oh, I think you are so right about that.

WEAVER: People talk about *The Iceman Cometh* and *Long Day's Journey into Night:* the great masterpieces of American theatre. But where was he building the resources for those plays? *The Great God Brown, Marco Millions . . .*

SHAFER: Now there's a play that is so interesting and Alfred Lunt was in it, but they didn't do it the way O'Neill had really written it. For economic reasons many things were eliminated.

WEAVER: Well, what happened to that, did they ever get it on?

SHAFER: They got it on, but it was not a big success, so they didn't run it very long. It's nice to hear somebody express interest in those plays. Also, people often express the idea that, well, he was just kind of fooling around with a lot of crazy stuff, and then he finally got reasonable and wrote these two good plays.

WEAVER: No, it's just simply not true. I think that they repay, simply just reading them without seeing them.

SHAFER: When was it that you were reading them?

WEAVER: I was at the University of Chicago, and I had just got interested in the theatre, and I played a couple of Shakespeare parts there. Somebody said, "You've got to read these O'Neill plays." And I'd always meant to. When I read them, I thought, "Jeez, these are really marvelous acting vehicles." I mean, they are great plays as well. Now *Days Without End*, has anyone ever done it?

SHAFER: That's one everyone thinks is a complete disaster—total failure.

WEAVER: Oh, that's too bad. I loved it.

SHAFER: Well, that is really fascinating. Were you a theatre major then?

WEAVER: No. I was a major in everything but the theatre. I was . . . well, I got the two-year bachelor degree there, that was Chancellor Hutchins's idea. Speed up that process, then you choose your specialty. So I went into the History Department, I went into the Philosophy Department, I even was in the Physics Department, but that was a mistake because I had absolutely no aptitude for that. I was just fooling around and I was doing theatre on the side. There wasn't even a theatre course at the University of Chicago, but a lot of people like Mike Nichols and Elaine May, we were just all there, sort of fooling around on our own. That is when I was reading O'Neill.

The Great God Brown was the first one I did. Oh! What a part, Dion Anthony. What a tremendous part it is. I remember saying, formulating, for myself, O'Neill asks for all that you have got as an actor, and then he asks for more. He knew to a hair's breadth about acting, and he knew how to design great acting roles. I don't know if that is your primary interest here, but the acting of O'Neill is the nearest thing I know to Shakespeare, where you simply are tested to the outmost by the roles. Dion Anthony, and then the next one that I played—there have been very few, although I've done some readings, but I acted *Touch of the Poet* on television.

SHAFER: That was a fine cast with Roberta Maxwell. I loved seeing it.

WEAVER: Yes, they were wonderful. That has become my favorite O'Neill part. That is a tremendous part and, I think, a tremendous play.

SHAFER: Were there any others after that?

WEAVER: No, I don't believe there were.

SHAFER: But, surely people wanted you to do *Long Day's Journey into Night*.

WEAVER: Oh, yes, many times. Gerry Fitzgerald called me many times. She was about to do her Mary Tyrone. But I'll tell you that this is the one part that I have never felt that I could bring anything to. That particular kind of actor does not resonate in me. The kind of man he was, I am sort of a little afraid of, to tell you the truth. I, who have played Lear, and I was afraid of Tyrone. Because you mentioned, for instance Peer Gynt. That play was utterly miscast with me as Peer Gynt. I did it as a favor to Stuart Vaughan. I think he wanted Chris Plummer, and he couldn't get him, so he said, "You have to step into this" at the last moment, and I said, "Hey, this is not a part for me," but I played it and fell on my face in the fire. It was not a success.

SHAFER: I don't remember hearing that.

WEAVER: Oh, if your memory was as long as mine, you would remember Walter Kerr and a few other people giving me the business. No, but back to *A Touch of the Poet*. Now years later, I am up at the O'Neill Center in Connecticut, and we are dedicating a new statue to O'Neill, the young O'Neill, that boy. And we were standing around the statue, and Jason Robards was there. And Jason and I fell into conversation. I'd known Jason on and off socially, and we both agreed that *A Touch of a Poet* is the finest acting role in the entire body of his work. It was his favorite play, too. Now that surprised me because he's played them all. The later ones, he didn't play the earlier ones, but all the later ones and he said that was it by all means. There's something about that play that is like the history of the country, in a single play we got the poet, the aristocrat of the first of the part, who turns into a man of the people with the coming of Andrew Jackson, and democracy really taking over from the aristocracy. In this one character, he goes through both of those changes. He is busy quoting Lord Byron in the whole first part and in the second part he is schizoid, he is totally schizoid. He goes into this plebian, peasant personification and the contrast of the action is just unbelievable. You know you run the whole gamut of emotions. But that's not what makes it a great play, I think. What makes it a great play, is it was part of this great vision he had of writing the entire history of a country, in play after play, and in that play he got the transition out of the first six presidents and into Andrew Jackson. Out of the silk pants and the silk stockings into the backwoodsman, and one character goes through that entire gamut. I just think that is fascinating.

SHAFER: Where were you working on that—where did you make that film?

WEAVER: We did it for Channel 13, in the days when they used to do that sort of thing.

SHAFER: I remember seeing that, it was early '70s, and I was in Connecticut. . . . Did Arvin direct that?

WEAVER: No, Stephen Porter directed that.

SHAFER: Oh, yes, of course. Such a fine director.

WEAVER: A wonderful man, and I particularly remember that in one of my more violent scenes I did what he called . . . I totaled three antiques that had been specially gotten for the production, and I smashed three tables. Stephen blanched off camera, and said "Oh, please!!" That role takes over. You don't really control that part, it takes you over. It goes on its own steam. Stephen paid me a great compliment because he said, "You know, you used a classic schizophrenic gesture in the second part of the play." Now, I had been aware of the schizoid nature of the man, it was the most incredible thing. But I apparently intuited, or I was deeply schizoid enough myself, that I went into this . . . they say this is true of schizophrenia patients, they do this a lot. [Makes a frightful gesture of clawing at his head.] It's almost as if you're trying to claw your way into your skull. It's almost as if you are trying to tear your head open. And I found myself doing that, and he said he had been to a mental hospital and noticed that.

SHAFER: That's really remarkable. It's a difficult role. It seems to me hard to try to decide how much sympathy you want the audience to have for the man. What do you think about that?

WEAVER: I'll let you in on an actor's secret: you always want the maximum sympathy because you're playing it from the character's own point of view and he doesn't think he's unsympathetic. He thinks he's carrying out his own destiny, whatever that is. And that's always been my philosophy, I don't try for sympathy but I tried to understand what he's doing, I try to think his thoughts.

SHAFER: In the relationship with the two women, it seems to me that the audience tends to feel that he's mistreating them.

WEAVER: Oh, very definitely. But I felt almost incestuously about the daughter. I think that this is a deep love for the daughter which expresses itself in a most horrible way, just blasting her, talking about her ugly hands, you know all of that, but all the time deeply, deeply attracted to her, sexually. It's a wonderful engine for the part, too, because that tension is playing in him all the time. It's not something I invented incidentally. I don't go around inventing these things. Stephen agreed, too, he thought it was there, father-daughter, feeling very strongly. Of course the mother . . . she's all by herself in a kind of little dream of . . . I don't know. She was not an important imaginative figure for me, but she was for O'Neill for the character. He called her a bog trotter. He despised her for the first part of the play, thought she was a peasant, but there is great wisdom in that woman. Great sympathy. I saw Helen Hayes play the part and she was wonderful.

SHAFER: That was the production with Eric Portman.

WEAVER: Eric Portman, I saw him, I didn't understand a word he said, I had great difficulty following his diction. I'll tell you what Thornton Wilder said. Thornton Wilder came backstage to see Helen Hayes. She told me this story. He came back and he said, "I am going to sue Eric Portman for playing my friend O'Neill's play in Chinese." When I heard it I said, "I'm glad you said it, because Eric was . . . he's a wonderful actor but he was just wahlyahlwa—I didn't know what he was talking about." And then Kim Stanley, of course, she was just wonderful.

SHAFER: Of course you talk to other actors, you were mentioning Jason Robards. It seems to me that actors, generally speaking, really like to act O'Neill.

WEAVER: As I say, Shakespeare's the only other experience I know where you dive into these parts and there's no bottom. It just goes forever, the fullest amount of energy you bring is not enough. The opposite is the kind of play where the material is so thin that there's nothing to do accept stand around, and, dig as you may, you don't find anything. Ibsen is another one where digging really repays.

SHAFER: Yes. And of course O'Neill was initially inspired so much by seeing Nazimova in *Hedda Gabler* ten times. Because of his father, he could go into any theatre, walk up to the box office, and they would let him in, so he saw a lot of theatre.

WEAVER: Well, that's right and they lived right here.

SHAFER: Isn't that something? May I ask you another thing? How did it come about that you and Stuart decided to do *The Great God Brown* at the Phoenix?

WEAVER: It was his decision completely. I had just done Hamlet at Stratford and he wanted a season. Oh, no, wait, it was the second season when we did *The Great God Brown*. In the first season we did *The Power and the Glory,* and T. S. Eliot's *Family Reunion.* In the second season we did first O'Neill and then *Peer Gynt.* It opened the season, and it, in fact, moved to Broadway.

SHAFER: Yes, I know. Everyone was talking about it.

WEAVER: It was something of a success. I can't answer your question because it was his decision but the mask idea was so fascinating to me—the idea of wearing masks.

SHAFER: What was the mask like?

WEAVER: It was a half mask, it came to here, which freed the mouth. It was wonderful, so stylized like the Greek plays. I wish I had the program because the front cover shows all four of us with our masks, on and then off. There again you see, O'Neill's son was a great Greek scholar, but O'Neill himself knew the Greeks. He knew how important the mask was. He tried everything, this man. He knew what some of the acting schools have been discovering, that when an actor puts a mask on, he is totally freed of inhibitions, his body tends to be very alive because this part of him is not working. I found this to be true just experimentally, when I was playing O'Neill with the mask. I was a different character with that thing put on my face, my body just exploded. Because that becomes the most expressive part of the body—of the total instrument. I loved it! That's why I think the early plays should be revived. He tried so many different things.

SHAFER: When you worked with Stuart and the rest of the cast, did you worry a little at all about whether the audience was going to be confused or unclear about the use of the masks?

WEAVER: Not for a moment, they all loved it and it was very clear. I don't know if other people have had this problem, but we didn't.

SHAFER: People who just read the play will say something like, "I don't understand it, when was he supposed to be this? Was that really a mask? When he dies does Billy really become him?"

WEAVER: To me its like that familiar O'Neill theme. Just what I was saying about *Touch of the Poet:* man is two people; with the mask and without the mask. I think in *Touch of the Poet* the mask comes off at the second part of the play and he goes wild in that part. That's the true spirit of this country. Threw off all that European-aristocratic thing and became America. That, too, is a mask, only in this case it's a schizoid mask. In *Strange Interlude,* where they speak their thoughts, there's another mask thing. It's like I am one thing to you and I have another message here. [Taps head.]

SHAFER: It must have been exciting to be playing that role of Dion Anthony, which is so associated with O'Neill in autobiographical details.

WEAVER: Oh, yes, my character is so much like the young O'Neill. A young rebel, very sensitive, wild and untamed.

SHAFER: It's interesting, Michael Kahn said to me a couple of weeks ago that when he first directed *Long Day's Journey into Night* that he read all he could get about O'Neill. Now he said that if he did the play again he wouldn't read anything.

WEAVER: That's good. I think that's very good.

SHAFER: I thought it was interesting. It's an artistic work and it should stand as an artistic work.

WEAVER: And O'Neill put it there on paper for you, all you need is there.

SHAFER: It's a very poetic kind of play, one would say it is not in written poetry, but there are a lot of poetic images and all in it.

WEAVER: Oh, yes. Well, O'Neill first wanted to be a poet, didn't he, and wrote poetry?

SHAFER: I think it's too bad in *Long Day's Journey into Night* that he says that thing about wanting to be a poet and not making it. A lot of people who don't like him use that to kind of beat him on the head. Yet I think actors find his language quite wonderful.

WEAVER: Acting language is very different from book language. This kid grew up watching his father onstage and as you say, not just his father, of course, but all of the great actors.

SHAFER: Well, certainly he had seen the great actors, and yet there's the popular impression that he didn't like actors. Why do you think that is?

WEAVER: I think it had to do with his old man, his bitterness about his old man. But he was compelled to stay in the business and write these great parts.

SHAFER: Have you ever worked with a playwright who was alive and had to do with rehearsals?

WEAVER: Oh sure.

SHAFER: I supposed you had. Did they seem to be satisfied all the time?

WEAVER: No, almost never.

SHAFER: I wish you'd speak to that point. So many people act as if O'Neill was somehow some kind of unpleasant person because he was not satisfied with the actors.

WEAVER: No, I think in his mind it was an ideal way to do his work; flesh and blood actors who couldn't live up to what was in his mind. But I think that all playwrights share that a little bit. They hear it in their heads and see it in their mind's eye and suddenly it's taken away from them. A director casts somebody, and they say, "Oh, no, please not that actor." It's an imperfect medium, it just is. I mean I played King Lear in Washington and sailed about seventy per cent of the time even though it was generally applauded as performed. I would come offstage and say, "Well, maybe I got twenty-five per cent of it that time." It's such a high electric voltage on those lines, you fall behind it for just a second, you lose the current of whatever the engine of the play is. I think that O'Neill hated his father's theatre, he hated the kind of theatre his father did. This is why he was so experimental and why he went so far afield to try and see what else could be done with it.

SHAFER: I think people tend to think these later plays are just realistic and straight realism. Do you think that?

WEAVER: Not at all. They're poems. They're just more disguised. You can think they are realistic and they really are on one level. But that is just because he got more and more skillful at what he was doing. Experimenting had been done, he had done all the things he had tried in different ways and now he just drew it all together in one seamless thing. Those plays are perfect.

SHAFER: So would you say on the whole, if you looked back on your career, that those two O'Neills were some of your most enjoyable work?

WEAVER: Absolutely, I think I learned more from them than almost anything else I've ever done.

SHAFER: That's interesting, one early and one late play and that's all there was after all the reading.

WEAVER: After all the reading, the desire is still there to do whatever there is that can be done. I would love to.

SHAFER: What would you play?

WEAVER: That is a good question because I am now seventy-three years old and I can't play Dion Anthony anymore.

SHAFER: You still don't think *Long Day's Journey into Night* is the role for you? It's funny, because I was just talking to somebody today and we were both saying we wished we could see you in the role.

WEAVER: Now you've started me thinking—maybe I should rethink that. I haven't even thought about it for a while. Thank you, I'll think about that.

Index